A Shared Future

A Shared Future

Faith-Based Organizing for Racial Equity and Ethical Democracy

RICHARD L. WOOD
AND BRAD R. FULTON

The University of Chicago Press
Chicago and London

Richard L. Wood is associate professor and chair in the department of sociology at the University of New Mexico. Brad R. Fulton is assistant professor at Indiana University in the School of Public and Environmental Affairs.

The University of Chicago Press, Chicago 60637
The University of Chicago Press, Ltd., London
© 2015 by The University of Chicago
All rights reserved. Published 2015.
Printed in the United States of America

24 23 22 21 20 19 18 17 16 15   1 2 3 4 5

ISBN-13: 978-0-226-30597-4 (cloth)
ISBN-13: 978-0-226-30602-5 (paper)
ISBN-13: 978-0-226-30616-2 (e-book)
DOI: 10.7208/chicago/9780226306162.001.0001

Library of Congress Cataloging-in-Publication Data

Wood, Richard L., author.
   A shared future : faith-based organizing for racial equity and ethical democracy / Richard L. Wood and Brad R. Fulton.
      pages cm
   Includes bibliographical references and index.
   ISBN 978-0-226-30597-4 (cloth : alkaline paper) — ISBN 978-0-226-30602-5 (paperback : alkaline paper) — ISBN 978-0-226-30616-2 (ebook)
1. Religious institutions—Political activity—United States.   2. Community organization—Political activity—United States.   3. Equality—United States.   4. Minorities—United States—Social conditions—21st century.   5. Democracy—Moral and ethical aspects—United States.   I. Fulton, Brad R., author.   II. Title.
   HN90.S6W67 2015
   306.60973—dc23
                                                              2015015810

♾ This paper meets the requirements of ANSI/NISO Z39.48-1992 (Permanence of Paper).

Rev. Joseph Forbes, an elder statesman of racial equity in faith-based community organizing at "Faith Voices Action" of Communities Creating Opportunity (Kansas City, February 2014). (Photo by Stacey Schmitz, Communities Creating Opportunity)

This book is dedicated

to

Elder Joseph Forbes

(Ebenezer AME Church and Communities Creating Opportunity in Kansas City)

and to all those who have given their best selves to work for

economic justice

racial equity

immigrant rights

and to building a shared future for us all

CONTENTS

President Obama, Vice President Biden, and faith-based organizing leaders at signing ceremony for the reauthorization of the State Children's Health Insurance Program (March 2009). (Photo by Gordon Whitman, PICO National Network)

Introduction: Exorcising America's Demons, Building Ethical Democracy

Three demons bedevil American society today. The first is obvious: We suffer levels of economic inequality not witnessed in the hundred years since the Gilded Age, with stagnant or falling wages for the large majority of American families. The second is often misdiagnosed: Political pundits decry the polarization within national political discourse and institutions, but the real problem is not generic "polarization." In the context of such high economic inequality, polarization is to be expected, for its absence would simply represent acquiescence to stagnant wages and the resultant decline in the quality of family life. Rather, the real problem results from *strategic* polarization from above, that is, from the manipulation of political sentiment and democratic institutions to produce paralysis within national democratic institutions.[1] Thus the second demon is *policy paralysis*: our national political institutions' inability to foster any shared prosperity or good society in the American future—their failure, in the context of strategic polarization from above, to effectively address a broad variety of crucial realities undermining a shared American future. Those issues include economic inequality and stagnant family wages, the underclass status of a large immigrant sector, the ballooning national debt, the corrosive influence of unregulated money on elections, and the unsustainable rise of health care costs despite recent policy reforms.

Closely bound up with the first two demons is the recrudescence of a third demon that has forever bedeviled American society:[2] racial inequity, the ways that racial and ethnic minorities—the emerging majority of American society in the near future—disproportionately suffer the consequences of economic inequality and policy paralysis. Indeed, minorities in general and African Americans in particular too often stand at the whipping post some politicians and political commentators use to flog the issues that drive policy paralysis.[3] Only by casting out these three demons can the United States hope to build a shared future for all. Yet American society struggles to find adequate democratic means to even begin to do so.

This book plumbs for a way forward against these three demons by analyzing the experience of one broad movement that directly addresses economic inequality, policy paralysis, and racial injustice in the United States. Faith-based community organizing has a decades-long track record of working to advance the ideals of shared democratic life.[4] The movement works in poor, working-class, and middle-class settings to advance the political voice and economic interests of those sectors; it has recently provided a high-profile voice in national debates regarding universal health care, immigration reform, the foreclosure crisis, racial profiling, and the effort to rein in Wall Street malfeasance.[5] Projecting that voice has required faith-based organizing to broaden its historic focus on local communities or metropolitan areas in order to build links between local organizing and influence on higher-level policy. Underlying this development has been a new, more ambitious set of political aspirations within some sectors of the field. As one prominent strategist in the field, George Goehl (executive director of National People's Action [NPA]) noted:

> I think we marginalize ourselves by thinking of [ourselves] as the "community organizing sector." I think that's just really small. We want to change the political terrain of the country in a way that creates opportunity and advances racial and economic justice. What do we need to do, to do that? What kind of institutions do we need to build? What kind of talent do we need to attract and train? What kind of infrastructure do we need? What would it take to shift the ideas at the center of American life? And what role does organizing play in that?[6]

We seek answers to Goehl's questions not in abstract theory, but by using ideas to illuminate the experience of faith-based organizing coalitions and networks as they address the three demons identified above. In particular, we probe the tension between two ideals of American democracy: the universalist ideal, embodied in the notion that the democratic promise of equal opportunity applies to all Americans regardless of economic class and social identity; and the multiculturalist ideal, embodied in efforts to actually *redeem* that promise vis-à-vis subaltern groups that have been historically excluded from it, with legacies that continue today.[7] As shown below, democratic theorists and legal scholars have long debated the notion of an inherent contradiction between universalist and multiculturalist democratic ideals—that is, between understandings and practices of democracy that emphasize universal principles and absolute equality of citizens before the law, and those that emphasize redressing the unequal status of different groups within a multicultural society. Our focus here will fall less on the *theoretical* tension between these strands of democratic thinking and more on how that tension-in-principle actually plays out within organizations struggling to advance democratic outcomes.

Thus the insight we offer emerges from a binocular view: one eye on the interplay of universalist and multiculturalist democratic ideals; the other eye on faith-based organizing's work to advance democratic voice and equality in multiracial settings, where the dynamic tension between the two ideals is played out.

We show that this tension, when handled effectively, can be politically fertile in the sense of producing new democratic energy for grassroots political efficacy. We show that faith-based community organizing offers an excellent setting for advancing this analytic agenda, because major sectors of that movement are embedded in highly diverse communities and are committed to sustaining internal multicultural pluralism and do so in ways demonstrably effective in external political terms. All of the above have been true of faith-based community organizing at the *local* level for some time, but two new factors make this analysis particularly timely. First, in the last ten years the field has become markedly more ambitious (and significantly more effective) at projecting power onto higher-level political terrain and into more substantive political fights at the local level. The field thus has greater insight to offer an American society struggling to find adequate democratic means to combat rising inequality. Second, in the past faith-based organizing had largely kept the linkage between multicultural pluralism and the struggle for racial equity *implicit* in its work, whereas today large sectors of the field now make that linkage *explicit*.[8] At a time when concerns are growing about deepening inequality between racial/ethnic groups in America, making this linkage explicit is critical for a society in which children of color already constitute a majority of those under eighteen years of age, a society on a trajectory to become a majority-minority country in those children's lifetimes.

This introduction briefly frames the theoretical and philosophical issues at stake in the tension between the democratic ideals of universalism and multiculturalism, introduces the social movement that offers a concrete setting for exploring and addressing that tension, and provides an overview of the book's chapters and central argument.

Democracy and Multiculturalism: Dilemmas
of the Democratic Public Sphere

Moral and political universalism . . . are not irreconcilable with the recognition
of, respect for, and democratic negotiation of certain forms of difference.

—Seyla Benhabib, *The Claims of Culture*

Seyla Benhabib, a leading social theorist, captures the complexity of the
struggle to preserve the promise of universalist democracy while simultaneously coming to terms with the multicultural reality of contemporary
society. The "forms of difference" for which strong multiculturalists argue
include those based on race, ethnicity, immigration status, gender, and sexual preference, as well as those carried in communities based on religious
affiliation or nationality. In arguing for a certain kind of democratic universalism, Benhabib takes seriously the legitimacy of particular claims emanating from these communities, but she argues that those claims best contribute to the long-term development of a democratic public sphere when
they are embedded within broader, more universalistic understandings of
democratic life, such as those derived from the work of Jürgen Habermas.[9]

Although not widely known to nonacademic American audiences,
Habermas provides the framework for much contemporary thinking about
the nature of democracy.[10] Central to his theory and widely adopted among
social theorists is the concept of a *democratic public sphere*: all those settings
in which people deliberate together regarding publicly relevant concerns.
Via the public sphere, the democratic will takes shape—that is, the building
up of sufficient collective will to impel shared civil initiatives and governmental action to solve problems faced by contemporary society. Also via
the public sphere, subcultures that unnecessarily restrict personal rights, opportunities, and autonomy can be interrogated and encouraged to change,
over time contributing to democratizing trends throughout a culture. Importantly, however, it is also via the democratic public sphere that those
subcultures can argue back in favor of the validity of their worldviews and
commitments—and why *society* should change.[11] Thus Habermas offers a
society-centered view of democratic life instead of the highly government-
centered and market-centered views more familiar to most audiences. In
providing a focus on cultural and institutional dynamics in civil society,
Habermas's framework offers a way to think about long-term political and
economic reform as partly a struggle to reshape the institutions and cultural
assumptions that inform political and economic decision making.

Benhabib and another feminist theorist, Nancy Fraser, were among the most cogent early interlocutors and critics of Habermas's initial analysis of the democratic public sphere, which was centered on the abstract notion of an "idealized speech community."[12] Both were concerned with the way Habermas's abstract conceptualization elided questions of power, especially the way powerful interests exclude or suppress marginal voices even within what is ostensibly a democratic space. But they developed their positions vis-à-vis Habermas in quite distinct ways. In counterpoint to Habermas's universalism, Fraser developed the concept of *subaltern counterpublic spheres*—alternative public spaces outside of the public arena that money and power dominate. Such spaces shelter subaltern groups from the stigmatizing assumptions that constitute them as outside public discourse. In such subaltern spaces, the marginalized can formulate their own identities and recognize their own dignity—and ultimately insist on that dignity in the wider society. Thus, in the past, men without property, women in general, racialized minorities, and subnational ethnic groups all built subaltern counterpublic spheres from which to contest their marginal status. Today in American society, we witness the same dynamic among undocumented immigrants and same-sex couples seeking a recognized, legitimate status.[13] Fraser's position, while not in principle hostile to universal democratic standards, in practice emphasizes insights in keeping with a more deeply multiculturalist version of democratic theory.[14]

In contrast, Benhabib's position remains grounded in the universalist democratic tradition derived from Habermas. Benhabib draws on that tradition to articulate a critique of what she calls the "four dogmas of multiculturalism." She identifies these as (1) the dogmas of cultural holism, (2) the overly socialized self, (3) the prison house of perspectives, and (4) the distrust of the universal.[15] We can summarize her concerns as follows: even when multiculturalists are motivated by a proper desire to advance the cause of justice for marginalized social groups, they promote understandings of society that ultimately undermine that very project. They often promote a view of each subculture as an integrated whole, relatively static and sufficient unto itself, with its own standards of justice held without interrogation by other views. However, subcultures are dynamic; they are embedded in history and inevitably shaped by interaction with other subcultures. In particular, each embodies its own forms of injustice and illegitimate power, which must be interrogated (in part from within, but also via critique from the standpoint of other subcultures). According to Benhabib, multiculturalists give culture such power over people that individuals and groups appear locked into culturally determined views rather than being capable of contesting and combining cultural views as they go about constructing their own political agency in the world. Benhabib argues that in rightly rejecting the claim to rational impartiality and universalism made by some white, male, heterosexual, Western perspectives, multiculturalists implicitly throw out any standards of fairness by which social policy might be judged. Ironically, they do so in the name of a multiculturalist project seeking precisely such fairness for marginalized groups. As a result, from this standpoint even the best-intentioned multiculturalists face what Benhabib calls "the fundamental dilemmas of multiculturalism"[16]—that is, the tensions between universal egalitarian democratic standards and the implications of their own appeal to particularist cultural identities.

Ultimately, Benhabib embraces Fraser's argument for recognition of marginalized identities and redistributive policies to benefit the least advantaged—but she does so while insisting that such policies be universalist:

> I would indeed agree with defenders of strong group identities that to redress entrenched social inequalities redistributive programs need to be in place, and that the democratic dialogue about collective identity should not result in the neglect of the needs of the weak, the needy, the downtrodden, and the victim of discrimination. Here again a more universalistic perspective suggests itself: In the allocation of distributive benefits, why not find programs and procedures that foster group solidarity across color, culture, ethnic, and racial lines? Why not universalize the entitlement to certain benefits to all groups in a society? . . . [she goes on to suggest high minimum wages, better access to health care and education] The public conversation would then be about redistribution as well as recognition. Yet the goal would be to redress socioeconomic inequalities among the population at large via measures and policies that reflect intergroup solidarity and cultural hybridity.[17]

By embracing and extending a core insight from Fraser's work, Benhabib moves beyond a caricature that would equate all multiculturalist positions as "identity politics" conceived in narrowly ethnocentric terms. She explains that when multiculturalist claims are reconceived as a "politics of recognition,"[18] they can be voiced and debated without simply "accepting that the only way to do so is by affirming a group's right to (unilaterally) define the content as well as the boundaries of its own identity." That is, multiculturalist claims *can* be asserted without dissolving the healthy interchange between cultures as well as the healthy contestation of inequality within them that produces democratic progress. Benhabib argues on theoretical grounds that this will occur only when multiculturalist claims are embedded within an overarching universalist aspiration.

Iris Marion Young adopts an even stronger multiculturalist position, insisting on the limitations of any universalist claim:[19]

> I agree with many of the points that Benhabib makes about the wide range of issues she takes up in this essay. Like many others who in recent years have worried about the dangers of group-based political claims, however, Benhabib wrongly reduces the differences that motivate such claims to culture. In these remarks I want to reinstate a more generic interpretation of a politics of difference in which culturally based claims are only one species. In this more generic understanding, the problems that motivate social movements around group difference have to do with dominant norms and expectations in the society. Dominant institutions support norms and expectations that privilege some groups and render others deviant. Some of these are cultural norms, but others are norms of capability, social role, sexual desire, or location in the division of labor. Most group-based political claims of justice are responses to these structures of privilege and disadvantage.[20]

Despite Young's protestations, her focus on "norms of capability, social role, sexual desire" seems to evoke precisely the kinds of cultural norms that Benhabib discusses. But Young's position does foster great clarity regarding the disadvantaged *power* position of subaltern groups in democratic dialogue. To the extent such dialogue occurs on cultural terrain defined by dominant institutions, subaltern groups are often marginalized or stigmatized *within* whatever dialogue occurs. She thus continues, "Attention to the issues of justice [that] many group-based claims raise, however, goes beyond principles of tolerance and openness, to the criticism and transformation of social structures that marginalize and normalize," and, later, "What is at stake in a politics of difference is *privilege* more than 'recognition.'"[21] Thus Young's framing more clearly marks out ground from which subaltern groups can question the terms of privilege across the boundaries of multicultural settings.

As fruitful as these ideas have been in exploring the dynamics of democracy and the struggles of subaltern groups to deepen democratic life, they have also generated sharply contested understandings of democratic ideals. Those debates have been especially sharp around the question of multiculturalism and democracy. We can locate our democratic growing pains at the tension between two questions: First, how can highly valued "forms of difference" be sustained in the face of the disruptive and (at times) homogenizing forces of modernity and globalization? Some communities attempt to sustain their difference by striving to wall themselves off from critique or influence from those who do not share and thus would reject their own commitments and construction of reality. Such "walling off" occurs in socially powerful groups because they strive to avoid engagement with those who might question their power; it occurs in marginalized groups as they seek shelter from the stigmatizing gaze of the powerful. In both cases, isolation can serve to avoid egalitarian and democratic pressures (for example, pressure to discard assumptions of white privilege among the powerful; or to discard sexist, anti-immigrant, or antigay assumptions in some marginalized groups). The second question therefore arises: How can full commitment to the egalitarian ideals of democracy be sustained if any self-identified "form of difference" can legitimately wall itself off from being questioned by the wider democratic dialogue? In the long term, how we answer these questions will determine whether democracy will be substantively deepened via the hard dialogue of differing worldviews, or simply fragmented into competing worldviews incapable of engaging one another constructively.

This book explores these questions while asking what a shared future for all members of American society might look like—not just any "shared future" but rather one that could be termed *ethical democracy*. Ethical democracy entails not simply the presence of a particular set of electoral institutions or political arrangements, nor does it assume that elected political representatives are ethical virtuosos. Rather, the term *ethical democracy* is rooted in the early democratic theorists of American pragmatism and marks off a particular way of living together and imagining ourselves as inhabiting a shared future in a free society.[22] Such a way of living together requires democratic institutions to channel shared desires into public policy and laws, but it also requires an underlying democratic culture that shapes individuals capable of self-government, of advocating for equal economic opportunity, of deliberating together and fostering political voice within all societal sectors. Ethical democracy thus demands attention to the cultural and institutional underpinnings of democratic life, not simply to partisan politics during elections; it involves habits of ongoing criticism of structures of economic or political domination and advocacy for movements that foster democratic agency from below.

We suggest that the struggle to construct a shared future of ethical democracy must take seriously both the universalist and multiculturalist emphases within democratic theory. We ask how—in a deliberative democracy in which elected representatives make ultimate political decisions,

yet are in principle accountable to all via a participatory society-wide dialogue—the workings of the democratic public sphere relate to the subaltern counterpublics rooted in particular communities of interest. We argue that the field of faith-based organizing offers important lessons for an
American public struggling to combine universalist democratic ideals with
an increasingly multicultural reality—in what will soon be a thoroughly
multicultural society, as new immigrant arrivals and demographic diffusion
spread diversity into settings that were once bastions of white subculture.

Those hoping to build a shared future of ethical democracy must also
struggle with questions of *power*. Dominant institutional and cultural patterns, even those that ultimately frustrate the best aspirations of all, also
benefit some societal sectors—and those sectors use their power to resist
change. As we argue in the concluding chapter, such hegemonic patterns
typically change through some combination of "top-down" initiatives (for
example, new legislation, new interests of economic elites) and "bottom-
up" transformation (for example, social movements, demographic changes,
and cultural change). All intentional efforts to foster social reform, including the struggle to build ethical democracy, must therefore generate forms
of counterhegemonic power. Thus while our analysis focuses on the creative tensions between universalist and multiculturalist democratic commitments, questions of power are never far from the surface—and we return explicitly to those questions in the conclusion.

One way the field negotiates the universalist-multiculturalist tension is
by thinking about social policy in terms of what john powell (he does not
capitalize his names) has called "targeted universalism" (see chapter 4).[23]
Targeted universalism involves setting universal *goals* for equal opportunities and social outcomes; its means of attaining those goals address the
particular needs and draw on the particular strengths of concrete communities with their specific histories. Such organizing by no means shelters
subaltern communities from the pressure of democratic norms and demands of responsible citizenship in a diverse society; indeed, when done
well it exposes communities to the full challenge of engagement in the
complex demands of public life in a culturally and racially diverse, scien-
tifically and technologically based, polarized society with rising levels of
economic inequality.

Significant sectors of faith-based community organizing use targeted
universalism to negotiate the tension between universalist and multiculturalist understandings of the democratic challenge. In studying their efforts,
we can most clearly see that tension's creative potential, rather than assum-
ing that it necessarily undermines democratic work.

Universalist and Multiculturalist Democracy in Action: The Scale and Strategic Ambition of Today's Faith-Based Community Organizing

Contemporary community organizing in the United States draws from a variety of figures in the history of grassroots American democracy, including Jane Addams, Saul Alinsky, Cesar Chavez, and Martin Luther King Jr., as well as from union organizing and the movements for civil rights of African Americans, women, and Hispanics.[24] Out of that broad tradition, Ed Chambers and the Industrial Areas Foundation (IAF) pioneered early elements of a model of organizing based more explicitly in community institutions—primarily but not exclusively religious congregations—a model that has been adopted and reworked by a variety of organizations. Today, most faith-based community organizing efforts are affiliated with one of several sponsoring networks. Nationally, these include the PICO National Network, the Industrial Areas Foundation, the Gamaliel Foundation, and National People's Action (the last does both institution-based and individual-based organizing). Important regional networks include Direct Action and Research Training Center (DART) in the Southeast and Midwest and the InterValley Project (IVP) in New England, as well as state-level collaborations (most prominently the Ohio Organizing Collaborative) and several statewide efforts internal to each network or collaborative efforts between these groups and other forms of organizing. In addition, a smaller number of organizations doing faith-based organizing exist independent of the formal sponsoring networks. Although each of the organizations mentioned above has developed its own organizing approach, they remain sufficiently similar to treat them as one field. Their "tool kits" of organizing practices overlap considerably, and all are built with *institutions* as their foundation—that is, participants are not "members" of the organization, but rather become involved via congregations, labor unions, parent-teacher organizations, neighborhood organizations, or other institutions.[25] More broadly still, a variety of other community organizing efforts built on individual rather than institutional membership also form part of this tradition. The Center for Community Change, the National Domestic Workers Alliance, the Center for Third World Organizing, and ACORN (before its collapse, with its work still carried forward in some states) represent important strands of this model. Other related organizing models include the work of Interfaith Worker Justice, Clergy and Laity United for Economic Justice (CLUE), and the Sojourners community. But all these differ significantly from the faith-based model founded on institutions that is analyzed here.[26]

The organizations studied here train grassroots leaders to push for public policy to improve the quality of life for residents of poor, working-class, and middle-class communities. They sponsor "political actions" or "accountability sessions" at which they call on political officials to support particular public policies; organizations based in religious congregations undergird that call by articulating a vision of a better community and a good society, drawing on the languages of faith traditions. Each member institution typically works on issues of concern in its local area and collaborates with the larger coalition to address issues requiring citywide solutions. This model of organizing has often helped produce policy change regarding city services, policing, low-income housing, health care, immigration enforcement, and public education; the fields' most sophisticated practitioners have organized and trained long-standing teams of leaders in communities that previously suffered from a lack of effective democratic representation.

Because each local coalition carries a unique name, and because until recently nearly all such organizing focused on local issues, the broad reach of faith-based community organizing in the United States often goes unrecognized beyond the local level. But in fact these organizations have built a significant presence in American society and faith communities. As of 2011, 189 local community organizing coalitions rooted in institutions existed in the United States, with a presence in forty of the fifty states. In order to see clearly the contours of that presence, we draw on our National Study of Community Organizing Coalitions, a new national census of all institution-based organizing efforts in the United States.[27] These coalitions, as reported in detail in subsequent chapters, are among the most racially, ethnically, and socioeconomically diverse civil society organizations in America. They also represent substantial religious diversity. Of the approximately 4,500 community institutions that provide the foundation for this work, more than 3,500 are religious congregations from a variety of traditions. The strong majority is from the liberal and moderate Protestant (32%), historic African American (24%), and the Roman Catholic (27%) denominations. But Jewish synagogues (5%) and Unitarian Universalist churches (4%) also have a growing presence, each having more than doubled their proportion of participating congregations in the last decade. Evangelical Christian (4%) and Pentecostal Christian (2%) churches also engage in this work, but at levels not nearly reflective of their presence in the wider field of American congregations—in which they represent nearly half of all congregations. This underrepresentation is particularly acute for white evangelical churches.

The religious composition of the field should be understood in the overall context of the changing demographic and organizational structure of religion in the United States. While beyond our purposes here to fully delve into that structure, a quick summary may suffice. First, the proportion of Americans who report no religious affiliation (religious "nones") has rapidly increased over recent decades, in part because they have been alienated by faith-based voices of religious exclusivism. Religious nones now represent about a fifth of all Americans—and almost a third of Americans under the age of thirty.[28] Combined with rising religious diversity, these trends may mean that faith-based community organizing will increasingly need secular allies and that the more tolerant and diverse faith voices associated with this field will have an easier hearing in the public arena. Second, the more liberal Protestant congregations and the core urban churches within the historic African American and Catholic traditions—all mainstays of the faith-based organizing field—have undergone fiscal and organizational decline in recent decades. Such decline may or may not continue, but it has clearly presented challenges to the field in ways we will later see. Third, white evangelicals and African American and Latino evangelicals of the Pentecostal tradition have all shown a growing propensity to address issues of inequality in society. Reflecting this trend, these groups have become more active in faith-based organizing, as have Jewish synagogues and Unitarian Universalist churches. Finally, sectors of American Catholicism that have long been committed to social justice and addressing inequality are showing new vigor under Pope Francis I. This new energy and the potential, under Francis's inspiration, for renewed institutional priority to Catholic social teaching may buttress Catholic involvement in faith-based organizing and, more generally, strengthen the Catholic voice on issues of inequality in society. All these contextual factors will shape the trajectory of faith-based organizing in the future, and thus its ability and desire to link public policy to universal and multicultural democratic priorities.

The most consequential example of faith-based organizing's effort to link universalist and multiculturalist democratic commitments—which also reflects the field's strategic ambition to effectively address inequality and policy paralysis at the national and state levels—lies precisely in what is arguably the most important domestic policy initiative of recent decades: health care reform. At the forefront of this effort is the PICO National Network.[29] The PICO National Network sponsors a particular model of faith-based community organizing in nineteen states, through the work of fifty local organizing coalitions that the network refers to as "federations."[30] We will see more of the PICO National Network later; here, we briefly profile its national work in order to demonstrate the field's emergent strategic ambitions. PICO first achieved prominent national-level influence during the debate under the administration of President George W. Bush regarding reauthorization of the State Children's Health Insurance Program (SCHIP), the primary federal program to provide insurance coverage to uninsured children (approximately fifteen million American children lacked health insurance at the time of SCHIP's enactment in 1997). In 2007 and 2008, PICO leaders testifying before Congress provided much of the faith-based moral voice in favor of reauthorization, and twice Congress passed the relevant legislation—only to see it vetoed by President Bush as unwarranted federal spending. As one of its first acts under President Barack Obama in 2009, Congress once again passed SCHIP legislation, again with testimony from PICO leaders. Those leaders were in the front row of invited guests at the March 2009 White House ceremony at which Obama signed SCHIP reauthorization, accompanied by Vice President Joseph Biden, other leaders in the administration, and the congressional leaders who had seen the legislation through.[31]

The PICO National Network continued its heavy involvement in the national health care reform effort during the 2009–10 debate to shape the signature domestic initiative of the Obama administration's first term: the Affordable Care Act (ACA, a.k.a. Obamacare). Through the ACA, the administration sought to universalize access to insured health care and bring down the long-term cost of health care provision in American society. Throughout this period, the final shape of the legislation was very much in doubt—as was its ultimate passage until the very end, as congressional Republicans emboldened by the "Tea Party" movement united to defeat it. PICO was a prominent part of the coalition seeking to shape the legislation in ways maximizing affordability and access: affordability for low- and middle-income families and individuals, and access to health care in poor communities. PICO leaders testified in Congress, met with administration policy makers, and rallied on Capitol Hill and in the home districts of key legislators around the country. Most of that effort went into pushing for substantial subsidies to help low-income workers afford health insurance in the new health care exchanges and coverage for immigrant workers; both items were eventually adopted in the final legislation.

Through this effort, faith-based community organizing demonstrated its capacity to work effectively for significant policy change, not only at neighborhood and metropolitan levels but also in state and national policy arenas.[32] Particularly important for the success of such higher-level organizing efforts are three factors: (1) the ability to mobilize "everyday folks" (in both home congressional districts and periodic national events) who are perceived as not the typical Beltway activists, and thus granted a certain credibility in policy circles; (2) the ability to do so over sustained periods (measured in years) in order to shape gradual policy emergence, build a political reputation, and forge lasting coalitions with other organizations in favor of pragmatic policies to benefit poor and middle-class Americans; and (3) perhaps the unique strength of faith-based organizing as a sector—the ability of religious leaders to fluently connect such pragmatic policy alternatives to the deep moral languages and ethical framing carried by their various faith traditions.[33]

While the health care debate represents the highest profile the field has attained on successful national legislation so far, faith-based organizing has come to play a salient role in the public arena at the local, state, and national levels in a wide range of settings around the country. As we shall see, the field built that influence on a foundation of universal democratic values, the mobilization of highly diverse constituencies, and an embrace of the multicultural reality of those constituencies. Furthermore, some sectors of faith-based organizing have made working for racial equity—both within their organization and in the public sphere—an explicit commitment. The field thus constitutes an ideal case study for understanding the tensions between the universal norms of democratic theory and the specific democratic demands our emergent multicultural reality generates. Such tensions represent a dilemma within contemporary democracy. But we argue that it is a dilemma fertile with constructive possibilities for building a shared future for all Americans, a future that narrows our yawning chasms of inequality and ends the strategic policy paralysis in the nation's capital. In so doing, such work might enable democracy to once again serve as a beacon to people the world over.

The Other Democratic Dilemma: Religion in the Public Sphere

Using faith-based organizing as a case study of universalist-multiculturalist tensions also introduces a second key theme that remains in the background for much of our analysis yet should not disappear from our sight: the complex role of religion in contemporary democratic debate and in helping the field of faith-based organizing manage its internal diversity.

Culturally defensive religious forms—and at times explicitly anti-intellectual and fundamentalist expressions of them—have come to dominate religiously framed public discourse, at least in the popular perception based on media coverage. That perception of blanket religious conservatism across issues from access to birth control to sexual behavior to gay marriage to tax policy to American and Israeli policy in Palestine represents a gross oversimplification of complex religious terrain, and the conservativism itself often oversimplifies complex religious teachings. But the perception is pervasive and has combined with public scandals regarding clergy sexual misconduct and irresponsible religious authority to undermine the credibility of religious voices within American political discourse. Although no doubt celebrated among strong secular fundamentalists, this weakening of public religion represents a significant democratic loss. Historically, religious actors played central roles in democratic movements, from the nineteenth-century abolition of slavery to Progressive-era urban reform to the movements for the civil rights of minorities to the struggles to end apartheid in South Africa and gross human rights violations in Central America. It remains an open question whether faith-based community organizing can contribute to reestablishing a credible religious voice for deepening democracy that is broadly accepted as legitimate in the American public arena.

Benhabib's argument for a political and moral universalism that exposes all human communities and cultural traditions to democratizing critique—and explicitly *against* those models of multiculturalism that would particularize cultural groups and shield them from the claims, opportunities, and challenges of shared democratic life—carries an important implication for this book's analysis of religion and public life. Whereas academic multiculturalists typically either exclude religious voices from serious consideration as democratic protagonists or see religion as simply another set of incommensurable cultural strands that can be tolerated by society, Benhabib's version of political and moral universalism must include religious traditions as potential democratic interlocutors. But how can they best play this role?

A given tradition or community (religious or otherwise) can certainly argue that some emergent democratic norm should not apply to them, on the grounds of the integrity and self-understanding of the tradition. But all such communities face rising democratic expectations, both among their own dissenting members and in wider American society; all face evolving societal standards of what constitutes the minimal acceptable norms of democratic life. So traditional arguments may or may not carry the day. Gradually, even the most traditional of religions change, driven by ongoing internal discernment and shifting societal priorities and standards. This need not be seen as giving up the founding religious truths of the tradition, but rather can be seen as the ongoing discernment of the implications of religious truth in light of new realities and keener insight—or even of ongoing divine revelation.[34]

Wood has written elsewhere more extensively about the role of religion in public life, not the focus here.[35] But given that faith-based community organizing is primarily comprised of religious congregations representing multiple traditions, it is worth noting that religion represents a key mechanism through which these groups live out their commitment to universalism within a multiculturally rooted social movement. For some readers, this will represent a sticking point. For those whose only real exposure to religion has been via the voices of fundamentalism emanating from strident factions of evangelical Christian, Catholic, Muslim, Jewish, Hindu, or Orthodox traditions in different countries, the very definition of a democratic public sphere seems to exclude religion from any democratic public role. Fundamentalist definitions of truth claim to lie beyond critical reason and thus are not open to deliberative debate. But this represents simply a caricature of religion's historical public voice and fails to capture the reality of much more sophisticated and nuanced voices of religion today. Over time, Habermas recognized the ways that religious traditions can open themselves to critical reason and thus become valuable actors within the democratic public sphere.[36]

The *reflexivity* of religious traditions is the crucial issue, as shown in the works of Michele Dillon and Jerome Baggett. Dillon embraces Habermas's democratic criterion noted above but argues that certain forms of religion—even those most deeply rooted in "tradition"—can embrace and practice a kind of ongoing self-revision that meets the demand for openness of all truth claims to critical evaluation and ongoing revision.[37] Using the Catholic Church as a case study of a religious tradition asserting a strong claim to fundamental truth, she analyzes how any given *specific* religiously defined truth is critically appropriated, interpreted, and potentially revised within the context of commitment to the *overall* tradition. Although Dillon certainly does not suggest that contemporary Catholicism is a paragon of such reflexivity, she argues that openness to such reflexivity is crucial for religious traditions to remain credible and legitimate interlocutors in a democratic public arena. More recently, Jerome Baggett shows how this kind of reflexivity undergirds the continuing engagement and vitality of American Catholics from across the political and theological spectra.[38] In this way, religious actors can participate in the democratic public sphere, both as active interlocutors in societal deliberation and by exposing their tradition's teachings and practices to ongoing dialogue and potential critique. Religious traditions thus become credible public actors to the extent they embrace the fundamental norms of democratic participation, such as willingness to listen to competing societal voices (including scientific claims, alternative political positions, and other religious voices).[39]

While this theme of religion in the public arena is not a central focus of this book, it does return in two important ways in the end. First, we show that religiously grounded cultural practices are crucial to how these organizations manage internal racial and ethnic diversity (as well as socioeconomic diversity). Second, we argue that religiously grounded capacities for reflexivity and deliberation represent key practices through which faith-based community organizing links its universalist and multiculturalist democratic commitments.

Thus the role of religion in public life reemerges in the conclusion for both analytical and ethical reasons: analytically, because the faith-based organizing field operates precisely at the intersection of religion and politics, and ultimately its democratic capacity draws important sustenance from its spiritual grounding; ethically, because faith-based organizing represents a concrete effort to deepen democracy in American life, which we consider a central ethical goal of our time.

It seems hard to disagree with the notion of "deepening democracy."[40] But in invoking this as an overarching need for our time, we mean something specific and more controversial. Deepening democracy involves reversing the rising economic inequality in American life while simultaneously improving the ability of everyday citizens to have an impact in shaping societal priorities. That is, deepening democracy involves increasing "equality" and "voice" in American society, in ways that build toward a shared future closer to the ideal we term *ethical democracy*.[41] Since some religious congregations are profoundly engaged in this work, we pay attention to religion's role in it while focusing primarily on the interplay of universalizing and multiculturalist strands within the democratic public sphere.

Outline of the Book's Argument

This book's central theme revolves around three key arguments. First, that a commitment to a certain kind of moral and political universalism can simultaneously sustain strong engagement with multiculturalism (in this case via practices of reflexivity and deliberation within a democratic public sphere internal to a movement). Second, that some sectors of the faith-based organizing field combine such reflective multiculturalism-within-universalism with the organizational infrastructure and strategic capacity needed to make a significant impact on economic inequality, policy paralysis, and racial injustice in American life. Third, that the field as a whole still falls short of living up to that promise. To defend those claims, we show: (a) that the field of faith-based community organizing has sufficient institutional scale to actually make a difference in civil and political society; (b) that at least a significant portion of the field succeeds reasonably well at linking universal democratic values and multicultural commitments; and (c) that the field effectively brings those values and commitments to bear on public policy, but could do so more widely than is the case today. If faith-based community organizing does so, we argue that it can indeed help shape a shared future through which American society moves closer to an ethical democracy less bedeviled by economic inequality, policy paralysis, and racial injustice.

The chapters of part I address the first issue. We draw on systematic new evidence to argue that faith-based community organizing today has the organizational infrastructure, diverse leadership, and significant elements of the strategic capacity and organizational culture to play this role. Chapter 1 lays the groundwork for the subsequent analysis by presenting the overall national profile of the field, especially its significant growth in scale and capacity over the last decade. The next two chapters present the results of the National Study of Community Organizing Coalitions, a census of essentially all faith-based community organizing efforts in the United States. Chapter 2 provides a detailed demographic profile of the local leadership within faith-based community organizing and highlights the emergence of a more diverse field of leaders (in part via the internal struggle to recruit, retain, and promote a diverse leadership base). Chapter 3 describes the field's organizational infrastructure and strategic capacity, suggesting that although the former is impressive, the latter is uneven and at times disappointing. The chapter closes with a brief comparative analysis of how the field handles a quite different dimension of diversity: the challenges associated with having diverse sponsoring religious traditions. In keeping with the quantitative data being analyzed, our writing in part I strives for a relatively objective tone, laying out the contours of the field and the organizational underpinnings of its work to address economic inequality, policy paralysis, and racial injustice.

Part II offers an extended case study of one particular network's shift to a focus on racial equity within its own structures and on racial justice in America. Because part II draws on ethnographic and interview data, the tone shifts to a more interpretive mode of analysis as we strive to understand the dynamics of organizational culture that accompany such a transformation. Chapter 4 discusses how the universalist moral and political orientation that underlies the political culture of faith-based community organizing plays out in the context of that shift, particularly vis-à-vis African American communities but with an eye toward how those communities intersect with predominantly white, Latino, and Asian/Pacific institutions. Chapter 5 analyzes the highest-profile national campaign for racial equity and racial justice within faith-based community organizing today. Chapter 6 offers a less "digested" view into these dynamics via a 2013 interview with a key national leader of that campaign. Chapter 7 steps back to suggest what these efforts to deepen democracy can tell us about the role of spirituality and creativity in democratic struggles, and how those struggles might be better grounded in American culture and institutions. Drawing on the concept of "ethical democracy" that Wood's previous work used to characterize the ethos that underlies faith-based community organizing, we argue throughout that efforts to sustain moral/political universalism and multiculturalism can learn a great deal from faith-based organizing's commitment to ethical democracy—but it will only do so if the field succeeds in embodying that ideal and projecting it more assertively into American political society. The conclusion reflects on the way forward into a more satisfying and democratic future shared by all.

PART ONE

The strategic infrastructure, ambition, and racial/ethnic diversity of faith-based community organizing

Figure 1.1 Gamaliel leaders including Rev. David Bigsby from Metro Chicago hear US Representative Sheila Jackson Lee of the Congressional Progressive Caucus. (Courtesy of Gamaliel)

ONE

The Scale of Organizing Today: The National Study of Community Organizing Coalitions

Despite the fact that community organizing has existed for decades, the broad field Saul Alinsky founded—drawing on strands of noncommunist labor organizing, the settlement house movement, the Chicago school of ethnographic research, and other preexisting forms of community engagement for promoting grassroots democracy—was not even really recognized as one field until recently. To the extent it was recognized at all, it was seen as a disconnected set of local efforts. The once high-profile work of the Industrial Areas Foundation (IAF) continued under the leadership of Ed Chambers, but by the mid-1970s it no longer commanded widespread public attention.

Following Alinsky's death in 1972, the field had splintered into competing training centers. As the community institutions that had provided the organizational backbone for Alinsky's work declined, innovative extensions of his organizing model were being tested in new organizing efforts around the country. The most important innovation—building tighter links to religious congregations and traditions, and thereby linking faith communities in poor communities to grassroots democratic work, in part inspired by the movement for African American civil rights—was pioneered initially by the IAF organization Communities Organized for Public Service (COPS) in San Antonio, Texas.[1]

COPS's innovative approach in San Antonio spread across the Texas IAF under Ernesto Cortés and Christine Stephens, and to the rest of the IAF under Ed Chambers via work by Mike Gecan, Arne Graf, Gerald Taylor, and Dick Harmon. Elements of that approach were adapted into the emerging organizing models of the PICO National Network via the work of John Baumann, Scott Reed, Stephanie Gut, José Carrasco, and Ron Snyder; the Gamaliel Foundation via Greg Galluzo and Mary Gonzales; the Direct Action and Research Training Center (DART) via John Caulkins and Holly Holcombe; and to a variety of smaller regional networks or independent organizations via a variety of figures including Tom Gaudette, Shel Trapp, Moshe ben Aron, Lew Finfer, Ken Galdston, and later via Eugene Williams, Kim Bobo, George Goehl, James Mumm, and others. Each of these organizing networks further innovated on the basic Alinsky model, generally with greater emphasis on religious congregations as the core of the organizing infrastructure—in part because other institutions in poor communities were hollowing out.

Given this organizational innovation and proliferation and due to the thin academic writing on the field for three decades, by the turn of the century few people appear to have been aware that such a "field" existed, other than its participants and the foundation program officers who funded their work. Some wider awareness had been generated by the work of the IAF in educational reform in Texas in the 1980s and by PICO's work on public education and health care in California the late 1990s. But otherwise, knowledge of such a field rarely transcended the very local work of particular organizations. Not until the early 2000s did the field of faith-based community organizing begin to receive extensive scholarly attention.[2]

We now know a great deal more about the field, thanks to much broader scholarly attention and recent writing by key professional organizers.[3] But other than one 1999 study (see below), we have lacked a comprehensive look across all such organizing efforts. That has now changed as a result of a recent comprehensive census of the entire field, the National Study of Community Organizing Coalitions.[4] This chapter draws on that census and the wider literature to portray the full terrain of faith-based community organizing in the United States, including its organizational infrastructure, leadership, strategic capacity, and the organizational cultures within it. In the concluding section, we argue that the field today occupies an impressive strategic position within American civil society and yet as a whole falls short of its potential role in helping to build ethical democracy by confronting the challenges facing American political culture and institutions.

Background

The National Study of Community Organizing Coalitions, conducted in 2011, extends and improves upon a 1999 national census of the field that was conducted by funders.[5] The 1999 study provided the first systematic national data on the field and thus offers a baseline for understanding changes in the scope and scale of this organizing model and its evolution over the last decade and a half.[6]

In that period, both the national context and the field of community organizing changed substantially. Economic inequality rose dramatically, money flowed into electoral campaigns virtually uncontrolled following the Citizens United decision by the US Supreme Court, and national political institutions grew more polarized. Furthermore, the three religious sectors that composed the membership core of the field in 1999—urban Catholic, Mainline Protestant, and historic African American churches— each experienced stagnant or declining memberships and in some cases significant institutional crises.[7] All these changes had important implications for community organizing efforts. Meanwhile, as documented below, the field evolved and grew by extending its geographic reach beyond the urban core and into new states and cities, by developing a broader base of member institutions, by increasing its collaborative work with other kinds of organizing efforts, and by leveraging its power beyond the local level to more systematically address issues at state and national levels.[8]

In recognition of these changes—and the opportunity they presented to study significant strategic and organizational shifts in a dynamic social movement sector with reasonable baseline data—we collaborated with Interfaith Funders in 2011 to conduct a major census of the entire field.

On Nomenclature: Faith-Based or Institution-Based or Broad-Based Organizing?

The field under study here has been known by various names, with some organizations believing "congregation-based" or "broad-based" community organizing best represents their work. Both are appropriate in particular contexts, but neither quite characterizes the field as a whole. The shift in the composition of member institutions described above, along with the differing mix of congregations and noncongregational institutions in different networks, suggests that the term *congregation*-based community organizing no longer represents the field. Yet all these organizations have significant congregational memberships, and most rely heavily on religious worldviews in constructing their organizational cultures.[9] Due to the cultural centrality of religious discourse and meaning in the field, and what we show elsewhere to be the important role of religious practices in how the field sustains its racial, ethnic, and class diversity, we use the term *faith-based community organizing* throughout the book to refer to the field as a whole and highlight its core cultural dynamic: the continuing centrality of faith communities, prayer practices, and religiously tied ethical framing of issues in most organizing work.[10] We refer to individual local organizations as faith-based community organizing *coalitions* to highlight their diverse base of member institutions.

Research Design

The National Study of Community Organizing Coalitions was designed to replicate and build upon the 1999 study by surveying the entire field of faith-based community organizing. Wood, Fulton, and key collaborators from within Interfaith Funders formulated the goals and contents of the study in consultation with local organizers, national organizing staff, foundation program officers, denominational funders, and scholars of the field.[11] In addition to asking identical questions from the 1999 study, several new items were added to better assess the work on specific issues, collaborative relations, and religious practices within the field. The final survey instrument was designed and implemented by Fulton, and it has two parts: an online survey that gathered extensive data on each faith-based community organizing coalition's history, constituents, collaborators, activities, finances, and issue work; and a set of customized spreadsheets that respondents used to provide detailed demographic information about their coalition's member institutions, board members, and paid staff.

The study defined a faith-based community organizing coalition as a local organization that practices the institution-based model of organizing (that is, its membership is composed of institutions rather than individuals), has an office address, and has at least one paid organizer on staff. Based on these criteria, 189 active coalitions were identified using databases from every national and regional faith-based community organizing network, databases from fourteen foundations that fund faith-based community organizing, and archived IRS 990 forms. The survey was distributed electronically to the director of every local faith-based community organizing coalition during the second half of 2011. The directors were informed that their responses would be kept confidential and that nothing would be published that identifies specific characteristics of their coalition unless they provided consent.[12] The survey achieved a response rate of 94%, gathering data on 178 faith-based community organizing coalitions and demographic information on the 4,145 member institutions plus 2,939 board members and 628 paid staff affiliated with those coalitions.[13]

The structure of the study allows the data to be analyzed at two levels.

The field level demonstrates patterns as a whole; the coalition level assesses similarities and differences among individual faith-based community organizing coalitions. In addition, the fact that we replicated items from the 1999 study and included the coalitions surveyed in 1999 means we can assess *changes* in the field (and in individual coalitions) over the last decade. This offers a more dynamic view than possible with only a one-time snapshot.[14]

As a result of these factors, this chapter presents the only available comprehensive data on the entire field of faith-based community organizing. The quality of data collection and the high response rate allow us for the first time to confidently portray the broad profile and specific characteristics of the field in ways scholars could only speculate on previously. We think our ability to do so is especially important in a context wherein some professional organizers seek to position themselves and their allies as doing the only good work; thus, a person's perception of the field may be highly distorted by working solely with any one coalition or network.[15] Through the new study, we can describe and analyze the field more accurately.

Organizational Infrastructure: The Changing Field of Organizing

Overall Growth in Organizing Infrastructure at the Local Level

Comparing the 1999 snapshot with the current state of the field reveals dramatic growth over the last decade in some key dimensions, including geographic reach and strategic depth. At the coalition level, the overall field grew by 42% from 1999 to 2011, with 102 new coalitions established and forty-six that had become inactive.[16] In most areas where a coalition had become inactive, another one has arisen to replace it.[17] Among the inactive coalitions, twenty-three had dissolved, eight are rebuilding but did not meet our criteria, fourteen had merged into another coalition, and one had stopped using the institution-based organizing model.

The overall growth of the field corresponds with its significant geographic spread. In 1999, thirty-three states had active faith-based community organizing coalitions; today, faith-based community organizing coalitions are active in forty states. New coalitions have been established in nine new states (Alaska, Alabama, Maine, Montana, New Hampshire, Nevada, Oklahoma, Virginia, and Vermont)—states characterized by dramatically different dynamics within the partisan political system, including reliably Democratic, reliably Republican, and "swing" states. The number of faith-based community organizing coalitions at least doubled in Hawai'i, Indiana, Kentucky, Mississippi, North Carolina, New Mexico, and Wisconsin. While the field has spread to new states and beyond its original base in core urban areas, it remains concentrated in metropolitan areas and in

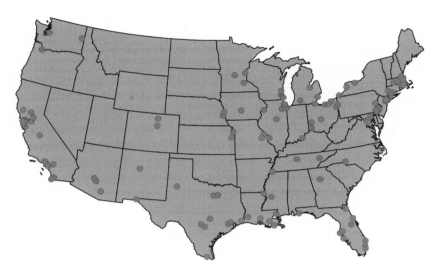

Figure 1.2 The state of the faith-based community organizing field in 1999 (N = 133).

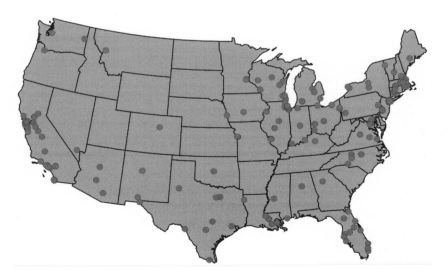

Figure 1.3 The state of the faith-based community organizing field in 2011 (N = 189).

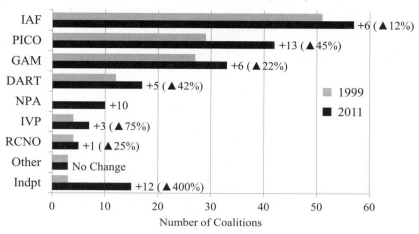

Figure 1.4 The growth of the faith-based community organizing field between 1999 and 2011.

populous states with a long history of this kind of work. Half of the coalitions reside in California, Illinois, Florida, New York, Texas, and Wisconsin.

Most faith-based community organizing coalitions are formally affiliated with a national or regional organizing network, and from 1999 to 2011 the number of local coalitions coordinated by each of these networks increased. The largest relative growth occurred among three networks that were comparatively smaller in 1999, most significantly the PICO National Network but also Gamaliel and DART. As a result, the field has become more evenly distributed among the various organizing networks. The number of coalitions not affiliated with any formal organizing network also increased during the same period but remains relatively small (fifteen coalitions, or 8%).

Expansion and Diversification of Mobilizing Structures

The foundation of the faith-based organizing infrastructure lies in its member institutions, which social movement scholars refer to as its "mobilizing structures."[18] The profile of the field's member institutions has shifted in important ways that collectively add up to a diversification of local mobilizing structures. In 1999 the field was comprised of roughly four thousand member institutions—of which 88% were religious congregations and 12% were noncongregational institutions. Even though the number of organizing coalitions increased by 42% over the last decade, the total number of their member institutions increased by only 12.5% (to approximately 4,500).[19] As a result, the median number of member institutions per coalition declined from twenty-three to twenty-one. The composition of member institutions shifted as well. Since 1999, the number of member congregations has remained the same (approximately 3,500, or 78% of member institutions), while the number of noncongregational members has doubled (increasing from approximately five hundred to one thousand, or 22% of member institutions).

Thus noncongregational community institutions—mostly made up of public schools, faith-based nonprofit agencies, labor unions, and neighborhood associations—now make up between a quarter and a fifth of all member institutions, and 70% of faith-based community organizing coalitions have at least one noncongregational member institution. Schools represent 18% of these noncongregational institutions (4% of all member institutions), faith-based nonprofits represent 16% (3.6% of all), labor unions 15% (3.4% of all), and neighborhood associations 13% (2.9% of all).[20]

In 1999, 13% of faith-based community organizing coalitions had at least one union as a member institution; by 2011 that had grown to 23%. In addition, roughly one-quarter had a school, faith-based organization, or neighborhood association as a member institution. The mix of congregations versus noncongregational member institutions varies considerably. For instance and as a broad generalization, coalitions affiliated with the PICO National Network and DART tend to be more heavily based in congregations (with some still having significant noncongregational members), whereas coalitions affiliated with the Industrial Areas Foundation and Gamaliel tend to have more noncongregational members (while still being primarily based in congregations). Coalitions affiliated with National People's Action tend to have both institutional and individual members, and some of the other networks have recently experimented with such an institutional/individual membership structure in an effort to adapt to declining institutions in poor communities.

Overall, 30% of faith-based community organizing coalitions have a member base comprised *exclusively* of congregations (down from 45% in 1999). Several networks have launched significant work specifically dedicated to using the practices of organizing to strengthen member congregations under the auspices of the Interfaith Organizing Initiative, local and national clergy caucuses, and/or training programs for future clergy and organizers.[21]

However, other changes over the last decade and a half are cause for concern regarding the state of the field. First, that the number of member institutions has increased only 12.5% while the number of sponsoring co-

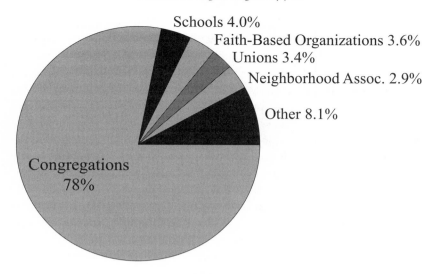

Figure 1.5 The types of member institutions.

alitions has increased 42% suggests some "thinning out" of institutional participation on the ground in local congregations. While this finding may partly reflect irregularities in the 1999 data analysis and relative decline in some of the denominations traditionally most involved in faith-based organizing, it likely also reflects the difficulties inherent in balancing vigorous local organizing and efforts to influence policy at higher levels.[22] Second, as discussed in chapters 2 and 3, while overall diversity has increased in the field, on some dimensions it has stagnated or decreased; sustaining and building upon that diversity will be critical if the field is to keep up with the changing demographics of American society. Third, the quality of staffing, local leadership development, local policy impact, and engagement in higher-level organizing all vary quite substantially from one coalition to the next. Whether the field can attain real influence on the American future and whether it can become a compelling model of civic engagement that broadly attracts people of faith and their institutions, and a new generation of young people both religious and secular, will depend significantly upon how well leaders can meet these challenges.

Scale and Scope of Organizing: The New Political Imagination

The most important change in the field in recent years—most important because it underlies and shapes the other changes, including the geographic expansion and new strategic directions documented here—has been the more ambitious political imagination that has come to characterize the best work in the field. Later chapters will evoke the touch and feel of organizing efforts informed by that new political imagination. Here, we focus on some initial evidence for it. The clearest evidence emerges from the field's efforts to change public policy at higher levels of government. In 1999 it was rare for these coalitions to address issues beyond the city level—though some strategic leaders in the field articulated the need to do so even then.[23] Since that time this organizing strategy has become much more common. The range of issue engagement now extends from the neighborhood level to the national level, and many coalitions are simultaneously addressing issues at multiple levels. Thus by 2011 over 87% of the coalitions reported addressing at least one issue at the state or national level.[24]

The issues most commonly addressed at the state or national level are immigration, health care, banking/foreclosures, public finances, employment/wages, poverty, racism, and public transportation. In other words, the field now engages many of the primary domestic policy challenges facing the country, and in its stronger versions does so at multiple levels simultaneously. They often use local organizing to build constituencies for policy change at higher levels and use advocacy in higher arenas to bring resources and policy change to local communities. To do so these coali-

Percentage of coalitions actively addressing the following issues:

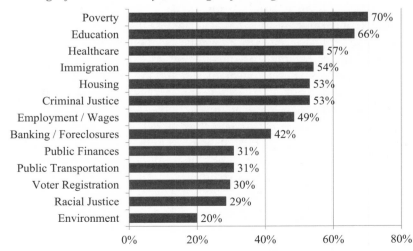

Figure 1.6 The primary issues coalitions have been actively addressing in the last two years.

tions have had to shed the earlier illusion that addressing socioeconomic issues only at the local level could fundamentally alter the reality of ongoing decline in the quality of life for working families.

Three caveats must immediately be registered. First, "in its stronger versions" means that a more ambitious political imagination has by no means spread to all corners of the field; nor has the capacity to act on such an ambitious agenda. Second, we must not lose sight of the potential trade-offs to the strategy of projecting influence in higher-level political venues, including the risk of undercutting local leadership development and local empowerment; we discuss these trade-offs in the conclusion. Third, the field's strength in focusing on socioeconomic issues affecting working families also represents a limitation; these organizations rarely engage with issues that might divide their base (same-sex marriage, gender and sexuality generally, climate change, issues of medical ethics, and such)—though note that immigration and racial equity would at one time have been on that list as well, yet the field has gained the capacity to address such issues quite head-on, as we will see.

Beyond "addressing" such issues, what kinds of success have these efforts produced, in terms of increasing the "voice" of middle- and low-income Americans or generating greater "equality" in American life? The following examples of specific accomplishments at the state and national levels that field directors reported give some sense of the kinds of gains that have been made:[25]

On health care reform:

We advocated for quality, affordable, accessible, health care for all people. National health care reforms were passed, and statewide mental health care reform legislation passed.

Our leaders worked tirelessly in support of health care reform and played a key role along with the [national network] in getting strong affordability standards. Our leaders played a key role in bringing health care reform home (that is, bringing money and policy changes flowing from health care reform down to the local level), and were successful in securing a site and full funding for a new clinic. It will provide health access to [the] critically underserved [part of our county].

On banking reform:

Our campaign played a key role in demonstrating public outrage at the role of large banks in the collapse of the economy during the debate over financial reform. We helped to initiate and orchestrate some of the largest actions around the country from April to June 2010 that helped to shape media coverage that emphasized the public outcry for stronger reform. This had a direct impact on strengthening financial reform legislation as it moved through the Senate and also contributed to our ability to win the new federal policy to provide assistance for unemployed homeowners.

From San Francisco to New York, Chicago to Charlotte, Kansas City to Washington, DC, we let Congress know that a broad cross-section of Americans would hold them accountable for passing real financial reform. We shut down the financial district in San Francisco, Kansas City, and Wall Street. We shut down K Street at the height of the process and told a new public narrative that declared decisively that the American people were angry at the abuses of Wall Street and were demanding change.

On foreclosure reform:

We played a strong role in pressing for the creation of a national loan modification program and were credited in the White House's online rollout of the "Making Home Affordable" program in April 2009. . . . Many of our members and their stories were featured in a series of local and national media coverage and served to generate pressure on the Department of Treasury

Figure 1.7 Interfaith leaders praying for House Speaker John Boehner to let an immigration reform bill come to a vote, June 2014. (Courtesy of Gamaliel)

to launch an audit and investigation which preceded the Attorneys General lawsuit.

[A particular meeting] generated national media coverage and our recommendations have been circulated to key administration officials, including Peter Rouse, the current White House chief of staff. Our meeting was also referenced by a group of US Senators in a letter to the Secretary of the Treasury where they supported the key points of our recommendations. The Treasury Department has made a series of policy changes in response to our recommendations.

On employment and public transportation:

We maintained state funding [for public transit] through a designated transportation fund. We won collective bargaining for transit workers. We won a commitment from two congressmen to solve a federal funding issue. . . . On the national level, we have been to Washington, DC, four times to speak with congressional leaders or their staff about the need for the reauthorization of transportation legislation and our interests around jobs and flexible funds.

On immigration reform:

We fought successfully to stop Arizona-style legislation from coming to our state; that fight will continue next year.
    We won passage of [the state-level] Dream Act (several instances of this).

On electoral influence:

[Our local congressman] came under heavy assault by the coal industry for his position against mountaintop removal mining. We have two large chapters in his district that registered, informed, and mobilized thousands of voters. He won by 647 votes.

These kinds of claims cannot simply be taken at face value—such victories in these higher-level arenas almost always involve broad collaboration between organizations and/or elected officials and are rarely the work of a single coalition or even network. But contemporaneous press coverage and insider knowledge from third-party analysts who track the activities of this field verify that these coalitions have been among the crucial actors in these and a variety of other high-level policy outcomes.

A second piece of evidence for this rising political ambition comes from the evolution of the field's core strategy of engaging with elected political officials to shape public policy and use it as leverage to influence the economic well-being of families. Fifteen or even ten years ago, it was rare for these locally grounded organizations to meet with elected officials beyond the city level; when they did, it was usually with their local representatives in the state legislature. That practice remains a core strategy. In 2011, 90% of the coalitions had met with a city-level political official about a particular issue within the last year. Some coalitions (about 10%) still restrict their level of issue engagement to a city, and 34% had not in the last year engaged any official beyond the state level. But most coalitions are clearly engaging higher-level political officials. In 2011, 66% had met with a national-level official and an additional 22% had met with a state-level official.

Thus good evidence exists that the rise of a more ambitious political imagination has indeed begun to generate active engagement and influence in higher political arenas. At the same time, it must be said: such impact has only begun to put a dent in the vast increases in socioeconomic inequality that have emerged over the last three decades. Other than on the national health care reform debate that led to SCHIP reauthorization and the Affordable Care Act, and to some extent on reform of the financial sector, this new political ambition has not broken down the policy paralysis that bedevils Washington, DC. Nor has it really lessened the racial inequality that overlaps with and undergirds the high levels of overall economic inequality in American society. Meanwhile, implicit racial bias is still mobilized to checkmate policy initiatives designed to address that inequality. Until democratic organizing successfully inserts the priorities of ethical democracy into the leading agenda of the national public arena— and achieves the scale needed to hold political representatives accountable

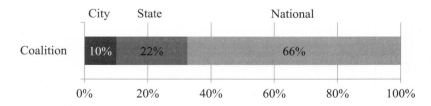

*2% of the coalitions had not met with any political officials in the last year.

Figure 1.8 The highest level political official faith-based community organizing coalitions have met with in the last year.

to those priorities—all efforts to address economic and racial inequality, including living wages, financial reform, and the extension of health coverage to millions of low-income Americans, remain vulnerable.

Collaborating for Ethical Democracy

Beyond their primary organizing base, many faith-based community organizing coalitions collaborate far more broadly and strategically than has historically been the case. These collaborative efforts take a variety of forms: local coalitions affiliated with the same sponsoring network working together on state- and national-level issues, those network-based efforts coordinating with other national organizations (often across the religious-secularist divide), or a single faith-based community organizing coalition collaborating with other community organizations on a local initiative. These collaborations are thus too heterogeneous to characterize easily. They may focus on a single issue during a short campaign, or may constitute long-term strategic alliances. The more substantial ones help coalitions broaden their constituency base, consolidate public influence, learn new organizing skills, extend their reach to new geographic terrain or new issue areas, and learn to work with secularly oriented organizations and with other faith communities, but the less substantial likely leave the coalitions unchanged.

What we can document is as follows: In 1999, only 20% of faith-based community organizing coalitions participated in statewide collaborations, and to our knowledge none participated in nationwide efforts. In 2011, although nearly all of these coalitions retained the field's historic focus (and in our view its ongoing source of greatest strength) on locally grounded organizing, 50% of coalitions linked that local organizing to statewide collaborations, and 25% to nationwide collaborations. Likewise, in 2011, 66% of coalitions reported participating in multiorganizational collaborations of some kind, and among these, over 95% collaborate with organizations *outside* their formal organizing network (either locally or through their sponsoring network's higher-level work). These are profound changes in a field of organizing once criticized as being narrowly local, parochial, and nonstrategic. Also, most of the more impressive examples of higher-level impact cited above involved such collaborative efforts. But it is also the case that some collaborative efforts bear little fruit. Thus collaboration for its own sake seems senseless; rather, *strategic collaboration driven by ambitious political goals* represents an important emergent property of today's most effective faith-based organizing. Today, at least some sectors of faith-based community organizing (i) transcend localized concerns while remaining embedded in local communities; and (ii) operate with a strategic vision that carries them into regional-, state-, and national-level work.

Some faith-based community organizing coalitions, however, eschew participating in multiorganizational collaborations or addressing issues at higher levels of government, arguing that doing so would undermine their local organizing work or lead their member institutions to become less engaged. Nonetheless, the trend within faith-based community organizing seems to be toward building collaborative ties "upward" through the national networks, "outward" through local collaborations, and/or "upward and outward" through national collaborations seeking to influence public policy at higher political levels.[26]

Two other dimensions of the new scope of organizing are harder to capture firmly but appear to represent significant evolution within the organizational culture of the field: new sophistication in how these coalitions exert power, and a new willingness within these coalitions to share credit for victories. One way to see the evolution of the field over the last decade is to compare the ideas of *hard power* and *soft power*.[27] The field for decades focused primarily on creating a "power organization" through what might be called hard power—"organized people" holding political officials accountable via the sheer weight of their numbers. This involved building power through internal relational work and then projecting that power into the political sphere. Today, the field has learned to extend that relational power externally in more systematic ways via a wider set of organizing practices more oriented toward what might be called *soft power*. Soft power involves cultivating relationships with political officials and other institutional leaders, negotiating policies, building long-term strategic alliances, and drawing on specialized policy expertise, then using these relational and cultural resources to prioritize social needs, propose possible solutions, and generate the urgency needed to ensure the swift implementation of those solutions. Linking these hard and soft forms of power appears to have bolstered the field's public influence and fostered its emergent higher-level influence.

Less substantial but also important: Leading organizers now often seem willing to share public credit for significant victories rather than adopting a posture that claims exclusive credit for one's own coalition (itself part of the one-dimensional hard power organizational strategy described above). In a field once widely given to the narrowest of relentless organizational self-promotion, we found it striking to hear multiple coalition directors sharing credit with others. For example, one director made the following unsolicited statement in response to the open-ended questions: "We would like to reiterate that many organizations and factors have contributed to these victories, but we believe that we played a substantial role in contributing to these important changes." More broadly, such willingness to acknowledge others' contributions to important victories emerged in many of our interviews with strategic leaders in the field. While perhaps not terribly significant in itself, the collaborative and reciprocal ties that underlie this shift in tone matter for the strategic capacity of the movement for deepening democracy in America as a whole—and long-time observers of organizing will recognize just what a cultural shift this represents.

Finally, the greater scale of organizing of recent years can be glimpsed in the number of people mobilized for political actions—that is, the "turnout" for public accountability sessions that are a key tool of influence. We assess this dimension of power projection via two measures: each faith-based community organizing coalition's *largest* turnout and its *total* turnout over the last year. Differences between the 1999 and 2011 studies in the way coalitions were asked to report turnouts make it difficult to confidently compare turnout figures, but attendance at the largest events appear to have decreased somewhat, while the total number of people mobilized annually in public actions increased. In 2011, summing the directors' responses indicates that over two hundred thousand people attended at least one faith-based organizing action in the course of a year. The typical coalition-wide public action drew roughly six hundred people, and the average coalition reported having one thousand different people participate in their events during the past year.[28]

We interpret these findings as follows: First, the decline in size of the coalitions' largest public action *may* be cause for concern. To the extent the field continues to seek to exert "hard power" on the local level, this decline might undermine its ability to do so. On the other hand, more sophisticated exertion of "soft power" and greater coordination of work at local, state, and national levels might counterbalance the decline. Second, a coalition that reliably turns out six hundred people for focused meetings with elected officials on substantive political issues is likely to gain attention in most American cities. About half of the coalitions achieve that turnout level, and some produce far larger public actions, up to five thousand or ten thousand people in attendance. While we do not have data on the quality of particular meetings with elected officials, extensive research documents the field's reputation for running disciplined meetings that foster constructive political problem solving.[29] Third, the overall increase in total annual turnout reflects the more ambitious political agendas being pursued by these coalitions. Rather than striving to increase political clout by doing more within their existing tactical repertoire of large-scale political actions—since it is not particularly evident how much greater political leverage a coalition gains by turning out say 20% more people at a single event—much of the field has instead *expanded its tactical repertoire*. We will later see this in more detail; here, we simply note that the more sophisticated coalitions now engage in far more negotiation prior to public actions; move multiple issues simultaneously into the public arena; advance legislation at the state or federal level, then link local actions to that legislation in order to "pull down" resources to benefit local communities; engage simultaneously with elected officials (state legislators and national congressional representatives) both in the state/national capitol and within their home district; link their standard repertoire of person-to-person organizing with sophisticated use of social media; link long-term organizing to short-term campaigns for voter turnout and other forms of civic engagement; engage youth and young adults as active leaders; draw on a more imaginative array of "performative" political actions for a media-driven public; and actively cultivate ties to the electronic and print media.

None of those approaches were widespread in the field even ten years ago, beyond pioneering efforts by the IAF in Texas in the 1990s and PICO in California in the 2000s, and more scattered efforts elsewhere. All that said, the field almost certainly has the potential to generate even larger turnouts and greater impact at the polls, considering that their member institutions can credibly claim to collectively represent over five million people. The ongoing credibility of that claim depends on assuring that serious local organizing continues, even as these organizations also strive to project power at the state and national level—an issue to which we return in chapter 7.

Overall, the picture that emerges of the field's evolution over the last decade includes issue work at higher political levels, carefully cultivated links with state and federal officials, a new capacity for exerting "soft power" backed up by "hard power" projection, new tactical repertoires, increased total turnout capacity, and more extensive collaborative ties both within networks and beyond them. That strategic activity combined with specific issue victories in those higher arenas provides strong evidence of intensified power projection in the faith-based organizing field over the last ten years. That power has been achieved despite a likely decline in attendance at the largest public actions, which had been the field's primary tactic for exerting its influence. Instead, faith-based organizing's combined hard and soft power strategies implemented at local, state, and national levels have helped coalitions develop the wider array of tactics just noted, draw on policy expertise more broadly and systematically, and as a result attain greater political capacity than in the past.

Political reality is harsh, however. Severe and growing economic inequality continues to be the defining reality of American life, and in a post–Citizens United context, money flows virtually unrestricted into the political arena. If faith-based community organizing and its "organized people"—along with its broader allies in other forms of advocacy—want to reverse economic inequality and counter the antidemocratic influence of "organized money," they will have to project still greater public influence in the years ahead. To do so, strategic leaders must continue cultivating a sophisticated mix of soft and hard power. But even as they embrace more relational, cultural, and negotiation-based mechanisms for exerting power, nothing can replace their ability to turn people out for public action and contested elections. If the field can sustain that balance internally, these coalitions may be positioned to make a crucial contribution to renewing American democracy in the years ahead. But they must also construct the structures needed to sustain such a balance over time; we turn next to that terrain.

Emerging Federated Structures: State and National

To see clearly the new strategic position of faith-based community organizing, it is helpful to understand the recent evolution of the field's structure. Much of the scholarly writing on this terrain was either done before this evolution became apparent or simply fails to analytically capture that evolution.

The best framework for understanding the field's evolving structure draws on two studies of social movements in American history. First, Theda Skocpol, Marshall Ganz, and Ziad Munson systematically studied the history of social movement organizations that have had a major impact on American social life and policy.[30] They find only a relative handful of such organizations and argue that the crucial characteristics of the most successful of them reside in a three-level "federated model" characterized by having organizational infrastructure at local, state and national levels. Thirty-four of forty-six total "successful" cases from throughout American history were built on such a federated model. That is, they argue that the sine qua non for social movements to achieve major national influence lies in having local organizational units (which often include religious congregations) that sponsor the primary organizing work, state-level advocacy groups that communicate organizational priorities to state governmental structures, and national-level organizational leadership that coordinates priorities and channels pressure for national policy change.

Second, in two seminal publications, Marshall Ganz analyzes the role of "strategic capacity" in social movement success.[31] Ganz notes that innovative and coherent strategy is crucial to such success, but he argues that studying social movement strategy directly offers little analytic leverage, because strategy itself is so context dependent.[32] Instead, he studies *strategic capacity*: what makes social movement organizations able to recognize strategic opportunities within a complex political environment and innovate tactically and strategically in the face of that complexity. He finds that having leaders with diverse social backgrounds and a variety of organizational paths into leadership fosters such strategic capacity.

The emergence of faith-based community organizing's higher profile in recent years results from changes well captured by these two analyses. First, major sectors of the field have begun to build—partially and unevenly, but quite significantly—organizational infrastructures that approach the "federated model." Originally in Texas and California and more recently in states such as Colorado, Minnesota, Ohio, Louisiana, Florida, Virginia, Arizona, and Massachusetts, something like true state-level coordination has emerged. Furthermore, as we shall see in chapter 4, the PICO National Network and on a smaller scale National People's Action (and in a more limited sense Gamaliel) have built national-level coordinating and advocacy. As a result, a federated structure for faith-based community organizing is being constructed, at least within some sectors of the field. To the extent that local organizing remains vibrant in the future, a truly sustainable national federated structure is now imaginable (albeit probably not one based on a single national organization).

Finally, in parallel with this structural shift, the emergence of wider collaboration and the advancement of female and minority professional organizers mean that local, state, and national network leaders now represent more diverse social backgrounds and have entered leadership positions through a variety of organizational paths rather than solely via this particular organizing model. We shall later see the evidence for these shifts; here we simply note that they contribute to rising strategic capacity and organizational innovation in the field.

Mobilizing Resources: Funding in the Field of
Faith-Based Community Organizing

The field has achieved this level of engagement and leadership development with fairly modest financial resources. Since 1999, the median annual budget for faith-based community organizing coalitions increased from $150,000 to $175,000, but adjusted for inflation, this represents a slight *decline* in revenue for the average coalition.[33] On average, 60% of a coalition's budget goes toward staff expenses.

Funding sources have shifted significantly. Even though faith-based community organizing coalitions prioritize raising funds from their member institutions in order to protect the coalitions' autonomy, the percentage of funding that comes from member dues decreased from 22% to 15%. The percentage of funding provided by the Catholic Campaign for Human Development decreased from 19% to 15%, and the percentage provided by other faith-based funders decreased from 12% to 7%. Meanwhile, the percentage provided by secular foundations and corporations increased from 30% to 39%. Of the latter, donations from corporations constituted 4.5% of total reported local coalition revenues in 2011, with secular foundations making up the remainder.[34]

The above financial patterns reflect several dynamics:

· Long-term commitment to the field from a core set of faith-based funders related to Catholic, Unitarian, Mainline Protestant, and Jewish denominational bodies and their ethical teachings regarding poverty (many of whom collaborate via the Interfaith Organizing Initiative and other initiatives), and secular funders interested in local community development and empowerment (many of whom collaborate via the Neighborhood Funders Group).

· Wide recognition among funders of the field's important recent impact at the state and national levels, particularly on health care reform, public education, economic development, and to some extent reform of the financial sector, in addition to the field's long-standing impact on local issues regarding poverty, inequality, and quality of life in poor and middle-income communities. As a result of this recognition, an expanding list of secular funders has shown heightened interest in this work, even as the field's institutional membership remains based primarily in an increasingly diverse set of faith communities.[35]

· Declining contributions to the liberal Protestant denominational units that previously provided significant contributions to the field. The same pattern emerged within the Catholic Campaign for Human Development (CCHD) following the 2008 recession, amid coordinated attacks on the CCHD by what appear to be small groups of sectarian Catholic critics, but in this case funding levels recovered as the recession waned and the Catholic bishops launched a "review and renewal" of CCHD.[36] The shift of tone and emphasis emanating from the Vatican since the 2013 election of Pope Francis might auger further emphasis on this dimension of Catholic public presence in American society.[37]

Note that the stagnation of average local-level funding for organizing can be read negatively or positively. On one hand, from the point of view of organizers, stagnation in funding is never a good thing—especially in a social movement field with the rising political aspirations documented above and at a time of enormously heightened inequality in American life. On the other hand, that the *average* local budget has nearly held its own while the number of local coalitions has grown by 42% means that *total* local funding aggregated across the country has grown significantly over the last decade. That it held onto that growth well into the Great Recession that began in 2008 represents a significant achievement.[38] Finally, as we see next, funding for local coalitions are not the only resources supporting this work.

Summary: Dynamics Underlying the Growth of Faith-Based Community Organizing

Over the last decade, the geographic expansion, heightened political profile, and higher aspirations of faith-based community organizing—including the push to explicitly address issues of racial justice and racial equity— appear to result primarily from several key dynamics, three of which we note here (others we characterize in chapter 7).

The three dynamics are primarily internal to the field: First, heightened access to *financial resources* for network-level structures clearly has mattered. That is, while total financing to local coalitions has only grown with the growth in the number of these local coalitions, with the average local budget staying constant, some networks have successfully raised substantial new funding to sustain work at state and national levels. That money, and the national staffing it makes possible, has funded much of the higher-level strategizing, training, and collaboration of recent years. This comes as no surprise; social movement scholars of the "resource mobilization" and related "political process" perspectives have long documented the influence of resource acquisition on the survival of social movement organizations.[39] Obviously, organizations that draw on professional staff need money to hire and retain the staff members—all the more so in a field that does intensive training in the skills of democratic life rarely taught elsewhere.

Second, the expansion of the field required new *organizing talent*, which we can think of as the human capital embedded in the professional organizers, religious clergy, and local leaders who do the work of organizing. In the last decade, a great deal of new work has been invested in recruiting and developing organizers with the required interpersonal, analytic, managerial, and political skills; deepening religious leaders' understanding and knowledge of organizing in their congregation and in the political arena; and cultivating lay leaders' democratic skills not only at the very local level but also for use in higher-level political arenas. As we shall see, the current pool of professional organizing staff (comprised of 545 people) is substantially more diverse and younger than the much smaller pool a decade ago. Recruiting and retaining these organizers has entailed not simply finding money to pay them professional wages but also reengineering the internal dynamics of local coalitions and sponsoring networks to make organizing both exciting and sustainable to a younger, more diverse generation. The latter has included addressing racial equity and racial/ethnic relations inside of organizing and in the wider American society.

Third, the expansion of the field also required cultivating *organizational cultures* that could sustain that growth in scope, scale, and ambition. The "cultural turn" in the study of social movements has helped scholars recognize the crucial role of cultural dynamics in sustaining effective mobilization.[40] The recent national influence of the PICO National Network and National People's Action on reform efforts regarding health care and malfeasance in the financial sector did not result simply from having more participants and greater access to resources. Rather, it required intentional effort to build an organizational culture that could undergird work at local, state, and national levels and across various issues simultaneously. The same is true of state-level work to influence public education, workforce training, economic development, and regional transportation done by the Industrial Areas Foundation and Gamaliel.[41] In all these cases—as well as when higher-level power is projected by other groups, such as DART, the Ohio Organizing Collaborative, the InterValley Project, Interfaith Worker Justice, and Clergy and Laity United for Economic Justice—professional organizers work with lay leaders and religious clergy to cultivate the symbols and stories, the ideas and identities that can help their coalition project power at multiple levels. They do so while also addressing the inevitable internal struggles that accompany intense political work. Perhaps most crucial in that work, as noted by Jeffrey Stout, is the cultivation of legitimacy, mutual trust, and accountability as moral resources inside each coalition and network through the core practice of one-to-one meetings.[42] When cultivated well, these moral resources facilitate the effective use of legitimate authority within the field. When this very localized work of building relationships is done well, the key up-front leaders can authoritatively represent their coalition vis-à-vis elected officials at large public actions and political negotiations, and a broader group of leaders can authoritatively deliberate regarding key organizational decisions.

Thus the field of faith-based community organizing has attained a level of public presence and political maturity few imagined possible even fifteen years ago, when substantial scholarly writing on the field first emerged. This chapter has presented the first systematic evidence to substantiate that assertion, showing the new capacities of this field: the growth of organizing infrastructure, the diversification of mobilizing structures, the new scale and scope of organizing, the initial construction of "federated" structures, and new resource mobilization.

In recognizing the expanded strategic capacities of the field, however, we do not want to suggest a sanguine picture. These new capacities are by no means spread evenly throughout the field but rather vary considerably depending upon local context, the talent of local leadership, the priorities of key strategists, and network affiliation. For faith-based community organizing to really contribute its full potential to reshaping public policy, those capacities (and others) will need to be multiplied and built out to new geographic sites and to all sectors of the field that are capable of embracing them and that desire to do so.

Crucial to *all* these developments has been the newly ambitious political imagination documented above. That political imagination—fueled by democratic ideals, stoked by prophetic strands of faith traditions, and fired by moral outrage at the human costs of historic levels of inequality in American life—created the hunger that has driven key strategic leaders to build the new capacities identified here. Thus for faith-based organizing to help American society exorcise its demons of vast economic inequality and grinding policy paralysis, it will have to cultivate wider cohorts of organizers with equally ambitious political imaginations.

In part II, we will introduce some of the key strategic leaders who have shaped the field in recent years and see how they have done so. But so far we have only made the case that faith-based organizing represents a form of democratic engagement on a scale worthy of the attention of those concerned about inequality and political paralysis. We have not yet explored what all that can tell us about the connections and tensions between the universalist and multiculturalist strands of democracy, and thus about ethical democracy—and whether a truly shared American future is possible. To excavate those insights, we need to see much more of the multiracial and multicultural realities within faith-based organizing. We turn now to that task.

Figure 2.1 PICO National Network staff at annual retreat, Applegate, California, June 2014. (Courtesy of Heather Wilson)

TWO

Leadership and Diversity

In the United States today, we have the appearance of racial comity, and Obama in the White House, and technological comfort like we have never had before. Yet [we] also have levels of inequality that rival any this country has ever seen, and racial inequality that remains scandalous. In housing, we have a version of the apartheid we castigated South Africa about a generation ago, and today have in our own country. We have an incarceration rate that rivals that after the Civil War and Jim Crow, affecting an entire generation of black and brown men. We need to build bridges of understanding, real relationships across race lines, for the sake of justice and the saving of our democracy. This will be the most important work I will do in my lifetime, the most important work I will have done when I go to meet my Maker.[1]

—Rev. Alvin Herring, *Deputy Director for National Training, PICO National Network*

To make the case that faith-based organizing offers insight and lessons for building a multicultural yet universalist democracy, it is not enough to show that these organizations' constituencies are diverse (as done in chapter 1). Rather, we must also ask whether minority groups once marginalized from the realm of legitimate democratic discourse represent themselves within the decision-making structures of these organizations and whether these organizations' internal social dynamics and decision making take seriously the particular cultures, histories, and struggles of those subaltern groups (even as they also embody universal democratic commitments). That's a tall order. This chapter explores the representation and leadership dimension of this question by examining the demographic profiles of local-level leaders within the field of faith-based community organizing. Later chapters explore internal dynamics and decision making within faith-based organizing.

Governing and Leading: Board Members, Clergy, and Leaders

As the field of faith-based community organizing has changed at the coalition level depicted in chapter 1, it also has changed at the individual level. Four groups of individuals are critical to the field: *clergy and lay leaders*, who participate actively in the organizing; *board members*, a subgroup of the first group, who typically sit on the "Board of Directors" for their local coalition, made up of representatives of its member institutions;[2] *staff organizers*, who provide training to leaders and are in many other ways central to the organizing process albeit not "up in front" during public events; and *directors* or *"lead organizers,"* who head up each faith-based community organizing coalition (in the smaller organizations, the latter may be the *only* staff).

Clergy and Lay Leaders

For decades, the field has stated that among its primary objectives is to develop leaders from within its member institutions. The underlying notion is that these leaders will mobilize their communities around a collectively determined agenda promoting better quality of life, and these leaders will in turn strengthen their member institutions from within (although the intensity of the latter commitment varies considerably).[3] The field currently reports having over twenty thousand core leaders playing active voluntary roles within local coalitions. Among these leaders, over five thousand had attended a multiday training event in the year prior to our survey.[4] This represents a 70% increase in the number of leaders receiving intensive training since 1999, suggesting that the field remains committed to developing a strong leadership base among its constituents. Because those in this broad leadership category vary enormously in their level of engagement and exact role in the organizing work, we chose to focus our data gathering instead on a subset of them: those playing the more defined role as members of the coalitions' governing boards.

Board Members

The profile of the board members within faith-based community organizing offers crucial data regarding the democratic potential of this field. Many organizations—civic groups, social movements, and both political parties—claim to speak in the interests of average Americans or the poor. Even if in some instances the substance of those organizations' policy work would arguably advance those interests, that is not the same as actually engaging poor, working-class, and middle-class folks in representing their own interests. The gold standard should be engaging those groups in actively representing themselves while simultaneously advocating effectively for substantive policies that will serve their interests—this is the essence of real democratic organization.

What do we now know about the members of faith-based organizing governing boards? First, some general trends: The total number of board members increased 18.5% (from approximately 2,700 to 3,200) from 1999 to 2011. Their average age increased from fifty-one to fifty-four. The broad trend thus appears to be that board members remain in place as they age or are replaced by people only slightly younger than themselves, rather than by being replaced by a significantly younger cohort. Male and female board members remain equally represented; the field apparently has avoided the patterns of female predominance in involvement in many faith communities and of male predominance in some forms of political engagement. According to the 2011 data, 14% of board members are immigrants, and among immigrant board members, 56% are Hispanic—both figures closely corresponding to the proportion of immigrants in the 2010 US population.[5]

The socioeconomic status of board members may be among the most important characteristics of these coalitions. The National Study of Community Organizing Coalitions provides data on the education level and the household income of board members: 23% have less than a bachelor's degree—not nearly as high a proportion as in the US population as a whole, but demonstrating that these boards are not composed solely of the highly educated. More impressive is the spread of household incomes on these governing boards (see figure 2.2): 23% of board members have a household income of less than $25,000 per year, placing their households only slightly above the 2011 federal poverty level for a family of four. A further 35% have household incomes between $25,000 and $50,000 per year, putting them a little above 200% of that year's poverty level for a family of four; at this income level, families typically struggle to meet their basic living expenses. Together, these two groups of board members closely match the proportion of all American households with incomes below $50,000 per year. The governing boards on average have majority representation from the kinds of "working families" that often take center stage in policy discourse without being much represented in those conversations.

Although no good comparative data exist that would allow us to rigorously compare the income levels of corporate boards or influential figures in the political system, coalition boards certainly include representatives of

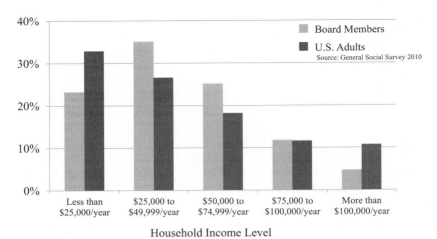

Figure 2.2 The household income level of coalition board members compared with all US adults.

low-income sectors of American society far more fully than either group—all the more so since the 2010 Supreme Court decision in *Citizens United v. Federal Election Commission*, allowing virtually unlimited campaign donations by deep-pocketed corporations and organizations. While we cannot be as confident regarding how coalition boards compare to the board members of other civil society organizations, and good comparative data again are conspicuously absent, what is clear is that faith-based community organizing coalitions have systematically included poor, working-class, and middle-class members on their governing boards in ways that appear rare among American civic organizations. Such strong low-income representation presumably arises partly due to the nature of organizing focused on issues of concern in poor and middle-class communities, which attracts institutions rooted in such communities; partly due to professional organizers' own ethical and political commitments and strategic calculations; and partly due to a specific policy of one of the key funders of the field. In order for a faith-based organizing group to receive funding from the Catholic Campaign for Human Development (the domestic antipoverty arm of the United States Conference of Catholic Bishops, which provides about 15% of total funding for local faith-based organizing work—see details below), at least half of its governing board must qualify as low income.[6]

Through this direct representation of low-income individuals on coalition governing boards, less privileged sectors claim "voice" in civil and political society in ways quite rare in American life.[7] Only labor unions—

with all their current problems, predicaments, and potential—similarly represent the economic interests of less privileged sectors, and even some unions often fail to address their broader social interests. Given the overlapping realities of socioeconomic status, race, ethnicity, immigration status, schooling, and family concerns in the United States, as well as the stark and unabated rise in inequality that currently bedevils American society, this ability to address broad socioeconomic concerns while staying focused on an agenda driven by the needs of less privileged communities represents the central distinguishing feature and achievement of this community organizing movement.

In considering this presence of low-income individuals on the boards of faith-based organizing coalitions, however, we should not overestimate the socioeconomic diversity of these coalitions. They clearly represent low-income Americans to a significant level, and better than most civil society organizations. Although truly systematic data are lacking, historically it appears to be the case that the field's base in *institutions* has meant that is has mostly engaged relatively less marginalized sectors of poor and working-class communities.[8] In addition, income levels of board members may not reflect the income levels of wider participants. Furthermore, at least as important as simple representation are the cultural dynamics within these coalitions, and whether they adopt hegemonic cultural assumptions and styles that disempower lower-class participants.[9] All that said, these coalitions bring impressive socioeconomic diversity to their work; certainly, their core policy issues address meaningful concerns of lower-class communities, and how well they represent the most marginalized sectors clearly evolves over time. As of 2014, those that have most strongly advocated issues such as mass incarceration and immigrant rights have reported stronger representation from marginalized communities.[10]

The racial and ethnic diversity of the governing boards of these coalitions offers a crucial way to assess the appropriateness of the field as a case study of multiculturally grounded yet universalist democracy. Although he studied only the Industrial Areas Foundation and thus fails to see the wider field of organizing, Princeton philosopher Jeffrey Stout has nonetheless made a compelling case that what he terms "grassroots democracy" is the most important ethical and political phenomenon going on in the United States, since it strives to reground our politics in the ethical and institutional resources of American democratic traditions. Furthermore, he argues that the kind of organizing studied here represents the most important instance of American grassroots democracy today.[11] But are these coalitions sufficiently diverse to offer a compelling case study for understanding the dynamics of multiculturalism and racial diversity within grassroots democracy?

The National Study of Community Organizing Coalitions finally provides data to undergird an authoritative answer. That answer begins with the racial/ethnic and immigrant-native profile of board members and organizers, but will ultimately hinge on deciding what constitutes a "compelling case."

Racially and ethnically, these governing boards are substantially more diverse than the US population as a whole, and dramatically more diverse than the boards of all nonprofit organizations in the country. While nearly half (49%) of the coalition board members are white, the US adult population as a whole is nearly two-thirds (64%) white. Meanwhile, the history of white dominance of associational life in the United States, along with dynamics of income stratification and educational attainment, have left a legacy in which 86% of nonprofit board members are white.[12] The difference is largely constituted by African American board members. Faith-based community organizing boards have Hispanic/Latino and "other" (either Asian/Pacific Islander, Native American, or multiracial) memberships that approximate their proportions in the overall US adult population but more than double the proportion of African Americans (32% of coalition board members are African American versus 13% of the US adult population). As documented below, while individual member institutions are sometimes rooted in a single racial or ethnic group, above that level the sponsoring coalitions and networks typically embody rich racial and ethnic diversity.

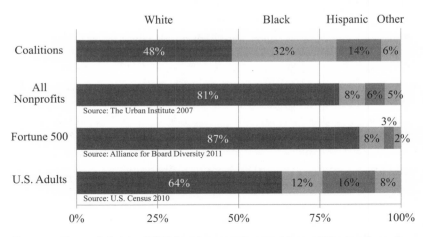

Figure 2.3 The race/ethnicity of faith-based community organizing coalition board members compared with the board members of other organizations and all US adults.

What does this level of racial/ethnic diversity mean concretely? Several things: First, in contrast to many civic sectors, Latinos participate in and lead faith-based organizing efforts at levels fully representative of their presence in American society as a whole. Indeed, although our study does not provide demographic data at the level of individual attendance at political actions sponsored by this field, we can surmise that Latinos participate in even greater proportions. Many of the large member institutions (those with one thousand to five thousand members) as well as many of the largest member institutions (those with more than five thousand members) are Hispanic Catholic churches.[13] When large political actions occur, these large and very large Hispanic Catholic churches often produce the largest turnout, disproportionate to their representation on governing boards.

Second, largely as a result of this involvement of Hispanic member institutions, immigrants are also strongly represented. Immigrants compose 14% of board members (and 13% of member institutions are predominantly immigrant member institutions, disproportionately in the large or very large categories).[14] More than two-thirds of immigrant member institutions are Hispanic; the other third are black (11%, mostly African or Caribbean immigrants); Asian (7%, mostly from Southeast Asia); or multiracial or "other" (14%).

Third, the very high rate of African American representation on governing boards—reflecting the large number of congregations affiliated with historic African American denominations plus newer nondenominational black churches, as well as high rates of urban black poverty and the rich social Christianity of the black church traditions—means that faith-based organizing both benefits from and cultivates significant black leadership.[15] As we will see in chapter 4, the initial push for greater multicultural/multiracial emphasis within organizing came from African American pastors, organizers, and lay leaders. The weight of black leadership on governing boards surely mattered in helping that push gain traction.

Fourth, since some local coalitions do embody relatively little diversity, racial and ethnic diversity increases as those coalitions come together at the state, regional, and national levels. This makes yet more important the higher-level political ambitions of some sectors of the field. Those ambitions matter not only because they hold promise to actually reshape state- and national-level policies that drive inequality, but also because they generate intense interaction across racial and ethnic groups that otherwise might remain isolated from one another within individual member institutions, where diversity tends to be lower.

Fifth, the continuing significant involvement of white Americans in faith-based community organizing—albeit at levels well below the white proportion of the American population—in our view represents an important *strength* of the field. For the foreseeable future, even when the United States eventually becomes a majority-minority nation, social power in American society will to a significant degree remain dominated by whites. White wealth and other socioeconomic power along with white positional strength in the corporate and civil society sectors will give white people disproportionate control over social policy. Thus having deep engagement from poor, working-class, and middle-class white people—and white allies from more elite social sectors and institutional leaders—will be strategically crucial. Equally important for this book's argument, and as articulated by Seyla Benhabib (see the introduction): If the tension between multiculturalist and universalist democracy is to be a constructive one, white people and various communities of color must rub up against one another, interrogate one another's priorities and commitments, and build solidarity and trust across lived racial lines. Only with substantial engagement from all racial/ethnic sectors will the struggle for greater socioeconomic equality and democratic voice in America adequately embody both universalist and multiculturalist strands of democratic theory—and succeed.

Other groups are relatively less represented in this field. Some of that absence is easily explained. Arab Americans and Americans of South Asian and East Asian descent are, on average, from higher economic strata than other groups, and thus less likely to engage in this form of organizing. Rural residents are also mostly unrepresented, due to the field's urban origins and continuing emphasis. Partly as a result of the latter factor, Native American institutions are less represented (although they may participate via member institutions that are not predominantly Native, which we did not measure). In particular geographic settings, some smaller racial/ethnic groups do participate at significant levels: Hmong refugees from Southeast Asia in California's Central Valley, low-income Chinese immigrants in New York, Haitians in Florida and New York, and so on.

Finally, the work of the faith-based organizing occurs in multiple languages. Three-quarters of the coalitions conduct some of their organizing in Spanish, and others (ranging from 2% to 5% of coalitions) conduct some organizing in Creole, Hmong, Arabic, French, Tagalog, or Vietnamese.

Before considering whether this level of diversity makes faith-based organizing the crucial case study of multiculturally based but universalist grassroots democracy, let us first consider the profile of the other key sector of the field: the paid staff of these coalitions.

Organizing the Terrain: The Makeup of Professional Staff

The profile of the staff members who are paid to train leaders and coordinate the organizing effort has shifted significantly over the last decade. Excluding the administrative staff of these coalitions, the number of paid organizing staff across the field increased 70% (from approximately 320 to 545).[16] If most coalitions today, just as ten years ago, have one or two professional organizers, what accounts for such growth in staffing? The biggest factor has been the growth of the field; with 42% more local coalitions in 2011 than in 1999, more professional organizers are needed simply to provide one or two staff people in each coalition. But 5% of coalitions today have more than eight paid organizers, whereas in 1999 no coalition reached that level of staffing. Two important developments appear to have driven staffing growth beyond that required for sheer geographic expansion. First, some sectors have increasingly linked their local organizing work to efforts at the national level (especially PICO, NPA, and to some extent Gamaliel) or at the state level (including those three as well as the IAF, the IVP, DART, and the Ohio Organizing Collaborative). Second, many coalitions now organize not only for influence in the political

Figure 2.4 Gamaliel executive director Ana Garcia-Ashley speaking to grassroots leaders and members of the Congressional Progressive Caucus, June 2014. (Courtesy of Gamaliel)

arena but also seek to use the tools of organizing to contribute to stronger organizational development *within* their member congregations and other institutions—on the argument that long-term thriving of the field and of American democracy generally requires strong institutions.[17] Both developments likely require a greater number of organizers on staff. Together, the demands of geographic expansion, translocal organizing, and intensive congregational/institutional development seem to have driven the increase in organizing staff. This growth, in turn, has combined with heightened emphasis on recruiting and retaining organizers of color and changes in internal decision making discussed in later chapters to create a context in which the racial/ethnic diversity of the organizing staff has increased.

Like the board members reported above, these professional organizers are substantially more diverse than the overall population of US adults— but in a rather different way. Again, the total population of organizers across the faith-based community organizing field is almost half (48%) white, compared to nearly two-thirds (64%) of all US adults. But the difference here is split between African American and Latino organizers; a fifth (21%) of organizers are African American and a quarter (24%) are Latino, whereas among US adults those figures are 13% and 16% respectively. Thus in both cases the professional organizers are represented at more than one and a half times their proportion in the overall adult population of the United States.

Meanwhile, other dimensions of the demographic profile of organizers have also undergone significant shifts. Religious diversity increased: in 2011, 20% of organizers identified as Mainline Protestant, 34% as Catholic, 14% as black Protestant, 22% as "other," and 10% as "not religiously

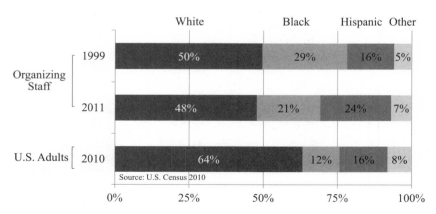

Figure 2.5 The race/ethnicity of coalition organizing staff compared with all US adults.

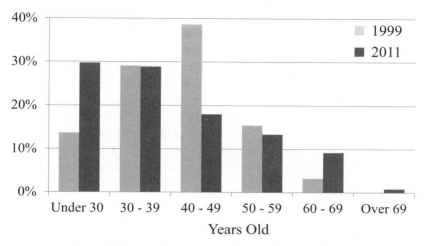

Figure 2.6 The age of coalition organizing staff in 1999 and 2011.

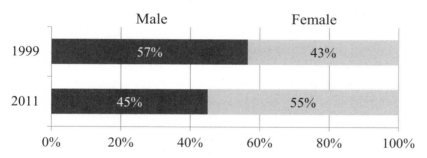

Figure 2.7 The gender of coalition organizing staff in 1999 and 2011.

affiliated." The average age of the organizing staff decreased: in 1999, the age of the majority of organizers was between thirty and fifty years old, while in 2011 the majority was between twenty and forty years old. The gender composition of the organizing staff flipped: in 1999, the majority (57%) was male, but in 2011 the majority (55%) was female.

Directors or "Lead Organizers"

Similar significant shifts have occurred among that subset of the organizing staff who serve as directors or "lead organizers." In 1999 the gender composition of this group was roughly 75% men and 25% women, which raised the question of whether a "glass ceiling effect" suppressed women's advancement into the higher reaches of this professional field, as in so many others. Today we can answer that question confidently "no" (though with progress still to be made). There is a nearly even gender split among lead organizers and directors, with 54% men and 46% women.

Most fundamentally for our purposes here, both the members of governing boards and the key professional staff within the field of faith-based community organizing embody substantial racial and ethnic diversity—significantly more than the demographic profile of American adults and dramatically more than the closest comparative group (the board members of all US nonprofit organizations). It is critical to recognize that high levels of staff racial/ethnic diversity did not just emerge "naturally" in the field. The field has always had significant numbers of professional organizers from minority social backgrounds, but it also historically carried an organizational culture that some organizers of color found excessively "white," that is, built on cultural assumptions from the dominant and hegemonic culture of white America.[18] As recently as fifteen years ago, network leadership was still almost uniformly white and predominantly male. Staff diversity—in this field as elsewhere—has grown through the struggle for racial equity and equal opportunity. As we shall see, that struggle has often been painful and difficult, has typically been pioneered by African Americans (and, for gender equity, by women), but women and men of all racial/ethnic backgrounds have advanced diversity initiatives in various ways at various times.

Given the widespread characterization of the field as embodying values of universalist democracy, this level of diversity indeed makes faith-based community organizing a strong prima facie case for understanding the dynamics of universalist multicultural grassroots democracy—although ultimately our argument will rest not only on individual demographic profiles but also on institutional characteristics and cultural dynamics within the field.

Retaining Professional and Diverse Staff: Salaries, Meaning, and the Shared Work of Multiculturalism

The complexity of the work of faith-based organizing requires professional staff with significant interpersonal, analytical, managerial, political, and pedagogical skills. This is especially true at the senior level, but even new organizers begin to exert such skills early on. This creates a need for sustained leadership in the field, to cultivate professional development and retain organizers. Once an organizer develops these skills, losing her imposes real losses and new training costs on the coalition; even raw talent capable of developing these skills is not easy to find, and developing them anew takes significant time. In addition, the racial and ethnic diversity of the member institutions and organizing base, documented in chapter 1, create a need for professional organizers who embody and promote diversity.

To meet that need, these coalitions have adopted a variety of organizational practices. In contrast to many organizations committed to social change, these coalitions generally pay middle-class salaries (especially those affiliated with networks). Although we did not collect systematic data on individual organizer salaries, years of conversations and interviews with organizers suggest that a typical salary scale pays early-career organizers something in the ballpark of a public schoolteacher's salary, and established lead organizers and directors may make two or three times that much. This practice presumably reflects these coalitions' commitment to social justice, but it also reflects their calculation that recruiting and retaining organizers with the diverse talents needed for success in this field requires professional wages, at least for experienced organizers.

In addition, some sectors of the organizing field have decided that retaining a talented and demographically diverse pool of professional organizers entails engaging more directly with internal issues of race/ethnicity, class, gender, and religion than was the past pattern in the field. As we shall see in chapter 5, this has sometimes entailed creating new internal structures focused on staff diversity; it has always entailed significant transformation of organizational culture, including difficult internal cultural work across these boundaries of difference.

Another form of cultural work in these coalitions—and a third mechanism for retaining professional talent in a competitive marketplace for talent—has been to pay greater attention to sources of *shared meaning*. This looks different in different settings. The Southwest region of the Industrial Areas Foundation pioneered deep engagement with prominent scholars and public intellectuals through its Institutes of Public Life. Similar endeavors are now widespread throughout nearly all the networks, often entailing serious intellectual work regarding the nature of democracy in a highly unequal and globalizing world and the strategic challenges this entails.[19] The PICO National Network and DART pioneered a more systematic approach to incorporating sources of spiritual meaning and theological reflection into its work. Gamaliel, the InterValley Project, the PICO National Network, and individual coalitions or regional groupings within other networks have drawn on "racial equity" perspectives to reflect seriously on racial and interethnic dynamics within organizing, and the field as a whole (including National People's Action, DART, and the InterValley

Project, along with PICO, Gamaliel, and the national IAF) has become more accommodating of family commitments and has pushed gender diversity up to higher levels in their professional staff structures (though unevenly). While significant "flow through" of organizers still appears to occur at lower points on the career ladder, once a person has been in the field for several years there appears to be a reasonable chance of building a long-term career. As a result, professional organizers in the field are often true "organic intellectuals": engaged in serious cultural, political, and even theological/spiritual analysis simultaneously and in dialogue with scholarly writing in those fields.

Finally, a fourth mechanism for retaining organizing talent has been to provide career development opportunities—including training focused on racial equity—to all professional organizing staff. At the high end, such opportunities sometimes include participation in recognized national training programs such as the Rockwood Leadership Institute and similar programs. However, our data show that the majority of coalitions still have only one or two organizers on staff, which complicates purely *local* career development and taking time off for high-end experiences. Thus the role of short-term training via translocal structures made possible by the organizing networks becomes crucial, and most formal professional development opportunities occur through their auspices.

When brought together successfully—by no means always the case—these changes have created an ethos that appears to be attracting more organizers of color and likely holds promise to better retain them. In the words of Michael-Ray Mathews of the PICO national staff:

> For me as a person of color, this exploration into race has allowed me to find my own voice and power in the context of our collective work. I'm thinking specifically about the training from Visions.[20] Their psychoanalytic approach had some real tools for people who live in excluded categories, ideas about internalized oppression behaviors, modern oppression, feelings as messengers were all very helpful. They helped me identify how suppression of differences, and how I behave, are the product of my own marginalization. And then see what more powerful behavior might look like, acting from a position of greater power. "Feelings as messengers" really helped me: how being mad, sad, or scared can be messengers about the danger you face because you are not coming from a position of power. . . . If I can interrupt this emotional dysfunction, name it, and get some agreement that I can talk about it without retribution, then I can speak about it and thus break open a new

space in the organization. Really helped me get beyond taking care of white people and operating out of my fear.

I've used that in mentoring other staff of color: how to operate in a context that feels oppressive, and interrupt it and be clear about what they need to be more powerful in that space: how can a young organizer see herself as a leader in helping undo the power of racial or gender oppression in our work. I think this is just crucial in our efforts to retain and advance staff. Staff [of color] have to see themselves as powerful players, have to see themselves as partners with our white colleagues and open up space for new thinking.

Rev. Alvin Herring, whose earlier words opened this chapter, links these commitments to the universal questions he sees facing American society:

It has meant a lot to me to work in an organization that has put so much of its capital into the fight for racial justice. Our organization is standing on the brink of doing what we have been waiting to do again for fifty years, ever since the Voting Rights Act: To stand shoulder to shoulder together across lines of race and answer together: Who is a person in this country? What kind of a democracy are we?

Conclusion

The field of faith-based organizing has long been known to successfully bring together poor, working-, and middle-class folks across racial groups —but there were long-standing concerns that it did not bring all groups equally into leadership roles. The shifting demographics revealed by the National Study of Community Organizing Coalitions show that the field today includes high levels of diversity among the staff and governing boards, across lines of difference including race/ethnicity, class, gender, religion, and the immigrant-native divide. Indeed, the data show that the field disproportionately mobilizes minority leadership, while still effectively engaging white Americans in work for social change. Those data reflect a dynamic field restructuring its internal leadership structure in light of new social realities—including the multicultural and multiracial dynamics of an increasingly diverse society. Whether and how this restructuring can be sustained, and its implications for the field's historic commitment to universalist democratic values, will occupy us in the coming chapters.

Yet this remains a field of political engagement built fundamentally upon the universalist ideals of democracy—that rights and opportunities should present themselves equally to all members of a society, regardless of race/ethnicity, class, gender, religion, and other nonmeritocratic characteristics. This combination of universalist foundations, long-standing racial and religious diversity, and newly emergent emphasis on explicitly cultivating a multiracial staff and leadership structure at all levels of these coalitions, with an emphasis on multiculturalism, is *part* of what makes the field of faith-based community organizing a compelling case study for learning about the strengths and challenges of linking universalist and multiculturalist democratic traditions.

However, we have not yet examined the field's actual base of constituents and member institutions. To what extent can the field legitimately claim to represent the broad array of social differences in contemporary American society? To what extent is such a claim true not just in the aggregate, in the field overall where people only rarely interact, but also *locally*, where the habits of the heart that underlie political culture are formed through regular interpersonal interactions over a lifetime? We turn next to these questions.

Figure 3.1 Leaders at a political action to launch "Cap the Rate/Raise the Wage" campaign, Communities Creating Opportunity (Kansas City affiliate of the PICO National Network). (Photo by Jonathan Bell, Communities Creating Opportunity)

THREE

Racial Diversity in Faith-Based Organizing

In arguing that the field of faith-based organizing offers an appropriate case for probing the dynamics of democracy in a multicultural society, chapter 2 offered a profile of the individual board members and professional staff who govern and coordinate these coalitions. But really delivering on the promise of insight into the interplay of universalist democratic ideals and multicultural social reality demands something more: some understanding of the cultural dynamics inside the member institutions and organizing structures that constitute the field of faith-based organizing. The next two chapters analyze those dynamics, institutions, and structures, with an eye toward generating such understanding of how a universalist, multicultural, and effective grassroots democratic movement might function. Because the twin democratic challenges of rising inequality and policy paralysis in national political life are deeply intertwined with racial inequity and implicit racial stereotyping, we focus on racial and ethnic diversity. But as in previous chapters we will occasionally draw attention to other dimensions of diversity as well.

Demographics of Institutional Diversity: Racial and Ethnic Diversity of Member Institutions

Recall from chapter 1 that the field of faith-based community organizing is made up of almost two hundred local coalitions typically (but not always) affiliated with one of the organizing networks and incorporated as a nonprofit organization under section 501(c)3 of the federal tax code. The formal "membership" in each of these local coalitions is composed not of individual people but rather of *institutions*. The almost two hundred such coalitions nationally vary in size, from less than a dozen to more than a hundred member institutions, and engage a total of about 4,500 member institutions. More than three-quarters (78%) of those member institutions are religious congregations from a variety of denominations; almost a quarter (22%) are public schools, parent-teacher associations, faith-based nonprofit agencies, labor unions, or neighborhood associations

An enduring characteristic of the faith-based community organizing field has been its capacity to bridge racial/ethnic divides across these member institutions. That capacity represents a remarkably rare resource in American society. The American experience of African American slavery plus systematic discrimination, racism, and de jure or de facto segregation—not only against African Americans but also vis-à-vis Native Americans, Hispanics, Asian–Pacific Islanders, and immigrant groups from elsewhere at least initially—has left a deep legacy. Very few civic associations build much "bridging social capital" across the resulting racial/ethnic divides.[1] Until now, claims of the faith-based organizing field's capacity to generate bridging social capital has been based on nonscholarly anecdotal portrayals or on scholarly case studies designed for other purposes, which thus could not claim representativity.[2] We can now portray with confidence the field's actual diversity of membership for the first time and thus characterize the institutional foundation for its linkage of universalist democratic ideals to a multicultural organizational reality.

The National Study of Community Organizing Coalitions defined the racial/ethnic identity of a member institution to be the racial/ethnic group that represents a majority in that institution. That is, rather than collecting data on individual participants in this work—data we were sure would be unreliable, given the fuzzy definitions of what an "individual participant" is in a field defined by *institutional* membership, and the obvious fact that we could not attend events nationwide to actually observe participants—we collected data on the primary racial/ethnic identity of each of the 4,500 member institutions. If no group represents more than 50%, then the institution was identified as being multiracial.[3]

The resulting picture shows an impressive level of diversity within the field: A little less than half of the member institutions (46%) are majority white. Some of these might well have significant numbers of nonwhite members or even be nearly multiracial by our definition. But given the substantial racial separation in American religion and the fact that three-quarters of these institutions are religious congregations, many would presumably be nearly monoracial. A little less than a third (30%) of the member institutions are majority black; one in seven (13%) is majority Hispanic; one in twelve (8.3%) is multiracial (that is, no racial/ethnic

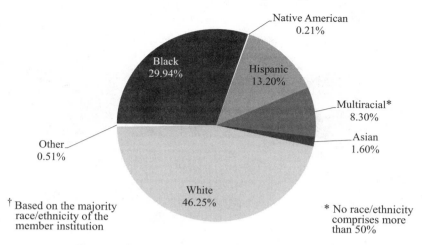

Figure 3.2 The race/ethnicity of coalition member institutions.

group composed more than 50% of the members); and 2.3% of the member institutions are categorized as "other" (that is, predominantly made up of Asian, Native American, or other ethnicities).

How does this level of racial/ethnic diversity compare with American society more broadly? Two comparisons seem most relevant: member institutions compared to the US population as a whole (figure 3.3) and member congregations compared to all US religious congregations (figure 3.4).

On both of these comparisons, the field of faith-based organizing emerges as significantly more diverse on racial/ethnic lines—and (as discussed in chapter 2) in comparison with the governing boards of all US nonprofits, which are 86% white, dramatically more diverse.[4] In this way, the field swims against the tide of deep trends in American civil society in which voluntary associations tend toward racial homogeneity.[5]

Note that the field has achieved this level of diverse membership *not* primarily by seeking diversity for its own sake, as if some racial/ethnic profile is in some fundamental sense "better" than another. Rather, the field has built a diverse institutional foundation through two fundamental commitments. First and most crucially, since its origins in Alinsky's work the fundamental *ethical stance* of the field committed it to addressing "quality of life" issues affecting the bottom half of the socioeconomic spectrum of American society. As a result, its constituent base reflects the fact that income—and even more so wealth—in the United States are skewed on racial and ethnic lines. Poverty, near poverty, and the economic vulnerability of the lower middle class all disproportionately affect African Ameri-

Percentage of member institutions that are *predominantly*...

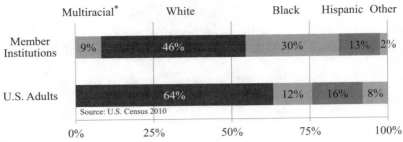

Figure 3.3 The race/ethnicity of coalition member institutions compared with all US adults.

Percentage of congregations that are *predominantly*...

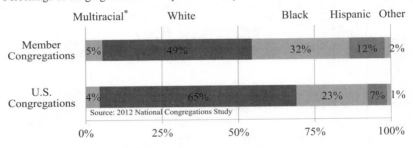

† Based on the majority race/ethnicity of the member institution/congregation

* No race/ethnicity comprises more than 50%

Figure 3.4 The race/ethnicity of coalition member congregations
compared with all US congregations.

cans, Hispanics, Native Americans, and certain groups of Asian immigrant populations. Relatedly, the field's origins and ongoing focus on urban areas, where African Americans and Hispanics—the two largest groups—are concentrated, reinforces these coalitions' diverse base. Second, key strategists in the field in recent decades appear to have calculated that among their coalitions' best strategic assets is the ability to speak credibly for a variety of sectors—not just for poor urban blacks but also for middle-class suburban whites; not just for middle-class blacks but also for poor Hispanic immigrants; not just for middle-class Hispanics in the suburbs but also for members of multiracial urban congregations. Thus for strategic reasons driven by their effort to build organizational credibility and power, they have sought to pull in institutional members across the various racial/

ethnic divides of American life. Together, these ethical and strategic factors have intertwined over time to construct the field on a highly diverse institutional foundation; *demographic* diversity is thus in a sense in the field's institutional DNA.

However, so far we have only seen that this is the case in the national aggregate—that is, we have shown only that the field of faith-based organizing nationally incorporates an impressive level of diversity. But for this field to authentically link universal democratic commitments to multicultural dynamics, there must be significant racial/ethnic diversity at the *local level*, where most organizing activity takes place.[6] Is that the case?

To capture the local diversity of faith-based community organizing coalitions, we use a more comprehensive measure of diversity that takes into account *both* the number of racial/ethnic groups *and* the proportion of each group represented within a coalition. As explored more fully below, this diversity scale can be used to measure and compare the diversity of coalitions that have different group configurations.[7] But most important here, it allows us to assess diversity at the local level as well as at higher levels.

The diversity scale calculates a *diversity score* that ranges from 0 to 1, and we can interpret the score as the probability that two randomly selected member institutions within a coalition will be of a different race/ethnicity. Based on this scale, a monoracial coalition has a diversity score of 0 (the probability that two randomly selected member institutions will be of a different race/ethnicity is 0). As the number of different racial/ethnic groups increases and as the proportion of each group becomes more evenly distributed, the coalition's diversity score approaches 1 (the probability of selecting two member institutions from different races/ethnicities approaches 1). Figure 3.5 shows the 2011 distribution of coalitions based on their diversity score, the percentage of the majority race/ethnicity, and the identity of the majority race/ethnicity.[8]

By using the diversity scale, the racial/ethnic diversity of faith-based community organizing efforts can be compared with the diversity of other community institutions. The average diversity score for faith-based community organizing coalitions was 0.47 in 2011. In comparison, the average diversity score for public schools is 0.33, for US counties is 0.28, and for all US religious congregations is 0.12.[9] Faith-based organizing coalitions thus tend to be significantly more diverse than public schools and US counties, and much more diverse than congregations. In an era of declining social capital, the faith-based organizing field clearly bolsters "bridging capital" by linking Americans across the divides that otherwise separate them.

Of the coalitions for which we have complete data and can thus calcu-

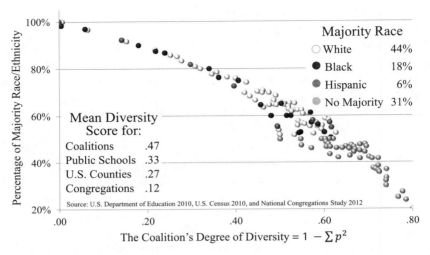

Figure 3.5 The racial/ethnic diversity score of faith-based community organizing coalitions.

late a diversity score (n = 166), 81% have a diversity score greater than the average diversity score for US counties, 80% have a diversity score greater than the average public school, and 56% have a diversity score greater than 0.5. These data show that faith-based organizing embodies high levels of diversity *not* just at the aggregate national level—as would be the case if many local coalitions were almost exclusively white and many others were almost exclusively black, to take a simple hypothetical example not uncommon in other settings, such as neighborhoods. Rather, faith-based organizing embodies high levels of racial/ethnic diversity *at the local level,* where most of its organizing work occurs. Thus when a local coalition brings together participants from its member institutions for training in democratic skills, for research meetings with public officials or academic experts, for political actions and accountability sessions, or to celebrate a victory, these gatherings typically bring racially, ethnically (and, as we saw in chapter 2, socioeconomically) diverse leaders into close interpersonal interaction.

Finally, two further notes: First, less than half of these coalitions (44%) have a majority of white member institutions, while 18% are majority black, 6% are majority Hispanic, and almost a third (31%) have no single racial/ethnic group that represents a majority of its member institutions. Second, faith-based organizing also increasingly embodies additional dimensions of diversity via extensive national-level organizing that introduces leaders to cultures not available locally: differing regional cultures,

Hispanic ethnic subcultures, minority religious traditions including Muslims, and so forth.

All this leads to one strategically crucial result. The racial and ethnic diversity underpinning the field is not simply the diversity of marginalized racial and ethnic minorities. Rather, it includes substantial representation of institutions in which white Americans also gather for worship, union organizing, school improvement efforts, and other purposes. Thus the close interpersonal interaction that occurs within one-to-one meetings and while strategizing together includes interaction with people of the "white" racial and ethnic identity that still holds dominant control of political, institutional, and especially economic power in the United States (even as it is gradually losing hegemony in many settings). There is a politically important sense in which such settings are *more* diverse than even highly diverse minority-only settings. In these settings, racial and ethnic minorities active in faith-based organizing gain experience in collaborating closely with one another *and* with white Americans in a cultural and institutional context wherein all participants are considered equals—at least, one in which organizational leaders often strive to hold themselves accountable to that ideal to a greater degree than is true in many American contexts. This is not liberal "interracial dialogue" à la efforts in the 1960s to heal the racial divide. Instead, this is shared work in the democratic public arena, in pursuit of shared interests.

Likewise, participants from the white racial/ethnic *majority* also gain experience in collaborating closely with colleagues from other racial and ethnic backgrounds. The white racial/ethnic majority may initially categorize those from other racial and ethnic backgrounds in generic terms as "people of color," but in the course of shared work they are rapidly pushed to see individual humanity rather than a generic "other." In this cultural and institutional context, as we see in detail in the next chapter, it may be harder to arrogantly or subtly assume a stance of superiority. At a minimum, one is more likely to have such a stance of implicit superiority challenged and unmasked (at least in some sectors of the field, where explicit commitment to racial equity has emerged).

Thus the internal world of faith-based organizing is not simply a "subaltern counterpublic" in which the racially marginalized gather to reclaim and redeem their humanity against the dehumanizing dynamics of racially tinged or openly racist cultural assumptions.[10] Faith-based community organizing, however, does include spaces in which subaltern racial and ethnic groups can gather to build their own spheres of democratic discourse. For example, some of the organizing networks have created regular venues in which professional staff members from communities of color discuss their experience and how to strengthen their work. But fundamentally the field creates cross-racial public spaces within the organizing process and links those internal public spaces *both* to these subaltern counterpublics *and* to the wider public arena that undergirds American democracy—"undergirds" it to the extent that American democracy has not been undermined by efforts to de-legitimize public institutions and egalitarian claims.

In all these ways—in its broad national diversity as well as its locally grounded diversity, and in the character of the cross-racial interactions that emerge through the work of organizing—the field of faith-based community organizing operationalizes its historic commitment to universalist models of democracy, but does so within local coalitions that bridge the divides that often separate the increasingly multiracial and multicultural communities of American life. This is so despite the continuing fact that the religious congregations that constitute the field's primary institutional base are not by and large very good at this kind of bridging on their own.[11] Faith-based organizing builds multiracial coalitions not by mobilizing the relatively small number of multiracial congregations that exist, but rather by linking a wide array of faith communities—the vast majority of which are far less internally diverse.

So far, so good. But what if the racial/ethnic diversity of the field is actually decreasing?

And Yet . . . Is Diversity in Faith-Based Organizing on the Decline?

All of the above offers a strong case that faith-based organizing constitutes a multiracially grounded yet universalist democratic movement and begins to show how the field addresses the resulting internal tensions. But pursuing that analysis must confront the following: in some ways, diversity in faith-based organizing appears to have *declined* over the last decade.[12] Consider the comparison of the best available data for assessing change over time in the diversity of the field illustrated in figure 3.6. As figure 3.6 shows, the racial/ethnic diversity represented by the predominant racial/ethnic identity of member institutions has shifted over the last decade. The percentage of majority white member institutions increased, and the percentage of black and Hispanic member institutions decreased.

Likewise, the racial/ethnic composition of coalition governing boards and organizing staff also shifted. We saw in chapter 2 the makeup of

Percentage of member institutions that are *predominantly…*

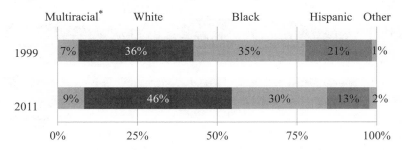

† Based on the majority race/ethnicity of the member institution/congregation
* No race/ethnicity comprises more than 50%

Figure 3.6 The race/ethnicity of coalition member institutions in 1999 and 2011.

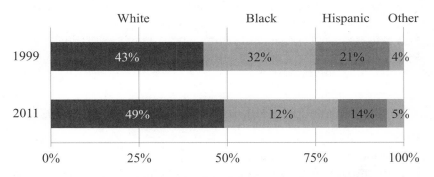

Figure 3.7 The race/ethnicity of coalition board members in 1999 and 2011.

boards and staff in 2011, but how has that picture *changed* over the preceding decade?

As shown in figures 3.7 and 3.8, the percentage of white board members increased, the percentage of Hispanic board members decreased, and the percentage of black board members remained the same. However, the picture among organizing staff differs: the percentage of Hispanic organizers increased, and the percentage of white and black organizers decreased.[13]

Thus while the field's overall professional staffing became more diverse over the last decade, the percentage of black organizers decreased (however, note that these data generalize by presenting field-wide trends; as we shall see in part II, some sectors of the field show significant increases in both Hispanic and black organizers). Meanwhile, the field's institutional base and boards of directors became *less* racially/ethnically diverse (by this

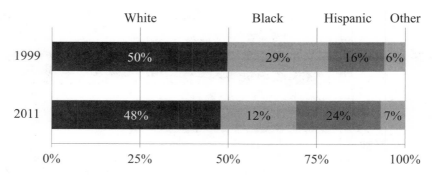

Figure 3.8 The race/ethnicity of coalition organizing staff in 1999 and 2011.

measure; see below for different results from the more sophisticated "diversity score" measure).[14] In sum, certain facets of racial/ethnic diversity have declined and raise legitimate concerns, which we explore shortly, but the changes in the field cannot be summarized simply as declining diversity. Rather, racial/ethnic diversity within the field is changing in complex ways and for complex reasons.

The Strategic and Institutional Origins of Changing Diversity

Why has the field become less diverse along certain dimensions over the last decade? It is important to parse this dynamic with care, to avoid caricaturing the complex changes occurring in faith-based organizing. We do so in two steps: First by discussing what dynamics *might* explain these patterns, then by analyzing our data to suggest which of those dynamics appear most significant. For example, it is *not* that those coalitions that existed in 1999 became less diverse. Indeed, the National Study of Community Organizing Coalitions data show that the coalitions that survived from 1999 to 2011 became *more diverse* on average.[15] Rather, the changing demographics of faith-based organizing partly reflect a key strategic dynamic in the field over the last decade that includes a deliberate effort to involve white constituents. Beginning around the start of the new millennium, strategists within the field arguing for the importance of projecting power into higher-level political arenas began to gain greater traction in some networks or sectors of networks. They also began to "think with" strategists from outside the network structures, and with scholars of social movement mobilization and democratic theory (see chapter 4). Among the critical insights that emerged and gained traction: That even high-quality community organizing at the local level—as crucial as this is in a field that wholeheartedly affirms the standard political adage that "all politics is local"—typically fails to affect the higher-level decision making that largely shapes economic flows, and that any serious effort to improve the quality of life in poor and middle-income communities requires gaining influence where those decisions are actually made. This insight is typically discussed as "getting to scale." In our interviews with strategic thinkers in the field, PICO executive director Scott Reed expressed the key insight as follows:

> One of the great things that has happened in the terrain of organizing is [the increasing number] of significant players in the field who recognize the need to collaborate, if not align their work. And that spirit is real important. If there's a remarkable change in the field of organizing over the last five or six years, it is this: Faith-based organizing comes out of a set of practices that were fairly stagnant and networks that were fairly stagnant, and individuals in the field were fairly isolated from one another. I think that is really changing. So it's a question of whether that can create scale. On the one hand, you've got talent. But how do we get to the scale that we win? I think that's the most complex and daunting problem.

The "New Voices" effort since 2005 (profiled in chapter 1) has been the PICO National Network's effort to really "get to scale" to affect national-level decision making, and the most ambitious such effort in the field to date. Other important efforts to shape national-level policy have also been undertaken by National People's Action and by Gamaliel, and all three of these plus the Industrial Areas Foundation, DART, and the Ohio Organizing Collaborative have significant projects shaping state-level policy in their regions of strength.

Over the last decade the networks have thus made major efforts to project power into higher-level political arenas. Once they made the decision to do so, significant strategic calculations came into play. Most importantly for the racial and ethnic diversity of the field was the following calculation: In order to shape policy making in state legislatures and in the US Congress, it is critical to have both a broad presence across many political districts (to speak credibly with and sometimes put pressure on legislators to support a given issue) and to be able to influence the key wielders of power—many of whom still represent relatively white districts (although this is changing). So the strategy of seeking to better shape the quality of life in poor and middle-class (and thus disproportionately nonwhite) neighborhoods and communities led many coalitions to expand beyond core urban districts into the suburbs. Although such suburbs today often

Figure 3.9 Leaders from across the Gamaliel network after holding a news conference on suppression of voter rights at the Martin Luther King Monument (Washington, DC, December 2013). (Photo by Heather Wilson)

include significant minority populations, they still typically have a larger white percentage than do the urban cores. The same strategic calculation led some networks to expand into regions and states that had not previously had much of a faith-based organizing presence. Thus the field has expanded into secondary cities of the upper Midwest (Wisconsin, Michigan), the Northeast (Maine, New Hampshire, Vermont, upstate New York), and the mountain West (Montana in 2011, and later in Utah). Paradoxically, while such choices potentially increase the field's strategic capacity to address the issues crucial to its lower-income constituents (including predominantly black and Hispanic communities), they simultaneously *increase* the field's membership base in predominantly white institutions.

For similar strategic reasons, some sectors in the field strove to increase the *religious* diversity of their organizing base. The strategic calculations behind this move included finding a stronger institutional base in a period when liberal Protestant, historic African American, and urban Catholic congregations are struggling; gaining the political credibility that might come with participation from broader faith communities; and a less strategically driven sense that welcoming minority faith traditions was simply a good thing to do. The resulting outreach was especially effective vis-à-vis Unitarian Universalist churches and Jewish synagogues (see chapter 2).[16]

However, given that all of the Unitarian Universalist and Jewish congregations represented in our survey are majority white, this strategic recruitment has led to a relative decrease in the proportion of nonwhite member institutions.

Alongside these strategically driven factors, other more contextual dynamics also may have contributed to the "whitening" of the field in some dimensions. First, changes within the Catholic Church in the United States may have decreased Catholic participation, which brings a large part of the Hispanic presence into the faith-based organizing field. These changes include fiscal challenges that have led to the closing of many urban parishes and a substantial shift in emphasis in the public voice of the national leadership structure of bishops. Over the decade prior to the 2011 data collection for the National Study of Community Organizing Coalitions, although the United States Conference of Catholic Bishops sustained a voice on issues of social justice and economic life, its leadership clearly placed far greater emphasis on its prolife/antiabortion work, high-profile fights against gay marriage, and teachings on issues of sexual morality, stem cell research, and end-of-life ethics. The resulting climate within church culture, along with the more "priestly" orientation and less working-class backgrounds of those entering seminary in recent years, appears to lead fewer young priests to see faith-based organizing for poor communities' interests as central to their calling—or as a route to advancement within the ecclesial hierarchy.[17] As of this writing, it remains to be seen whether the shift of Vatican tenor under Pope Francis will produce changes in priestly incentive structures or training that might affect these trends.

Second, the intense hostility toward undocumented immigrants that predominated in American public life in the years leading up to our data collection may well have suppressed Hispanic involvement in faith-based organizing.[18] Thus the drop in membership by Hispanic institutions might reflect Hispanic immigrants' insecurity regarding public engagement.

Third, important national institutions within Jewish, Unitarian Universalist, and Lutheran denominations chose to use faith-based organizing as a key vehicle through which to reinvigorate congregational life and reemphasize their respective social justice ethical traditions.[19] Thus the field's strategic outreach to Jewish synagogues and Unitarian Universalist churches noted above was met by a reciprocal outreach (and funding) from these religious sectors toward faith-based organizing, and strategic "in-reach" from denominations toward their own congregations, in favor of faith-based organizing as a tool of congregational development.

Fourth, the widely documented disparity in wealth between white and nonwhite sectors of American life—the legacy of generations of inequality in America—likely makes nonwhite institutions more vulnerable to failure during economic hard times. Thus the whitening of the field may also reflect the fact that our data collection occurred in the wake of the Great Recession that began in 2008.

Detailed analysis of the data from the National Study of Community Organizing Coalitions partially supports these arguments, but cannot unambiguously prove them. First and most clearly, religious factors drove at least part of the increased white presence in the field. Whereas 21.5% of the member institutions overall (including congregations, labor unions, public schools, and neighborhood associations) were predominantly Hispanic in 1999, of the member institutions who joined a coalition between 1999 and 2011 only 11% were predominantly Hispanic. Most of this was driven by a significant decrease in the presence of Hispanic congregations, which fell by over 13% the decade-plus after 1999. This decline reflected lower participation of Catholic parishes generally—and Hispanic Catholic parishes particularly—after 1999. Catholic parishes made up 40% of member congregations in 1999, but among the congregations that joined thereafter only 23% are Catholic. And of all the Catholic parishes that were members in 1999, 50% were Hispanic, but of those that joined after 1999, only 28% were Hispanic. The combination of these two dynamics means that only 6.5% of congregations joining after 1999 were Hispanic Catholic parishes, whereas 20% of congregations involved in faith-based organizing efforts in1999 were Hispanic Catholic parishes.[20] Thus some of the "whitening" of the field resulted from the withdrawal of Hispanic Catholic parishes, which was driven partially by the dynamics discussed above.

Several factors linked to religion, including this decline in Hispanic Catholic participation and an increase in Jewish and Unitarian participation, probably account for much of the 1999–2011 increase in the white presence in faith-based organizing.

But, second, the increase in white presence may also have resulted from the greater vulnerability of nonwhite institutions to failure in the face of economic crises, due to the far thinner accumulated wealth held by minority communities. Our data might capture such vulnerability in either of two ways: In the attrition of *entire* coalitions or in the attrition of member institutions *within* coalitions. Regarding the former, greater internal diversity did decrease a coalition's likelihood of surviving. We know this because the coalitions that did not survive the 1999–2011 period—that is, existed in 1999 but not in 2011, and thus plausibly may have fallen victim to the "dot-com" or the "Great Recession" economic crises—were more diverse than those that survived those downturns.[21] However, our data cannot disentangle whether these coalitions failed due to economic pressures, internal conflicts, or for other reasons.[22]

Regarding attrition of individual member institutions *within* faith-based community organizing coalitions, the vulnerability of nonwhite member institutions also mattered. Within coalitions that existed throughout the 1999–2011 period, predominantly minority institutions were more likely to discontinue their membership than were predominantly white institutions.[23] In addition, in the ongoing gain and loss of member institutions that occurs within all coalitions, black member institutions that discontinued their membership were the least likely to be replaced by a new member institution of their same racial/ethnic profile.[24]

Thus disproportionate institutional failure at the level of coalitions or member institutions likely contributed to the increased white presence over the last decade. However, the differences between surviving and nonsurviving institutions are relatively small, so institutional attrition likely accounts for less of the 1999–2011 changes than do the religious dynamics discussed above.

Third comes the question of how the field's strategic geographic expansion influenced its overall racial/ethnic composition. Here, dynamics are complex. Counties that lost a faith-based organizing presence after 1999 on average were 53% white in 2000 and had a diversity score of 0.57. Counties that *gained* a faith-based organizing presence between 1999 and 2011 on average were 61% white in 2010 and had a diversity score of 0.47. Likewise, in 1999 the average coalition had 36% white member institutions and had a racial/ethnic diversity score of 0.47, whereas the average coalition established after that year had 49% white member institutions and a diversity score of 0.43 in 2011.[25] These dynamics alone would "whiten" the field and might reflect the strategic expansion discussed above. However, this interpretation is complicated by the fact that some counties host more than one coalition *and* the fact that underneath all this, American counties generally were diversifying rapidly during this period. Because of these factors, the overall shift in the field looks different. The average county that hosted a coalition in 1999 was 61% white, 17% black, 15% Hispanic, and 7% other, whereas by 2011 the average county hosting a coalition was 59% white, 15% black, 17% Hispanic, and 9% other. Thus, despite the strategic expansion into new counties that were often whiter than existing coalition-host counties, the average host county was less white in 2011 than in 1999, and the average county diversity score rose from 0.47 to 0.49 during that decade.[26]

All told, the field's geographic expansion (into new counties and new states) does not appear to have been a primary driver of the whitening of the faith-based organizing field, though it may have contributed. In any case, in interpreting these dynamics, we do well to compare all this diversity data to the average US county, which is 78% white and has a diversity score of 0.28.

Taken together, these data argue strongly that the factors identified above substantially drove the partial "whitening" of the field of faith-based organizing over the decade between 1999 and 2011. Institutional dynamics within the Catholic Church that likely suppressed Catholic participation disproportionately affected the Hispanic presence in faith-based organizing; religious dynamics within Unitarian Universalist, Jewish, and Lutheran religious sectors, and strategic outreach toward the first two; and perhaps the strategic effort to expand the field's geographic base, all combined to paradoxically "whiten" the field's institutional base—by the measures we have considered so far. Whether this represented a net strategic gain in strategic capacity, or a net loss, depends crucially on other internal dynamics in the field. Before examining those dynamics, however, we must consider a rather different reading of the diversity picture within faith-based organizing.

Better Measures? Capturing the Complex Diversity Picture

The above analysis represents one reasonable way of assessing racial/ethnic diversity in the faith-based organizing field. But recall that when a local faith-based community organizing coalition moves to exert influence in the public arena, all member institutions are asked to turn out large proportions of their constituents. When done well, depending on the size of the local coalition, this regularly produces meetings of a few hundred to several thousand people; these are the "accountability sessions" or "political actions" that represent the field's central source of political influence at the local level.[27] By focusing on the majority makeup of member *institutions*, the above analysis misses the fact that some institutions turn out far larger numbers of *participants* than others—especially to the accountability sessions and public actions that are central to this form of grassroots representative democracy.

To see how this might matter, note that Catholic institutions *and* Hispanic institutions are heavily overrepresented among the largest member institutions across the field of faith-based organizing. Tables 3.1 and 3.2 show this clearly, breaking out large (1,000–4,999 constituents) and very large (5,000 or more constituents) member institutions (MIs).[28]

Table 3.1 Large and very large member institutions (MIs) by religion

Religion	All MIs (n = 3,454)	MIs with 1,000 - 4,999 constituents (n = 736) 21.31 %	MIs with >5,000 constituents (n = 179) 5.18 %
Catholic	24%	57%	59%
Secular	16%	13%	27%
Black Protestant	19%	10%	3%
Mainline Protestant	26%	10%	3%
Jewish	4%	5%	3%
Evangelical	4%	1%	3%
Muslim	1%	1%	2%
Unitarian Universalist	3%	1%	0%
Pentecostal	2%	1%	0%
Other	1%	0%	0%

Table 3.2 Large and very large member institutions (MIs) by race/ethnicity

Race/Ethnicity	All MIs (n = 3,377)	MIs between 1,000 - 4,999 (n = 720) 21.32 %	MIs 5,000 or more (n = 167) 4.95 %
White	46%	46%	43%
Black	30%	17%	19%
Hispanic	13%	27%	31%
Other	11%	10%	8%

Catholic parishes make up just under a quarter of all faith-based organizing member institutions, yet they make up nearly three-fifths of the large and very large member institutions. Similarly, whereas predominantly Hispanic institutions (mostly churches) make up 13% of all member institutions, they make up over a quarter of the large member institutions and nearly a third of the very large member institutions. All told, churches that are both Catholic and predominantly Hispanic are heavily represented among the largest institutional sponsors of faith-based organizing. Thus even after the declines of the last decade, Hispanic Catholic parishes in 2011 represented about a quarter of the large (23%) and very large (27%) sponsors, whereas they constitute only 8% of all member institutions.

The above analysis of institutions—the only level at which we have data to compare the racial/ethnic composition of the field in 1999 and 2011—tells us a great deal about changes in the field but may greatly underestimate the field's actual racial and ethnic diversity at the individual level of analysis. This cuts two ways, however. On the one hand, as reflected in many ethnographic accounts, the actual racial/ethnic diversity at public actions is likely far greater than might be assumed based on institutional profiles alone.[29] On the other hand, this also implies that the falloff in Hispanic Catholic parishes' involvement over the last decade has probably disproportionately affected the Hispanic presence in public actions.

Two other factors complicate our assessment of the changing racial/ethnic diversity in the field. First, even though the faith-based organizing field as a whole has become less racially/ethnically diverse in the sense described above, the percentage of coalitions that are monoracial (that is, all of their member institutions had the same racial/ethnic identity) has decreased. In 1999, 11% were monoracial; by 2011 only 8% of coalitions were monoracial. Furthermore, "monoracial" looks different in different settings. Three of the fourteen monoracial coalitions in 2011 were all black and practiced a model of organizing that focused explicitly on organizing in African American congregations. Two of the fourteen were Hispanic and located in the Rio Grande Valley of Texas, an overwhelmingly Hispanic region. The remaining nine had only majority white member institutions and organized in Maine, Vermont, small-town Wisconsin, Oregon, upstate New York, eastern Washington, and suburban California, some but not all of which have relatively small nonwhite populations. Thus while problematic questions can legitimately be raised about monoracial organizing in an increasingly diverse America, many of these cases can readily be attributed to local demographics. Also, in 2011 three-quarters (77%) of local coalitions had at least one black member institution, and two-thirds (68%) had at least one Hispanic member institution (nearly all had at least one white member institution). Compared to 1999, the percentage of coalitions represented by only two racial/ethnic groups decreased from 41% to 35%, while the percentage of coalitions represented by three or more racial groups increased from 48% to 57%.[30]

Second, the more nuanced "diversity score" approach outlined above shows a quite different pattern. Recall that a coalition's diversity score can be interpreted as the probability that any two randomly selected member institutions will be of different racial/ethnic groups. This provides a more quantifiable and more nuanced way of measuring diversity than simply assessing whiteness, in part because it implicitly counts all racial/ethnic groups as contributing equally to diversity, and in part because it takes into account both the number of different racial/ethnic groups and the proportion of each group. On this measure, the diversity of faith-based organizing coalitions has actually *increased* over the last decade, albeit marginally. The mean diversity score for coalitions was 0.455 in 1999 and 0.467 in 2011.

Furthermore, as shown in figure 3.5 on page 72, the spread of diversity scores also shows that many "less diverse" coalitions were predominantly made up of minority institutions. Thus, in both 1999 and 2011, considering the entire field of faith-based community organizing, if two member institutions were randomly selected from a coalition there was an almost 50% chance that they would be from different racial/ethnic groups. In coalitions where two randomly selected institutions were more likely to be from the same racial/ethnic group (toward the left side of figure 3.5), they were as likely to be black or Hispanic as to be white.

No simple summary can fully capture the complex patterns of racial/ethnic diversity within faith-based organizing. By some measures, the field has become less diverse in the last decade; by other measures, it has held its ground or become more diverse. The picture also changes if one considers the field as a whole versus individual coalitions.

But by all measures, the field of faith-based community organizing is more racially/ethnically diverse than America in general—and much more diverse than corporate and nonprofit boards, congregations, and most neighborhoods. That this is broadly true at the local level and not only in the aggregate means that in much of the field participants regularly meet, collaborate, strategize, and hash out political differences with people from across lines of difference—most importantly here racial/ethnic difference.

This finding is further buttressed by the many ethnographic studies of the field that have documented significant cross-racial and cross-ethnic interaction.[31] However, those ethnographic studies have focused mostly on urban settings. Cross-racial contact may be more likely to occur in such settings, so we cannot say for certain just how common substantial cross-racial contact is throughout the field. Given American residential segregation at the neighborhood level, such contact is most likely in settings where metropolitan- or state-level organizing work is substantial, and less likely where organizing focuses at the very local level.

All in all, the field's capacity to bring Americans together across racial and ethnic divides is extraordinary, and extraordinarily important in its potential impact on American political culture, institutions, and politics. Some sectors of the field are enacting that ability regularly, as we shall see in part II. Other sectors of the field are not: that capacity remains latent, due to a more local focus of organizing, lower strategic ambitions, or the challenges of organizing across racial and ethnic divides. In the next chapter, we turn to understanding the internal cultural dynamics through which one network has systematically begun to take on the challenge of bringing people together across racial and ethnic divides in ways that explicitly address racial identity.

Brief Contrast Case: Religious Diversity in Organizing

The new ways that some sectors of faith-based organizing are approaching racial/ethnic differences—to be explored in the following chapters—will come into starker relief if compared to the field's previous practices on this terrain and current practices regarding another axis of internal difference: religious diversity.

At one time, the field handled racial/ethnic and religious diversity in similar ways: *not* by talking about them much, but rather by working together across those axes of difference in shared efforts aimed at advancing equality and democracy in concrete ways, through improvements to neighborhood and city life. That is, the culture of organizing that these groups inherited from Alinsky focused historically on things that united the groups, in the fear (and no doubt some experience) that focusing on racial and religious differences would divide organizations and distract them from the concrete work of improving social and economic conditions in poor neighborhoods.

The thinking that underpinned this approach was articulated by a variety of interviewees, perhaps most fully by Scott Reed, now executive director of the PICO National Network following a four-decade career in organizing:

> I began my organizing career in the early 1970s. This was a very different country in those days. Our vision of organizing was also very different. Much of the community organizing was very local and neighborhood based. *Issues* were thought to be the vehicles that linked folks together. As organizing shifted to project power across neighborhoods in cities, we thought that in order to win, issues needed to be framed to appeal to broad segments of the population by *de-emphasizing race specific agendas.*
>
> This approach is what is now often referred to as "race neutral" thinking. It never meant that organizers were blind to race and class. Every good organizer I have ever known has profoundly engaged race and class in their relationships with leaders. Yet [at that time] we thought it strategically smart to *not* bring such narratives into the public domain. For many of us, issues and campaigns were proxies for race and class in the public narrative of our work. For much of PICO's life, our scope of interest was local and our vision of the work was to equip people to enter into public life by building organizations that could win on local issues.
>
> With that thinking in mind, we often chose issues that united diverse racial communities, and we created public narratives about our work that would build the largest and most diverse base in that community. We believed that this base was built by *focusing attention on the pain experienced in communities* [rather than on race] while also knowing that such pain was more disproportionably felt in communities of color and in low income communities.

That is, PICO—like most of the faith-based organizing field descended from Alinsky's work—often implicitly recognized the racial dimensions of inequity in America, but strategically chose to de-emphasize any explicit discussion of those dimensions in its public narrative about its work or in its internal organizational culture.

Faith-based organizing continues to handle *religious* diversity in a similar way, rarely focusing on lines of difference in order to focus on shared ethical commitments and social priorities. But the field's handling of *racial* difference has changed significantly in the last ten years. Indeed, Reed's next sentence following the above quotation was, "We are now wrestling with a different vision of our work." We shall see much of that vision and work in part II of this book. At the same time, we must also recognize that new practices for explicitly addressing race, ethnicity, and white privilege are by no means spread evenly throughout the field; some have moved in that direction systematically, while others have moved hesitantly or chosen not to do so at all.

Perhaps the most accurate characterization is to say that PICO's work analyzed in part II represents the field's boldest experiment in systematically addressing race, ethnicity, and white privilege, but that a variety of other networks and local coalitions are simultaneously moving in this direction. We cannot yet know the ultimate outcome of those experiments, or even their precise contours. But clearly the field is changing. Most coalitions in the National Study of Community Organizing Coalitions reported discussing racial/ethnic differences either "sometimes" or "often." Coalitions that were more racially/ethnically diverse, as well as those with at least one black member institution, reported discussing racial/ethnic differences more often. Diverse coalitions were also more likely to indicate that racial/ethnic differences complicated, prolonged, hindered, *and* enhanced their planning meetings. The overall culture of faith-based organizing has clearly shifted, in that many coalitions no longer attempt to be "color blind" in their operations. Rather, they appear to be cognizant of racial/ethnic differences, they focus on addressing those differences, and these differences influence their organizing activity.

In contrast, these coalitions reported talking less often about religious differences, and that religious differences tend to have little impact on their planning meetings. Moreover, this opposite way of responding to religious differences becomes amplified as the religious diversity of the coalition increases. Based on these results, it appears that coalitions respond to religious and racial/ethnic differences in contrasting ways. Yet that contrast does not seem to be driven by a lack of religious diversity. As outlined in chapter 1, the field also brings together a high level of religious diversity, with its member congregations including Catholic parishes (27%); Mainline Protestant (32%), black Protestants (24%), and conservative Protestant (7%) churches; Jewish synagogues (5%) and Muslim mosques (1%). The religious traditions active at the local level vary considerably, but nearly always include Mainline Protestant, Catholic, and black Protestant congregations. Fifty-three percent of all coalitions include at least one member congregation that is Evangelical or Pentecostal; 47% include at least one that is Jewish; 49% include at least one that is Unitarian Universalist; and 22% contain at least one that is Muslim.

Our recent collaborative research with Ruth Braunstein on how faith-based organizing coalitions draw on cultural practices to bridge racial and socioeconomic diversity also illuminates the field's contrasting way of handling racial and religious diversity.[32] Across the field, as the racial/ethnic or socioeconomic diversity within a coalition increases, their incorporation of religious practices within the organizing work also tends to increase. Furthermore, coalitions use such practices more as they experience more internal challenges related to racial/ethnic and socioeconomic differences (but not as they incorporate greater religious diversity). We draw on ethnographic evidence to argue that racially and socioeconomically diverse coalitions use religious practices to bridge nonreligious lines of difference that might otherwise undermine internal organizational coherence. Shared commitments to faith—even across lines of religious difference—thus appear to be part of what enables these coalitions to confront the challenges associated with racial/ethnic (and class) differences without tearing themselves apart.

Given the evidence reported here, it is hard to argue that what has driven changes in the practices of organizing vis-à-vis racial/ethnic identity is simply the fact of diversity. If it were so, the fact of religious diversity should also drive increasing focus there, but has not—and in any case the level of racial/ethnic diversity in faith-based organizing has remained at a similar level for over a decade (a high one, compared to most groups in American civil society). Rather, the next chapter shows that it was particular dynamics within the organizing world, particular political and social trends in the wider society, and the agency of particular actors that moved specific parts of the field onto new terrain, which made it possible to focus explicitly on racial identity, racial equity, and (as we shall see more briefly) the rights of immigrants.

Conclusion

Earlier chapters discuss the foundations of faith-based organizing in universalist conceptions of democracy, and document the field's political scale and the diversity of its local-level leaders. This chapter documents the field's racial diversity, including why it has changed and yet remains quite striking. It shows that by some measures diversity has decreased, while by other measures it has held steady or increased—and that these changes are driven both by societal dynamics and by the field's pursuit of political influence. We argue that the continuing significant white participation *and* the rich internal diversity of the field constitute strategic strengths if the goal is to exert influence to change social policy. And we show that racial and ethnic diversity is relatively high even at the local level where it matters most.

While the diversity documented here is impressive, two patterns should cause concern for leaders in the field—at least those committed to addressing economic inequality effectively in ways that overcome national policy paralysis. First, the decline of participation by predominantly Hispanic institutions can only be sobering. Although we have sought to understand that decline in the context of religious, financial, and political changes within and beyond the field, understanding the sources of decline does not reverse it; ongoing declines in participation among the largest minority group in the United States would surely constitute a strategic liability. Since our data collection in 2011, that decline might already have been arrested by the field's vigorous involvement in advocating for comprehensive immigration reform from 2011 to 2014. Or it might in the future be arrested by Pope Francis I's advocacy of a more socially engaged Catholicism.

The second pattern of concern is the field's limited progress as of 2011 in diversifying its local organizing staff. While it has succeeded in diversifying on gender lines, it remains an ongoing struggle to recruit and retain organizers of color. The evidence presented in part II suggests that successful recruiting and retention entails significant transformation of organizational priorities, including explicit attention to racial equity both within coalitions and in the public sphere.

So far we have empirically shown only that the field's social composition and structural position in public life make it a compelling study of racial equity and multiculturalist democracy built on universalist foundations—that is, we have shown that its composition, scale, scope, and political imagination give the field sufficient weight to be of national interest for those interested in deepening democratic voice and equality in America, and that its institutional base, leadership, and professional staff are sufficiently diverse across a variety of dimensions (including gender, immigrant-native, and especially racial/ethnic divides) to offer a compelling case study of universalist-multiculturalist dynamics of political culture. That is as much as the quantitative data from the National Study of Community Organizing Coalitions can give us. We now turn to additional ethnographic and interview-based accounts of the internal lives of these coalitions and networks to understand the dynamics of political culture that color the day-to-day experience of community organizing. We argue that those dynamics allow some of these coalitions to offer a case study in building a shared American future—a future that our political institutions alone currently seem incapable of creating.

PART TWO

Ethical democracy on the ground— organizing, democracy, and the challenges of diversity

Bishop Edgar Vann, Rev. Michael McBride, Dr. Iva Carruthers, Rev. Troy Jackson, and Rev. Jeffrey Brown: Religious voices for ethical democracy (African American Christian Clergy Consultation, August 2012). (Photo by Heather Wilson)

Introduction to Part II

In the introduction to this book, we drew on democratic theorists including Jürgen Habermas, Seyla Benhabib, Nancy Fraser, Iris Marion Young, Jeffrey Stout, Jean Cohen, and Andrew Arato to identify the tension between an emphasis on universal democratic norms—the basis of most historic democratic projects—and an emphasis on a specific commitment to addressing the particular claims embedded in different sectors of a highly multicultural and multiracial society. Then in part I, we argued that the faith-based community organizing sector under its various nomenclatures has today attained sufficient institutional scale to make a significant difference in the dynamics of civil and political society. On the basis of the field's organizational infrastructure, impressive diversity of leadership, and emergent strategic capacity, we showed that at least some sectors of the field have come to occupy a structural position in public life that can—and, we argued, should—aspire to profound influence on our democratic future. That is, that faith-based organizing can be one component of a broad movement toward ethical democracy in America, a constructive response to the ills of our contemporary political, economic, and cultural dynamics.

When Wood first adopted the term "ethical democracy" as a descriptor of the fundamental ethos underlying the work of the best exemplars of faith-based community organizing, little had been known about the field as a whole.[1] Indeed, it was rarely treated as a field at all, with each network and often each local coalition cultivating a separate identity. Today, a decade of scholarly attention and writing by practitioners of the arts and disciplines of organizing has provided much greater insight into the internal dynamics and policy achievements of this field. Various case studies examine particular coalitions and networks, and several books analytically compare this field's organizing model with other forms of organizing; together, these two sets of writing offer substantial depth of insight into the dynamics of grassroots democratic organizing in practice.[2]

Furthermore, two national studies supported by Interfaith Funders—the *State of the Field* study in 1999 and the *National Study of Community Organizing Coalitions* reported in the first three chapters here—provide a detailed picture of the field's changing profile at the level of individual demographics, member institutions, and the local coalitions that coordinate the day-to-day, on-the-ground work and train the participants.

On the basis of previous research, and in anticipation of what follows in subsequent chapters, we summarize the overall profile of the field of faith-based community organizing as follows:

First, each of the sponsoring networks has developed its own specific emphases within its own model of organizing, together with a preferred self-descriptive name for that model: faith-based organizing in the PICO National Network, broad-based organizing in the Industrial Areas Foundation, congregation-based organizing in DART, with Gamaliel alternating between broad-based and faith-based as a self-descriptor.

Yet, second, the real strength of faith-based organizing lies in its nascent capacity to coordinate action as a coherent field and collaborate with other sectors; only in doing so can the field achieve its full democratic potential. Yet too many scholarly analyses and practitioners' writings still embrace the notion that individual networks will somehow manage to make a significant difference on their own. Such analyses do the field and American democracy a disservice.

Third, each network's core organizing model brings its own strengths and limitations, rooted in the structure and staff of the local coalition and the organizational culture of each network.

Fourth, a weak local coalition in any of the networks tends to reflect the less-developed sides of the network to which it belongs, plus idiosyncratic weaknesses of particular local organizing staff.

Fifth—and most importantly for our purposes here—the work of the stronger local coalitions in each of the networks tends to look rather similar, having converged on a set of practices and an overall ethos of organizing. While this convergence has lessened somewhat as some networks have developed in the innovative directions analyzed in part II, a fairly consistent set of best practices continues to undergird the core organizing of strong coalitions. The local dimensions of those practices have been well described by recent accounts, by both scholars and practitioners;[3] less documented are the higher-level practices of the networks through which they generate political influence at the state and (particularly in the case of the PICO National Network) the national level.

Sixth, the term "ethical democracy" still best describes the overall ethos of the stronger exemplars of this work, from local work in towns and cities from the South Valley of Texas to the Twin Cities of Minnesota and from the Central Valley of California to the Gulf Coast of Florida and the river valleys of New England; in state-level work in states including Arizona, California, Nevada, Colorado, Texas, Louisiana, Ohio, Florida, and Massachusetts; and in projecting national-level influence on health care, financial reform, and immigration policy.

Ethical democracy involves the cultivation of grassroots democratic organizations via face-to-face relationships. Through those very local relationships, wider networks of political mobilization are constructed through which consultation regarding problems, issues, and potential policy solutions can occur. In the course of those consultations, some leaders are constituted with the credibility and legitimate authority to speak for wider groups of people—and in particular for people within member institutions and subaltern communities that the local coalitions strive to represent. In this way, this grassroots democratic structure rejects a pure "participative democracy" with its concomitant risk of descending into endless discussion, and instead links up with the existing structure of representative democracy—but in a form capable of focusing on real accountability: elected and other officials held accountable to democratic needs within society, and organizational leaders themselves held accountable to expectations of integrity, transparency, and right-dealing within the organizing structure. In the past, Wood has identified participatory democracy as the core of the *internal* organizing process and representative democracy as the core of the *external* political work of the field, and tried to capture the ethos of ethical democracy via a metaphor:

> Imagine the complex political culture of faith-based organizing, with all its variations and subtleties, as a musical composition as complex as jazz; one can pick out notes and subthemes from many of the political currents at play in American culture today, including strong strands from various religious cultures plus periodic fragments of shallow pragmatism, therapeutic culture, and antigovernment populism. But as the main theme in a jazz masterpiece is constantly reinvoked, the dominant themes in faith-based organizing are participatory democracy and representative democracy. . . . I term [the field's] ethos *"ethical* democracy" because the participatory and representative com-

ponents of its ethos function within the context of a set of orientations regarding the good life and how human communities can thrive; organizers explicitly draw upon these ethical orientations to question the social status quo. In this way, alternatives that in an ethically neutered setting might be considered simple "social choice" material are highlighted as connected to fundamental values of the organization and thus as morally charged.[4]

We would largely stand by that description today, but add that the contemporary field's political culture often more fully embraces and embodies the explicitly socioethical dimensions of its constituent religious traditions *and* sometimes a new emphasis on multiculturalism.

Of course, the above constitutes an ideal. Some organizations fall so short of it so regularly that the term *ethical democracy* simply fails to describe their work. Furthermore, *all* these coalitions periodically fall short of the ideal; at such times, participants draw on their internal cultural resources to right their path. For most, this especially involves spiritual resources of their multiple religious traditions, on which they draw to seek mutual forgiveness and regenerate hope for greater integrity, transparency, and right dealing in the future. At such times—even more than when they draw on religious imagery, stories, or music during public actions—the "faith-based" characteristic of this organizing most comes to life and most undergirds the ethical dimension of the work.

Ethical democracy also entails systematically addressing at least some of the most central democratic challenges that bedevil the American polity today. That is, good organizing can certainly still be done by faithfully addressing local issues facing poor, working-class, and middle-income families. But the ethos of the type of work we suggest constitutes "ethical democracy" aspires to something greater, in addition to such local organizing: Such work dares the ambition to *matter* in larger-scale societal terms by influencing the decisions that actually shape the quality of life in these families and their communities—including decisions that contribute to vast economic inequality, policy paralysis, and racial injustice. If those decisions occur locally, local work is the right venue—but for many years, community organizing settled for only that level of influence. In recent years, some faith-based organizing coalitions and networks have become significant players in shaping health care reform, financial reform, criminal justice policy, and immigration reform at higher levels of government, all with the aim of benefiting such working families. Thus the better work in the field links ethically grounded local relationships to addressing some of the most substantive issues that bedevil the American policy, via work in both local and higher-level political arenas. On this count, too, the term *ethical democracy* seems appropriate both to describe the best work in the field and to challenge the field to live up to its promise.

But, finally, for participative democracy to really matter in deep ethical and longue durée political terms, it must not only address current issues of economic inequality and policy paralysis, it must also engage in reshaping the deep dynamics of political culture that have bedeviled American society from top to bottom for generations—indeed, since before the founding of the American republic. This most obviously means addressing how work to decrease inequality and policy paralysis interacts with questions of race and racism in American institutions and the American psyche. To this we now turn—no easy turn, for such dynamics are not only "out there" in American society but also "in here" within the internal cultures of even carriers of ethical democracy.

Thus part II takes on a different issue: Does at least some significant sector of the field successfully link commitment to universal democratic values with work in marginalized communities—and do so in ways that explicitly engage in the "politics of difference" that matter for racially and culturally diverse constituents? When they succeed, how do they link their commitment to universal democracy with their multicultural organizational reality? In what ways does such work undergird or complicate work against economic inequality and policy paralysis?

In answering these questions, we draw primarily on our research in the national organizing network that has most aspired to combine local organizing with state- and national-level influence and to systematically address racial equity in its work: The PICO National Network. As briefly noted and now to be explored in depth, PICO's work in placing racial equity front and center on its organizational agenda constitutes the boldest experiment on this terrain within the field of contemporary faith-based organizing. It is by no means the only such effort, with Gamaliel as a network and a variety of local coalitions and regional or statewide organizing efforts having incorporated a priority on explicitly addressing racial equity. Thus work for racial equity has broad contours across the field, but in PICO's work we can see it in its most developed form and most systematically linked to local, state, and national organizing.

We now turn to explore the organizational dynamics involved in linking universalist and multiculturalist models of democracy, and in inserting the direct promotion of racial equity into the battle against rising inequality and political stagnation. To explore those dynamics, we draw on ethnographic and interview data, primarily but not exclusively from within the

PICO National Network. In keeping with this kind of data, so different from the survey data at the core of part I, part II shifts to a more interpretive mode of analysis in order to probe the cultural and institutional dynamics within PICO's complex organizational transformation. Understanding those dynamics will allow us to better understand the achievements not just of PICO but also of the broader field *and* the ongoing challenges inherent in work for racial equity, reduced inequality, and more effective democratic policy making. In providing a clearer picture, we hope to help advance the project of ethical democracy.

Figure 4.1 Rev. Jennifer Jones-Bridgett (PICO-Louisiana) and Dr. Iva Carruthers (Samuel DeWitt Proctor Conference). (Photo by Heather Wilson)

FOUR

Transforming Institutions:
The Strategic and Ethical Dynamics of Commitment to Racial Equity

In this chapter we follow a rather different angle of analysis than in the previous chapters. Up to here we have explored primarily the "objective" diversity that undergirds the efforts by faith-based community organizing to link universalist and multiculturalist democratic commitments. Here we explore the *internal dynamics* through which key actors in the field have sought to embody those democratic commitments. Only if that effort finds some measure of success can we really speak of this organizing vehicle as carrying the ethos of ethical democracy onto the terrain of racial and ethnic claims-making in American life.

In the crucial case analyzed below, the central network and key leaders, clergy, and organizers took up initial forays on this terrain fairly quickly (albeit with much soul searching). So here we focus primarily on organizational dynamics at the network level, which provide the key nexus of the struggle over how to link racial equity and work against inequality.

In the course of the following analysis, we will meet many individuals who have advanced racial equity work within the field of faith-based organizing—that is, efforts to assure that all racial and ethnic groups in American life have full access to the benefits of American institutions, despite the historical legacies and ongoing dynamics of racial and ethnic bias. We analyze the hard work that went into—and continues to go into—building institutions and organizational cultures capable of doing such work while remaining grounded in an overarching commitment to universalist democratic principles. That entails hard work in part because the community organizing tradition descended from Alinsky had assumed that universalist democratic commitments could best be built by eschewing any focus on race. As a result, advocates have struggled to convince people in this field (as elsewhere in American life) that embodying democracy requires explicitly addressing the racial dimensions of economic in-equality. That difficulty may arise partly because poverty and race are so deeply intertwined in America, such that virtually *any* serious antipoverty work can be interpreted as already contributing to racial equity; it may arise also due to the internal defensiveness of those who experience them-selves as nonracist but have not come to terms with the dynamics of im-plicit bias discussed below. In any case, explicitly addressing the linkages between inequality and racial bias has come neither easily nor via consen-sus. Rather, particular agents of transformation have led the way to chang-ing how faith-based organizing approaches race, often against opposition. By probing their experience—their achievements and their struggles—we can gain important insight for a broader project of transforming the cul-tural and institutional foundations of American democracy to better serve the multiculturalist realities of twenty-first-century America.

We begin by explaining why we focus on the work of the PICO National Network and by analyzing the dynamics of leadership and organizational change behind the network's embrace of racial equity. The chapter then presents the conceptual and analytic framework undergirding PICO's com-mitment to racial equity and racial justice, and closes by describing the issue work that concretely expresses that commitment. The theme that uni-fies this analysis is the way key thought leaders within the PICO network (i) drew on emergent understandings of race in American culture, in order to (ii) craft a process of organizational change addressing racial equity and (iii) raise their network's capacity for concrete political work against eco-nomic inequality and racial injustice. The three processes were interlinked and, at least at their best, mutually reinforcing.

Getting Real: Building a Culture of Engagement on Racial Equity, Preserving Political Efficacy

The PICO National Network focused for its first twenty years almost ex-clusively on organizing at the *local* level (as some organizing efforts con-tinue to do today). Such purely local organizing has been widely criticized, sometimes justly, but should not be caricatured. Engaging Americans in the public realm—especially those previously marginalized by or apathetic about political life—requires some prospect of making a difference. Since building and sustaining influence is far more difficult at the state and na-tional levels than at the local level, exerting local power represents a more reliable way of delivering immediate results. So, like most community organizing efforts, PICO had concentrated on influencing decisions at the neighborhood, city, and metropolitan levels.

However, like many community organizing projects, by the mid-1990s PICO had discovered that while they continued to wield influence over local decisions, such influence was increasingly inadequate to meet the challenges facing their working class constituents. In the context of municipal dependence on monetary flows controlled at state and federal levels, local decision making only kicks in after more substantial decisions are made; the decisions that the local coalitions previously could influence only occurred within vast constraints imposed by those higher-level decisions. To take but one example from a city where we will later see examples of racial equity work in organizing: In Philadelphia, today neither the city's budget nor its educational system is locally controlled. Rather, due to prior fiscal problems, a state-level commission ultimately controls the city budgets; a five-member School Reform Commission—three of whose members are appointed by the governor—controls the local school district.[1] This represents a more extreme example of the broader national reality that local quality of life depends mightily on state and federal decisions. While Philadelphia represents an extreme case, the widespread pattern of little local control over key decisions led network leaders to conclude that influencing state and federal policy was necessary if PICO wanted to respond adequately to the challenges faced by low- and moderate-income communities and the nation as a whole.

PICO's initial effort drew on its strong presence in California to shape education and health care policy in that large and complex political arena. Beginning in 1995, PICO California (originally the PICO California Project) built its profile through regular large-scale political actions and coalitional work focused on educational, health care, and housing policy. With a small staff under the leadership of Jim Keddy and by leveraging the work of eighteen PICO-affiliated coalitions throughout the state, over the next ten years PICO California became one of the most prominent organizations—and the single most salient religious voice—on these issues within California politics.[2]

Meanwhile, PICO's national executive director Scott Reed (then associate director) was learning from PICO California's experience and began to imagine how to project influence from PICO's nearly four hundred member congregations into crucial *national* policy debates. The effort to do so, originally called "PICO New Voices," was launched between 2002 and 2005, through a gradual process of convening internal leaders and organizers to discuss the possibilities and risks.[3] Early on, grassroots leaders from around the country who participated in PICO New Voices, advised by the national staff, chose education, health care, immigration, housing, and public safety as potential areas of policy focus for the national effort, and ultimately chose to make national health care reform the central arena for their initial work. Under the Bush administration, the key battle involved the renewal of SCHIP, the State Children's Health Insurance Program: whether it would be renewed at all, and if so whether it would be expanded to cover a larger portion of uninsured children. As noted in the introduction, through a series of hard-fought congressional battles a coalition of organizations succeeded in getting SCHIP reauthorization and expansion approved in 2007 and 2008—only to see President George W. Bush veto both bills.[4] PICO New Voices provided the key religious constituency and a significant grassroots presence during those battles, framing the claim for children's health coverage in moral terms rooted in a broad language of faith.[5] This effort strove to reclaim national politics from unproductive squabbling and partisan deadlock in favor of workable coalitions that could pass legislation. Through congressional testimony, coalition formation, press conferences, and events back in legislators' home districts, the effort gained sufficient bipartisan support to twice pass the SCHIP reauthorization and expansion, but ran aground at the presidential level.

One of Congress's first acts after the election of President Barack Obama was to once again pass SCHIP legislation. Recall the photo from the Introduction of PICO leaders seated in the front row of invited guests at the March 2009 White House ceremony at which Obama signed SCHIP reauthorization, flanked by Vice President Joseph Biden and the congressional leaders who had seen the legislation through.[6]

That experience along with PICO's subsequent role in health care reform, financial reform, and other national issues *and* the success of faith-based community organizing coalitions in advocating for policy reform in multiple areas at local and state levels around the country (see chapter 1) demonstrate the political efficacy possible through this model of organizing. Of particular interest here, however, is that PICO continues to build on this political capacity on universalist democratic terrain while simultaneously undergoing an intentional organizational transformation to embrace multicultural and multiracial democratic priorities.

In this chapter, we use PICO's intentional effort to cultivate an organizational culture of explicit engagement with racial equity as a case study to illustrate the cultural and institutional dynamics involved in making such a transition. Multiple groups in the broad organizing sector have made or attempted to make such a transition. We analyze PICO's transition not because it is "typical" of all sectors of the field; finding a "typical" example would be nearly impossible given the diverse ways organizations have taken up or decided not to take up the challenge of racial inequity in America. In fact, of the national faith-based organizing networks, the PICO National Network and the Gamaliel Foundation have been most systematic in linking racial equity and economic justice—and Gamaliel today is rebuilding itself from the divisions and organizational schism that arose during that effort (which coincided with the normal challenges of leadership succession in the organization). As we shall see, the PICO National Network has struggled mightily with the challenges of incorporating a commitment to racial equity into its work, and its embrace has been uneven across different local coalitions. Individual coalitions across the other networks and independent organizing groups have undertaken similar efforts. But overall the PICO National Network has sustained the most focused effort on this terrain, with relative success in incorporating racial equity into its internal culture and external work without fracturing its internal cohesion. PICO thus offers the most analytically revealing case study for understanding the dynamics involved in linking multiculturalist and universalist democratic commitments over time, while preserving organizational efficacy in addressing economic inequality and policy paralysis.

But none of this account should be read idyllically. Like the nation as a whole, PICO and the rest of the field will be wrestling with how best to address the American realities of economic inequality and racial inequity for years to come. The analysis here strives to offer insight that can inform that ongoing national project, culled from one organization's experience as nested within the larger field of faith-based community organizing.

The annual retreat for all the professional organizing staff of PICO affiliates nationwide offers a good window into the kind of self-understanding and strategic thinking behind the network's self-transformation. In June 2012, nearly 150 people—about a fifth African American, a third Latino, less than half white, with a handful of Asian–Pacific Islanders, American Indians, or multiracial individuals—gathered at a rustic mountain retreat center in Applegate, California. Scott Reed had become executive director of the PICO National Network in 2009, upon the partial retirement of longtime founding director John Baumann SJ. We quote here at length from Reed's opening address at one such weeklong staff retreat, as it represents his effort to capture the insights, challenges, and spirit bound up in PICO's ongoing work on this terrain. While it may seem odd to start a chapter on racial equity in this field with an extended quote from a long-established white male organizer, this choice allows us to capture some flavor of PICO's internal cultural work. It is also driven by three considerations. First, it is in keeping with the analysis advanced in recent years under the label of "white antiracism," which argues that it is the particular moral and political burden of whites in America to undo the profound distortions of racism.[7] Second, Reed has gained much of his insight from African American colleagues via dialogue with African American pastors, via agitation for change by African American organizers within PICO, and via learning from prominent African American scholars. Reed here articulates the insights learned from them, and this speech and the week of intense staff discussions that followed were pivotal in PICO's turn toward emphasizing a racial equity analysis. Third, it remains a simple social fact that much of American civil society remains dominated by white Americans.[8] If American politics are to be transformed from below, that effort will have to include articulate and dedicated white leadership of the kind described here, as well as the parallel black leadership we will subsequently discuss.

But first a clarification: The *origins* of PICO's push onto racial equity terrain lay neither in the national staff nor in john powell's intellectual work (presented below). Rather, its origins lay in advocacy by particular clergy leaders and professional staff on the front lines of organizing. Not coincidentally, they were nearly all African American; they ranged from relatively young recruits new to organizing to established organic intellectuals serving as pastors to senior clergy with links back to the civil rights movement. Thus, beginning this discussion with Reed and powell risks creating the illusion that PICO's push onto racial equity terrain was inspired centrally and intellectually rather than via the visceral experience of living black in a racialized society. Ultimately, the prospering of the network's racial equity work has been due in part to central staff commitment and strong intellectual underpinnings, but it originated in the lived realities of African American clergy, staff, and leaders within local organizing coalitions and the wider network. We later meet some of those individuals.

Reed introduced the 2012 annual staff retreat by noting that organizers are "blessed by the opportunity to do the work we do and anxious about this time in America," and that his work allows him "to live out my faith and serve my country."[9] He went on to note, "We sit in a special place with a unique view of the American social, political, and economic landscape; it is a view from the margins," and then to tell actual stories of people victimized by predatory financial institutions or Medicaid cuts that place their lives at risk. He voiced outrage at both banks and politicians behind such policy decisions, and cited the realities underlying the Great Recession: fourteen million unemployed Americans; the highest number of deportations ever; the credit system frozen for millions of families and small businesses, even at a time of record corporate profits and companies holding $4 trillion in cash reserves. He dramatized the social pain behind these figures by quoting the classical Greek poet Aeschylus:[10]

> Even in my sleep,
>
> pain, which cannot forget,
>
> falls drop by drop upon my heart,
>
> until, to my despair, and against my will,
>
> comes wisdom through the grace of Almighty God.

Reed noted that the week would be dedicated to asking *why* such pain exists, saying, "We want to better understand how racialization is creating and maintaining public systems and policies that are crushing dreams and putting lives at risk." He said that answering "why?" would include attention to the ways that economic distress intersects with the racialization of American society—the dynamic through which people are (often subconsciously) ascribed into racial categories and their competence and behavior interpreted in light of those categories.[11]

Reed's introductions of several speakers who would address the organizers during the week's retreat offer some insight into what PICO hoped each would offer the organization:

We have invited john powell to help us develop such understanding [of racialization and its impact on inequality]. john is the executive director of the Kirwan Institute and the Williams Chair in Civil Rights and Civil Liberties at Ohio State University.[12] john has written extensively on issues related to structural racism and racial justice and has, I believe, some profound insights about racialization, about anxiety and about our unconscious. . . . I have been transfixed by his profound wisdom on numerous occasions.

With that introduction, Reed signaled his personal commitment to helping lead the fifty local PICO coalitions and the national network into a frank and personal conversation about race. This signal from the top of the organization would be crucial in sustaining the resulting cross-racial dialogue within a field that, as we have seen in part I, draws on impressive racial and ethnic diversity on the national level but whose local member institutions often reflect the racial segmentation of the broader American society.

Reed's next introduction strove to challenge any complacency among these 150 dedicated community organizers:

> Every single person in this room, irrespective of your age or your professional tenure, must own the following statement: "During my career as an organizer, poverty in our country has become worse. During my watch." During your watch. So we want to better understand how the economy is fundamentally changing and the consequences those changes are producing. We have invited Heather McGhee to help us develop such understanding. Heather directs the Washington Office of Dēmos—a think and do tank. Heather is responsible for developing and executing strategy that impacts federal policy debates on issues of the economy, and was an important partner [for PICO] in the fight for the Dodd-Frank financial reform bill that passed last year.

Reed's final introduction signaled that PICO's move to systematically link its long-standing work against economic inequality to an explicit analysis of racial inequity would involve *change*; that is, such a move could not be built on more of the same work, but rather required new insight and new work on the organization's political culture:

> We are organizers. When we listen to stories, we imagine what we can do to respond. We want to expand our imagination to better understand how explicit racial and economic justice frames can build more powerful organizations. We have invited Doran Schrantz to help us develop such imagination. Doran is an organizing colleague. She directs ISAIAH in Minnesota—a faith based organization of 100 member congregations in the Metro region of the Twin Cities—and is at the heart of shaping a statewide effort. I have come to know Doran and her work well over these past two years, deeply admire and respect her and her organization.

Reed concluded with a standard "credentialing" of his own organization: "Welcome john, Heather, and Doran. You are with PICO—a powerful organizing network rooted in 150 towns and cities committed to developing a more just and equitable country." Note that Reed framed the coming week's meetings around themes of racialization and the anxieties and unconscious dynamics underlying it, rising economic inequality in American society, and the linkage of racial justice and economic justice within a movement long committed to holding democratic institutions accountable for social outcomes. In doing so, Reed strove to articulate a political culture in which racial equity, economic justice, and participative democracy

Figure 4.2 Scott Reed, executive director of the PICO National Network, and Dr. Robert K. Ross, CEO of the California Endowment, (Applegate, June 2014). (Photo by Heather Wilson)

jointly take center stage in a political drama that seeks to make public policy responsive to poor, working-class, and middle-income communities of all racial and ethnic backgrounds. He went on to expand on the theme of faith-based organizing's "unique view of the American social, political, and economic landscape." We quote his articulation on this theme at length, to capture some flavor of the political culture the PICO National Network is striving to construct:

> PICO has a view from a place of power. We have earned this vantage point through decades of strong organizing and a willingness to risk and innovate. We have built and are building powerful local organizations throughout our country, organizations rooted in faith institutions able to project power and solutions to chronic problems facing residents in our communities. Each organization embraces a similar discipline characterized by leadership development. The core aspect of our network is our deep commitment to equip people to embrace their own liberation in a confrontation with power that is oppressing them. Amazing work, and we know it is not good enough.
>
> We have built and are building powerful state networks that amplify local voice in state policy and resource battles, state networks created because we understand that we need to contest decisions being made in state capitals

that impact families in local municipalities. Amazing work, and we know it is not good enough.

We have built and are building a national voice, a voice that contests the big debates about our country's future. [We have done that through] solid organizing that influenced the extension of the State Children's Health Insurance Program and the passage of the Affordable Care Act; organizing that pressed passage of financial reform, organizing that fights to protect Medicaid. . . . Amazing work, and we know it is not good enough.

Reed thus embeds PICO's commitment to racial equity within universalist democratic intentions that center on core moral commitments that transcend but also incorporate racial, ethnic, religious, or other more particular identities—commitments to children, families, economic opportunity, political voice, freedom, and liberation. In an organization highly diverse across racial, ethnic, religious, geographic, and local cultural lines, these overarching commitments can be embraced regardless of such lines of difference, and they can help hold the organization together amid the tensions of cross-racial dialogue on difficult realities.

Reed reinforced this emphasis as he went on to highlight the public influence PICO federations at local and state levels wield, describing their underlying approach as "building a trans-local network" that promotes "a discipline of leader development strongly rooted in local community"; one that is "driven by faith and values, projects those values in the public domain, and unites communities across difference." Finally, in contrast to faith-based organizing's historic approach of addressing issues at only the local level, Reed noted that PICO now strives to "project power in city halls, state rotundas, and our nation's capital in a way that our efforts add up to more than the sum of our parts."

Reed thus *embedded* his articulation of racial equity as lying at the heart of the network's commitments *within* a broader narrative of participative and universalist democracy. In doing so, he affirmed a multicultural and multiracial America not as a stand-alone good unto itself, but rather as a reality that must inform the movement's ambition to transform American society in service of democratic ideals. He then reiterated the broad democratic crisis facing the country, described the "learning culture" that confronting that crisis would require, and evoked the popular alienation produced by rising inequality (via his reiterated theme of "what country are we living in?"):

We sit in a special place with a unique view of the American social, political and economic landscape. It is a place that invites learning and reflection.

Learning requires this interesting mix of humility and confidence: Humility that admits "I do not know enough"; confidence that what I learn will matter. As good as our work is—as significant as the many victories have been—we are losing. Our economy has doubled in size the last forty years—yet wages for most of us and our leaders have stayed flat. Where did the wealth go? This is our economy . . . and we are watching as it is stolen from us. What country are we living in?

We watch as investments in education for our kids are slashed and cut; investments in infrastructures to propel our economy and give us jobs are slashed and cut; investments in public institutions that serve our communities are slashed and cut. What country are we living in?

Our future is still to be determined. We *can* win. Most in America do not want this current reality. Yet, for this [win] to happen, we must renew our commitment to see ourselves as agents of that change. We must bring new tools and new strategies to our work, to complement existing good work. And so this week we will consider a set of ideas and strategies that we believe can extend leader development, grow organizational power, and further equip PICO to contest the direction of our country.

Reed went on to describe the arc of PICO's analysis that led the network to begin thinking more explicitly about racial equity and economic justice, and some of the concrete steps taken in the effort. At the heart of this description was his rhetorical question: Given current American realities, "how can we authentically change our country without explicitly tackling race and class?"

I want to place one such idea and strategy inside a historic perspective. I want to speak for a minute about race and why we are now intent on bringing racial and economic justice frame[s] explicitly into our work. There is a pattern of our internal work as network staff to embrace race and difference more fully and authentically. We have recognized that we need to change and develop new practices if we are to grow into our aspiration that the staff of our network reflects the diversity of our communities. We need to change and develop new practices to nurture the leadership voices of our staff of color and to see those voices in positions of leadership.

So we have launched new strategies: Three years ago we spent this [retreat] week with [organizational consultant] Visions to better equip us to engage relationally across difference.[13] We have established racial identity caucuses as a venue for nurturing staff and equipping our network to more effectively build powerful multicultural organizations. And we have launched a special yearlong leadership seminar for organizers of color. We are on a journey. We have embraced the need for change and taken steps on that pathway. We have not arrived. More and different is needed; more and different will be done. . . . The question we now ask is how can we authentically change our country without explicitly tackling race and class?

In an article in the *American Prospect*, William Julius Wilson eloquently articulates a similar pathway.[14] Wilson explains that he no longer holds to his previous position [of commitment to race-neutral social policy] given our current reality. Neither do I. The challenge in front of us is how to build powerful organizations capable of explicitly engaging racial and economic justice frames and winning policy and resource fights that change our country.

I believe it is increasingly clear that what is happening in the economy as well as in public policy and political domains requires an urgency to move new strategies and to live into new understandings. . . . If our unique practice of organizing truly cares for the whole person—not simply viewing people as means to an end—then we must *create the spaces for leaders to also nurture and express identity.* If we are serious about changing fundamental systems that create inequality and crush opportunity, then we must *build campaigns through the lens of economic and racial justice.*

Lest his audience hear triumphalism and easy confidence in those words, Reed concluded his remarks with some realism and a challenge:

We are organizers, living in the space between "what is" and "what ought to be." We know schools can educate our kids, because we are creating those schools. We know banks can modify loans, because we have forced some to do so. We know health care can be accessible and affordable, because we are making it so. Yet, when you step away from the boutique nature of these victories, *we are losing this country.* But we have choices. We can win. There is urgency to this moment. We sit in a special place with a unique view of the American social, political, and economic landscape. Let's seize this moment.

How Hard It Is: The Intellectual Work
behind PICO's Transformation

The scholarly underpinnings to Scott Reed's words above come from a variety of sources, but the most foundational emerged from the work of john powell, now executive director of the Haas Institute for a Fair and Inclusive

Society and holder of an endowed professorship at the University of California at Berkeley. powell's writing and speaking have profoundly shaped the work on racial equity within the PICO National Network and the Gamaliel Foundation, as well as other faith-based organizations around the country (important examples include ISAIAH in Minnesota, the Ohio Organizing Collaborative, the InterValley Project, National People's Action, and some individual organizations within the Industrial Areas Foundation and DART). In order to understand the internal organizational transformation of PICO, we focus on those dimensions of powell's work that concern racialized culture and attitudes in America, and their implications for cross-racial relationships. Other dimensions of his work focus on economic and political questions of regional inequality and the "geography of opportunity" and undergird some of the external policy analysis in the field, especially in Gamaliel but also more widely.[15]

At the core of powell's framework for thinking about racial equity lie the concepts of racialized structures, schemas, implicit bias, and targeted universalism.[16] powell treats societal structures—whether political, economic, educational, legal, or other—as complex systems. That is, structures are nonlinear systems functioning via iterative feedback loops. Structures operate routinely when those feedback loops confirm their underlying assumptions. Structures falter—or at least must adapt creatively—when those feedback loops contradict underlying systemic assumptions. Ideally, such contradictions force systems of thinking to adjust to reality by rejecting biased assumptions that do not reflect reality—for example, racial prejudices, gender stereotypes, or religious biases.

powell draws on recent research in cognitive science to show how humans process information in ways that obstruct such systemic adjustment to reality. Instead of revising our learned assumptions, we often show a remarkable ability to embrace only information that confirms our bias and to filter out information that otherwise would force fundamental revisions in our views. How does that work?

Given the vast quantities of information we must process daily, we do so mostly subconsciously via three mechanisms: we *categorize* information quickly (mostly using binary codes);[17] we *create associations* between things; and we subconsciously *fill in gaps* whenever our information is partial or ambiguous. In turn, precisely *how* each of us categorizes, links, and fills in gaps of information is driven by what cultural sociologists and cognitive scientists call *schemas*, more popularly thought of as the "frames" through which people interpret their experience and the world. Those schemas are largely learned from either our formal socialization within families, schools, religious congregations, and the like, or our informal socialization via friends, music, movies, books, news reports, and social media.

So far, so good. All this research simply describes the current understanding of how the human brain necessarily works as a product of our biological makeup and social nature. If our internalized schemas adequately reflected reality, and if our lived experience adequately encompassed the diversity of people in our society, none of this would have much to contribute to thinking about racial equity. But as powell shows, we live in no such ideal world. Because cultures take shape over long periods and change only slowly, the cultural traditions that shape our families, the media, and the nation developed in a context of racism and negative attitudes toward racial and ethnic minorities. So our internalized schemas distort reality via unconscious stereotypes of other groups. Because most of American society remains socially and residentially segregated, many people experience only very constrained interaction with people from other racial and ethnic groups. For many, what interracial interactions do occur happen mostly in situations lacking any real reciprocity, such as hierarchical interactions within the service economy. Beyond this, interracial and interethnic impressions are formed via the media, with their own distortions and stereotypes.

Such constrained and "mediated" interactions provide rich fodder for the subconscious workings of internalized schemas. Often the only obvious information about the other person—their skin color and other phenotypical characteristics—serves mostly to place them into racial/ethnic categories. Other information is often missing or ambiguous, so our internalized schemas kick in to impose some interpretive clarity upon the situation, often via subconscious associations carried to us via biased socialization processes. Those categories then readily translate into judgments of "we" and "they," "us" and "them." We then act on the basis of that interpretation; depending on who "we" and "they" are, our actions may be driven by collaboration, avoidance, deference, dominance, negative judgment, or a host of other patterns. Through many iterations, these patterns become habitual and, importantly, often self-confirming.[18] The implicit bias that results from these subconsciously structured interactions produces skewed expectations about racial "others" within many cross-racial and cross-ethnic interactions; these serve both to confirm the supposed accuracy of the originating schemas and to constrain interactions to narrowly defined scripts (say, friendly service delivery) so as to contain them and avoid unpleasantness or unpredictability. Note that implicit bias affects not only minorities but also can function in both directions across racial hierarchies—of course, with the most deleterious effects on those on the underside of hierarchy. When the psychological dynamics of implicit bias are manipulated for strategic political gain or to undermine effective public policy formulation, those deleterious effects are multiplied many times over for those communities and for the nation as a whole.

In the resulting "cycle of implicit bias," historical and continuing segregation produces racialized schemas and (often subconscious) stereotyped assumptions driven by implicit bias, which in turn generate self-reinforcing expectations, which also reinforce structural and systemic inequalities that contribute to ongoing segregation of social experience (and ongoing plausibility of negative cultural stereotypes). This cycle of mutually constituting cultural and structural dynamics results in different groups holding highly divergent perceptions of one another and of American society—because their *experiences* differ even within the same interaction.[19]

Note that Americans' perceptions of others are not driven solely by racial and ethnic categories. Perceptions of "blacks" differ according to their economic status, with "poor blacks" perceived as part of the category that Douglas Massey labels "despised," while "professional blacks" are "envied." These dynamics of implicit bias can occur across a variety of social divisions (for example, divisions based on religious beliefs, the native-immigrant divide, gender, sexual preference, political affiliation, and nationality), but in American life they appear especially powerful in driving perceptions of racial and ethnic minorities. The powerful structuring role of race and ethnicity in these perceptions is obvious. Americans on average see Asians, professional blacks, and Jews as highly competent but do not feel warmly toward them, and these groups are thus envied but not esteemed. To be "esteemed," one must on average be not only middle class but also white (and typically Christian).

Implicit bias, rather than a product of consciously held racist attitudes, is instead rooted in subconscious schemas through which we interpret our experience. As a result, implicit bias deeply shapes our perceptions of others and of ourselves and is regularly reinforced by our experience. Undocumented immigrants, black and white Americans, Latinos, Jews, and middle-class Christians, when placed in identical situations—say accused of committing a crime, or victimized by crime, or caught in a public scandal, or in need of public assistance—will each be perceived differently: some as more culpable than others, some as individuals, and others as exemplars of their "group" (thus often confirming group stereotypes).

Given these realities, powell argues that the democratic project is well served neither by universalist policies (which fail to adjust for the particular barriers faced by specific groups) nor by goals tailored too closely to group-specific needs (which serve to balkanize society and are too easy to interpret in ways that confirm negative stereotypes). He argues instead for social policies that are neither "universal" (that is, blind to individuals' particular situatedness and context) nor specified in a way that leads to zero-sum competition for public resources. powell suggests that our historical commitment to universal democratic ideals and emerging insight into the deeply structured bias and disadvantage suffered by some groups more than others demand social policies driven by "targeted universalism."[20] Targeted universalism involves identifying universal goals to which all should be able to credibly aspire, then identifying the specific obstacles that make it more difficult for particular groups to attain those goals. Such obstacles may be internal to a given social group or may be embedded in social structures, public policy, or others' perceptions of that group. Targeted universalism strives to design social policies through which those obstacles can be overcome by individuals, communities, and society as a whole.

powell emphasizes that social reform efforts guided by targeted universalism must consider both groups' situatedness with respect to social structures and how groups are situated vis-à-vis one another and the cultural schemas underlying society. The former means social reform efforts must change people's concrete opportunities and chances for a decent quality of life. The latter means social reform efforts must create forms of interaction and networks of relationships that bring different groups into *substantive* and *meaningful* interaction with one another. Only then will cross-group relationships and institutionalized cultural schemas begin to shift in light of actual experiential relationships.

These ideas from powell and others have been foundational for many social movement activists as they have wrestled with the mutually reinforcing dynamics of race and inequality in American society. We now turn to consider how one national organizing network, PICO, has drawn on this kind of thinking as it works against rising economic inequality and stagnant working-class and middle-class wages. That is, in its organizing, the PICO National Network consciously seeks to dismantle racialized cultural schemes by generating personal interactions and social networks across racial and ethnic lines, but it does so not as a single end in itself, but rather in the context of addressing American democratic challenges at local, state, and national levels. That's a tall order. PICO's effort has not been seamless, nor has it drawn solely on powell's particular analysis of our historical moment. But it has been relatively successful and has been shaped significantly by the framework described above.

Conclusion: Envisioning and Rebuilding a "Land of Opportunity" in America: Can Americans Deal with America's Racial Legacy?

By the time Scott Reed brought it center stage via the national staff retreat in 2012, the kind of thinking outlined above had been gestating within the national staff and locally grounded leadership of the PICO National Network and its affiliates for several years. Several PICO-linked clergy and organizers had been central to this early gestation of thinking regarding racial equity within the network and racial justice in American society. These pioneers included Elder Joseph Forbes of the African Methodist Episcopal Church; Rev. George Cummings, theologian and pastor of Imani Community Church in Oakland and a leader in the original PICO affiliate, the Oakland Community Organization (OCO); Joe Givens, then the longtime PICO lead organizer in New Orleans; Jennifer Jones-Bridgett, a pastor, organizer, and more recently executive director of PICO-Louisiana; and Michael-Ray Mathews, originally a pastor and board member in the San Jose affiliate and subsequently the national PICO staff person for organizer recruitment-and-retention efforts and clergy organizing.[21] Beginning in the early 2000s, as the position of working-class African Americans continued to deteriorate, these people challenged PICO staff and leaders to deal more forthrightly with race. The first substantial collective conversations occurred in Oakland and New Orleans. Those conversations included a frank assertion of the need to think about and engage with not only black-white relations but also with the black-Latino and black-Asian relations that had gained importance in the face of increased immigration and ongoing settlement of new immigrants in settings that had not previously been receiving locations. In the internal dialogue that ensued, Cummings and others also raised concerns about OCO's difficulties in retaining young African American organizers—a struggle reflected in the national field of faith-based organizing as a whole (see chapter 2 for national data on the decline in African American organizers during the 2000–2010 decade).

By all accounts, those were hard, sometimes acutely painful, conversations, as leaders—African American, Latino, White, and Asian—struggled to come to terms with one another's experiences of bias, privilege, and hurt, not only across the historic American racial divide but also across racialized views imported from other societies by immigrants or absorbed

Figure 4.3 Rev. George Cummings (right) and organizer Nelson Pearce
(Applegate, June 2014). (Photo by Heather Wilson)

in this country in the competition for jobs. Simultaneously, these conversations also forced leaders—black *and* white—to confront anti-immigrant sentiments being staked out in some sectors of American political culture at that time, and sometimes reflected inside their organizations. The organizational challenge was acute, as OCO's and PICO's long-standing ways of doing things came into question, including via the explicit indictment that "race neutral" ways of training organizers contributed to the organization's failure to hold onto talented young African Americans who wanted careers in organizing.

Over time, the internal Oakland dialogue—and its broader implications—made its way into the wider PICO National Network, a process facilitated by OCO's status as perhaps the most central node in the PICO network: the founding PICO federation in 1972, the training ground for many young organizers for decades, the originator of the idea of creating a state-level PICO California Project that eventually inspired the network's current national-level influence, and for many years the site of PICO's national headquarters. PICO's executive leadership began to reflect more carefully on questions of racial equity and how they could better train and retain organizers of color in a field that had once been widely criticized for having a staff structure that did not reflect its impressively diverse base. As the conversation took hold, PICO staff also began reading powell's writings and those of other prominent African American scholars, including Michelle Alexander, Rev. Cummings and his mentor James Cone, and William Julius Wilson.[22] The original internal challenge and PICO's response eventually gained sufficient traction that by the time of PICO's national "clergy summit" in November 2011, convened under the theme of "Creating a Land of Opportunity," powell and Alexander were two of the keynote speakers (in New Orleans with approximately five hundred clergy from around the country, which included clergy from the historic African American Protestant, Catholic, liberal and moderate Protestant, Jewish, Unitarian, Evangelical, Pentecostal, and Muslim traditions).[23]

At this national clergy gathering, the social analysis underlying the PICO

Figure 4.4 Organizers from local coalitions of the PICO National Network in intense discussions at annual retreat (Applegate, June 2014). (Photo by Heather Wilson)

Figure 4.5 An organizer shares his thoughts in staff discussions (Applegate, June 2014).
(Photo by Heather Wilson)

National Network's strategic thinking clearly centered on racial equity and economic justice, with a focus on "cleaning up the mess" of the financial sector in a way that would foster economic opportunity for working- and middle-class Americans. The rhetorical center during the two-and-a-half-day event was the repeated call to create a "land of opportunity" for all. The event launched PICO's emergent programmatic campaign linking organizing at the local, state, and national level around the five areas detailed below; note how these nationwide initiatives intertwine both the multiculturalist and universalist strands of the democratic tradition:

- "Let My People Vote," which later became the "Campaign for Citizenship":
  The network's major initiative in favor of comprehensive immigration reform, launched well before any clear prospect for movement on this front looked likely (and obviously before those hopes ran aground on the shoals of national policy paralysis). This effort highlights a particularly noteworthy outcome of the intensive cross racial and cross ethnic relationships developed within PICO in the years leading up to it. The official goal of the

effort was framed as follows: "We demand full citizenship for all Americans regardless of race, income, or immigration status. President Obama and Congress should move immediately to make citizenship legislation a top priority for 2013 and to make citizenship for all Americans the focus of that legislation." Note the strong, explicit language—perhaps not remarkable among immigrant rights organizations with narrower demographic bases, but noteworthy in a field with high levels of diversity across socioeconomic, racial/ethnic, and immigration status. In particular, endorsement of such a proimmigrant position by sectors of PICO's base that in the wider society were and *remain* strong opponents of immigration reform—especially white, lower socioeconomic status (SES) Americans, but also many lower-SES African Americans—suggests the impact of PICO's "equity" conversations in building cross-ethnic and cross-class trust and reshaping political culture inside the organization.[24]

·   "Bringing Health Care Home": An effort to capitalize on the passage of major health care reform via the Affordable Care Act to particularly benefit the poor, working-class, middle-class, and immigrant communities with high uninsured rates that form PICO's membership institutions—in other words, to leverage the network's involvement in national health care reform in order to generate local benefits.

·   "New Bottom Line": The centerpiece of the network's campaign to effect some measure of economic justice in American life, via foreclosure relief, major banking reform, and regulation of predatory lending. This ongoing campaign is a strategic collaboration between National People's Action, the Alliance for a Just Society, Right to the City, and the PICO National Network.[25]

·   "Great Schools": PICO's national effort to build upon innovative school-reform work by its affiliates in Denver, Sacramento, and Oakland, in ways that strengthen rather than undermine the public school sector. With the goal of raising graduation rates and assuring that every graduate is prepared for "college or meaningful work," the Great Schools effort focuses on promoting student-based budgeting, teacher home visits, and small autonomous schools.[26]

·   "Lifelines to Healing," which later became the "LiveFree" campaign: This campaign addresses the causes and impact of "pervasive violence and crime in our communities." Within that framing, it represents PICO's most direct focus on racial equity via a particular focus on communities of color. Its official statement of purpose notes, "We believe that the criminalization and mass incarceration of people of color, coupled with the lack of meaningful and quality opportunities, have contributed to a state of crisis in our country."

Since the Lifelines to Healing/LiveFree campaign most directly focuses on the terrain of racial equity, in what follows we pay particular attention to it. But two overall elements are noteworthy here: First, all five campaign areas are framed in universalist terms and address universal goals, such as the aspiration for full citizenship in pursuit of "the American values of freedom, fairness and family"; the slogan of "health care for all people" that undergirds the effort to bring health care home; judging financial reform according to "the level of economic opportunity we create for everyone"; the effort to support public schools as a resource for all; and most broadly the fight against mass incarceration as part of overcoming the general "state of crisis in the country" under the slogan "increase the peace, stop the violence, create opportunities."[27] These universalist goals provide focus and overarching direction to the campaigns, but embedded within each campaign are policy directions that reflect the needs and obstacles confronting a variety of particular sectors—including racial/ethnic minorities but also immigrants, middle-class homeowners, the working poor, labor, those who rely on public assistance, and others. This is "targeted universalism" at play in the field of public policy. Second, as of mid-2013, with the debate regarding Trayvon Martin's killing and George Zimmerman's acquittal raging, and immigration reform either at midstream or rapidly sinking (but in either case very much in the news), PICO's national communications efforts focused centrally on the first and last campaigns—that is, on immigration and on racial equity. The fact that PICO's decision to place priority and resources on both areas substantially predated the emergence of those issues as foci of media attention suggests something deeper than opportunism at play.

This chapter has suggested that this "something deeper" included the heightened strategic capacity within the national network, such that network leaders were in new ways assessing the broad picture of American political culture and the historic challenges facing the country; the ethical and political challenge regarding racial equity presented by key African American clergy and staff; the emergent ethical commitment—one might say moral conversion—of key national staff from a broader array of social backgrounds; and new analytic tools for understanding the dynamics of racialization and how they intersect with the reproduction of inequality. All these factors were brought together via concrete issue campaigns built around a racial equity analysis, but addressing broad issues of inequality that affect all Americans (albeit some racial/ethnic groups more than others). Those campaigns sought to invigorate PICO's long-standing work for greater economic equality by simultaneously tapping into powerful identities rooted in people's experience of faith, race, and ethnicity—and in so doing, to disrupt policy paralysis in the public arena. The next chapter portrays the emergence of one such campaign, focusing on how PICO's structure, culture, and leadership affected the network's decision to take the risks entailed in the Lifelines to Healing/LiveFree campaign.

Figure 5.1 "I Am Faith in Action" and "Love Is Our Weapon": Protesters in Ferguson, Missouri, after Michael Brown's shooting death (August 2014). (Photo by Heather Wilson)

FIVE

Lifelines to Healing: Betting Resources and Reputation on Racial Equity

We share a deep commitment to what it means to our work as faith-based organizers that embrace a race-based framework, and we strive for honesty about
our diminished humanity [resulting from racialized assumptions about one an-
other]. Who gets to lead? Who gets to inform our best thinking? We're going deep
in a different kind of way, and I'm very excited about it. We have some gaps in
the speed people are willing to implement these new ways of thinking, but we're
moving forward, and I'm deeply hopeful about it.

—anonymous PICO staff person

The PICO National Network's efforts described in the previous chapter—
national campaigns for health care and foreclosure protection for poor,
working-class, and middle-class Americans, for a path to citizenship for
immigrants, and for racial equity—were the fruit of a decade-long project
by the network to build a national structure capable of coordinating such
initiatives. As a result, PICO is now widely viewed by funders as a leading edge of strategic innovation within the field of community organizing
nationally—at least among those who see strategic importance in organizing to influence policy both at and beyond the local level. The Lifelines
to Healing campaign (a.k.a the LiveFree campaign) has allowed PICO to
put its work for racial equity front and center within its external organizing agenda even as it was simultaneously working to advance racial equity
within its internal organizational culture. By emphasizing "targeted universalism," Lifelines to Healing also demonstrates how faith-based organizing links universalist democratic commitments and multicultural realities of American society. But that achievement—still an imperfect work in
progress—only comes fully into view if we see how it came about via the

fusion of a specific organizational structure, internal culture, and approach to leadership. This chapter analyzes that fusion and the organizational dynamics underlying it.

A Campaign for Racial Equity: "Targeted Universalism" in Action

The Lifelines to Healing campaign helps local coalitions advocate for social policies that, in PICO's analysis, will address urban violence by helping less privileged Americans—especially young African American and Latino men—overcome the obstacles that make it harder for them to achieve goals nearly universally shared in American life. This represents an especially good case study for exploring the universalist-multiculturalist tensions within a diverse democracy because, among PICO's five national campaigns, it is perhaps here that those tensions are most acute. African American and Latino boys from less privileged families and disorganized local settings face some of the greatest hurdles to "making it" in American society, and the gulf between their social reality and that of other segments of PICO's base—in better organized urban neighborhoods and in more prosperous suburban congregations—is cavernous. If this type of campaign can succeed within this diverse organizational context, perhaps the tension between universalist and multicultural emphases within the democratic tradition need not permanently subvert the dream of a more egalitarian America.

The Lifelines campaign emphasizes four approaches to this kind of "targeted universalism." First, to address the particular forms of violence that engulf inner-city youth, Lifelines promotes the "Boston Ceasefire" approach the Rev. Jeffrey Brown and others in that city pioneered. The Ceasefire approach engages coalitions of law enforcement officials, clergy from congregations in the affected areas, and community leaders jointly in pursuing a strategy of both personal intervention with at-risk youth and targeted enforcement and suppression of the most violent actors. Second, and relatedly, Lifelines encourages policy makers to adopt a "public health framework" for assessing how best to address violence in the community. This essentially means thinking about how to intervene to change the social determinants that drive violence-generating community dynamics and is intended to contrast with approaches driven more narrowly by law enforcement frameworks.

Third, Lifelines advocates against the policies that have driven mass incarceration of young men of color, such as the widespread "Three Strikes" laws. Lifelines favors policies that in the experience of local PICO leaders and the analysis of PICO strategists do less damage to the social fabric of urban communities. Such policies include alternative sentencing and community diversion programs for nonviolent offenders and programs targeted at the specific needs of those who do end up incarcerated, both while in custody and at the time of reentry. Again, the fact that national discourse on these issues had shifted significantly by 2013–14 makes PICO's stance seem less controversial and politically risky than it was when internal work on these issues first began years before that and also suggests that the broader coalition behind criminal justice reform, of which PICO was a part, succeeded in shifting national discourse on this terrain during the intervening years (partly due to the high costs of incarceration).

Fourth, Lifelines advocates for "opportunity creation"—that is, for economic development tied to good jobs in poor neighborhoods and for decent job placement programs for those leaving prison, thus reducing recidivism.

In all four areas of the Lifelines to Healing campaign, PICO strategists argue that they simply do not care about the standard liberal and conservative pieties about how to address particular social issues. Rather, in interviews they say they seek the best, most thoroughly tested approaches to violence prevention, jobs creation, and lowering recidivism rates, and to implement those approaches in ways best adapted to local realities. Echoing this stance, the Lifelines website specifically claims that it pursues the "best evaluated strategies" for violence prevention, notes that "local communities are free to identify specific violence prevention strategies that meet their particular needs," and notes its "opportunity creation" efforts include both direct government-funded jobs provision and probusiness development policies.[1] Implementation thus looks different in African American, Latino, and Asian neighborhoods in Oakland, Camden, or Detroit than it does in mixed-race neighborhoods of Denver or New Orleans or in immigrant *colonias* of semirural southern New Mexico.

Note that the Lifelines campaign consistently reflects the kind of "targeted universalism" analysis for which john powell has argued, discussed in the previous chapter: arguing for goals that plausibly represent universal aspirations—access to economic opportunity, full citizen participation, reduction of violence, home ownership, stable neighborhoods in which to raise children, and so on—while insisting that efforts to advance those aspirations must take into account the particular realities of those who are least privileged, most affected, and often face the highest barriers to attaining them.

For present purposes, this outline of the Lifelines to Healing campaign must suffice, as our focus here is less on the campaign itself than on its organizational underpinnings. But before exploring those underpinnings, we consider a key question: Just how widely has racial equity work been taken up within the PICO National Network and within the field of faith-based community organizing generally?

Although we cannot definitely answer this question, the survey data from part I offer a place to start. As shown in figure 1.6, between a quarter and a third of local organizing coalitions reported working directly on issues of "racial justice" in American society. This certainly underestimates the adoption of racial equity work in the field, for two reasons. First, across many of the networks that coordinate most local coalitions in the field, at least some of the key strategists have argued for greater attention to the racial dimensions of public policy, and staff organizers have often raised racial equity analysis and sustaining diversity as key internal priorities. Second, a great deal of work on issues other than racial justice goes on in the field in terms explicitly framed in racial equity terms. As also shown in figure 1.6, local coalitions work extensively on poverty (70% of coalitions), education (66%), health care (57%), immigration (54%), housing (53%), criminal justice (53%), and a host of other issues that are sometimes addressed very directly as issues of racial equity (as in the Lifelines to Healing campaign's work on criminal justice), but certainly not always so.

Beyond this, our survey data cannot tell us exactly how widely such internal or external work on racial equity has become. Our broad knowledge of the field suggests that explicit work for racial equity is more common in some networks than in others, and that within those networks that have not chosen to emphasize such work, some local coalitions still focus significantly on racial equity and racial justice. But neither our survey data nor our ethnographic research allows us to confidently characterize those patterns.[2]

Internal data from the PICO National Network provide further insight into how widely racial equity work has spread among its affiliate coalitions.[3] Those data show just over half (52%) of PICO coalitions have incorporated a racial justice framework into their leadership development curriculum, and are using that "with every organizing leader." The vast majority of coalitions (88%) are approaching their issue work in ways that consider and promote racial equity. Each coalition articulates a "theory of change" that underpins their organizing work; exactly half of the PICO coalitions were characterized as having an evident "racial analysis" embedded in their theory of change. Seventy-one percent of coalitions were said to have "HR policies and practices [that] reflect a commitment to racial diversity and inclusion—e.g. recruitment and hiring practices; organizational norms, etc." Almost half (48%) indicated that either their coalition director or a "strong second" (staff person capable of leading the coalition in the absence of the director) was a person of color. Much less robustly, only one in eight (12%) of coalitions indicated that it had an "executive director performance evaluation by the Board [that] includes racial diversity and inclusion benchmarks."

These data are consistent with the picture portrayed by our interviewees—and together they suggest an organizing effort in which commitment to racial equity has taken substantial but partial hold, with continuing work to be done on this front. PICO national leaders' strong advocacy for internal racial equity, their efforts to infuse racial equity thinking into all external issue campaigns, and their decision to track each coalition's progress with incorporating racial equity and racial justice into its organizing work provide strong evidence that they see racial equity as a core commitment and are striving to institutionalize it for the long term.

The Symbiosis of Structure, Culture, and Leadership: Campaigns within a Network

The organizational underpinnings of PICO's ability to launch national campaigns in five areas and begin to infuse a racial equity analysis across those campaigns are to be found in the network's structure, culture, and leadership—and particularly the more-or-less symbiotic relationship among them.

We consider structure first. As shown in chapter 1, over the last fifteen years, PICO has built a structure that now approximates the kind of three-level "federated model" that Theda Skocpol and her colleagues argue has historically been the sine qua non for civic groups to achieve major national influence.[4] Such a model involves having organizational infrastructure at local, state, and national levels. In this case, that infrastructure includes:

· Local congregations and other institutions. These most local organizational units sponsor the primary organizing work that make faith-based organizing an example of grassroots civic democracy rather than simply another advocacy structure without an actual base of mobilization. In the case of the

Lifelines campaign, these most local units "develop and support the capacity of local congregations to advocate for policies and resources that create opportunity for young people of color."[5]

- Coalitions (which PICO terms "federations") at the level of a city, county, or metropolitan area, and (in some places) state-level organizations linking those coalitions for statewide campaigns and advocacy vis-à-vis state government. Within Lifelines, the local- and state-level structures support front-line leaders "as they advocate for policies and resources that reduce violence in their communities and create opportunities for young people of color."

- A strong national-level staffing structure (forty-three people as of early 2014) that coordinates the national network, scans the societal environment for strategic opportunities, provides a sophisticated communications infrastructure via a variety of social media platforms, and catalyzes the long-term and network-wide strategic thinking required for building influence over time—including how racial equity fits into a broader organizational agenda that reflects the diverse concerns of front-line leaders in local coalitions.

At present, while the structure is national in ambition and vision, it is not national in scale. With a formal organizational presence in nineteen states and emergent or exploratory work in several others, PICO can legitimately claim a real organizing capacity in much of the country including nearly all the most populous states and many of the politically crucial swing states and contested congressional districts.[6] But it is uneven in its geographic spread and in the quality of organizing work it can produce at the local and state level. Overall, the PICO National Network can draw on a sophisticated capacity to act nationally, but cannot always produce political pressure in all the settings needed to move state- and national-level discussions in the direction it would like to see. Nonetheless, its track record remains impressive, having been widely recognized as a significant actor in national policy regarding health care, immigration, foreclosure and financial reform, and (perhaps emerging as of 2014) criminal justice policy.

The network has gained this reputation not by dropping its long-established focus on local organizing in favor of mass mobilization for national causes, but rather by iteratively linking action at the local, state, and national levels on particular issues. Periodically—at times once a year, at times several times a year—the network brings groups of local leaders, ranging in size from a few dozen to several hundred, to Washington, DC, to educate congressional representatives on specific priorities and to learn from congressional staff about the current state of policy development or from national think tanks about potential policy alternatives. But in between, the local network affiliate organizations work on local issues and local facets of the national work—for example, on local implementation of health care funding newly available under the Affordable Care Act (ACA), or local protection of immigrant rights while simultaneously working to advance federal action on comprehensive immigration reform. Simultaneously, the state-level collaborative structures may be pressing for efficient set up of the health care insurance exchanges enabled by the ACA or calling for implementation of "Dream Act" legislation in that state.[7]

PICO's interlocking federated structure has been one crucial innovation within the field that has enabled the Lifelines to Healing and other campaigns of recent years (and has emerged partly through those campaigns). A second crucial organizational innovation has been cultural: the network's new willingness to form substantial interorganizational partnerships. While such partnerships are hardly innovations on the political scene, they are certainly innovative within the Alinsky-derived organizing tradition that long eschewed collaboration with other organizations. In the case of Lifelines, such partnerships are intended "to amplify issues of youth violence, mass incarceration, and lack of meaningful opportunity" in the public arena.[8] Partnerships with "policy, philanthropy, government, academy, practitioners, faith-based organizations, and industry" sectors are all mentioned explicitly. An example of such a partnership can be seen in the campaign's coordination with Ryan Coogler, director of the Hollywood movie *Fruitvale Station* that depicts the New Year's Eve killing of Oscar Grant by the rapid transit police in Oakland, California (subsequently ruled an unjustified police homicide). The film was released in the summer of 2013, just after the acquittal of George Zimmerman for the killing of Trayvon Martin, with the firestorm of media attention and outrage it generated in the African American community and allies nationally. Lifelines used PICO's sophisticated social media presence to promote the film widely. One example among many: Michael McBride, the national director of the Lifelines to Healing campaign since early 2012, sent the following message to campaign contacts nationally, with links to blogs, Twitter feeds, and Facebook:[9]

In my work with PICO Network's Lifelines to Healing Campaign, I've seen first-hand the deep pain that Saturday's verdict about Trayvon Martin's death has caused in communities of color in just the last 48 hours. But that pain didn't begin here. As a pastor, I've witnessed week after week, year after year, African-American and Latino youth who are struggling to believe that they are truly valued in our country. I've talked with people across all racial lines who are trying to figure out where we go from here. Saturday's verdict ignited a national conversation on race, humanity, violence and justice. As people of faith, I believe we are called to channel these conversations into action now.

This posting thus initially framed the issue within the immediate pain and moral outrage provoked by the Trayvon Martin killing and subsequent acquittal. In doing so, the posting tapped into deep resources of anger rooted in the particular experiences of sectors long on the underside of American society and sought to channel them into meaningful political engagement.[10] But it went on to frame the issue quite explicitly within universalistic democratic and faith-based terms:

Our Lifelines to Healing Campaign is working to ensure that all of God's children are alive and free, whether they're black, brown, or white, wearing a hoodie or a business suit. Long after the news cycle shifts to the next story, we will continue to organize, mobilize, and train people of faith to lead in our own neighborhoods. Across the country, people of faith are already leading campaigns to create safer communities through sensible gun laws, pressing for sentencing reform and other measures to keep youth of color from filling up our jails and prisons, and working to create more educational and employment opportunities in the communities that need those opportunities most. Join us in this moment of turning pain and confusion into a national movement that will heal our nation.

The post then directed recipients to a movement-building website that allowed PICO to be in contact electronically.[11] Finally, recipients were encouraged to see the movie and invite their friends:

"Fruitvale Station" will be opening in a city near you soon. It's based on the shooting death of 22 year-old Oscar Grant, by Bay Area police officers in 2009, and is an example of what happens when human life is devalued. . . . Check out the trailer here after signing up for Lifelines, and then invite a group of friends to see it with you.[12]

The Lifelines to Healing campaign has made clear the organizational advantages of a federated structure. As the verdict approached, PICO made available via its website, and promoted nationally via its social media links, a tool kit of organizing resources to assure that the high-profile case would help to catalyze a conversation about racial equity in America—regardless of what verdict emerged from the trial. This occurred under the catchphrase, "It's not about the verdict. It's about our values," and was framed online as follows:

> Awaiting the verdict in the Zimmerman/Martin case has ignited a national conversation on race, humanity, violence and justice. We are compelled by our faith to proclaim that the value of life among our young men has greatly been diminished. And people of faith have something to say about it! We are calling on everyone across the country to **preach, pray, and act** to heal our nation. This tool kit is designed to give clergy and faith leaders action steps to implement in congregations and communities. (Emphasis in original.)

Note the call to locally grounded action via the network's base in religious congregations, as well as that call's expression in the religious language native to those faith communities. McBride's fluency in the spiritual vernacular of faith communities emerges from his own background and status as an ordained pastor, and it is clear in how he presents himself publicly as "deeply committed to empowering urban communities, families and youth using the principles of a relevant and liberating Gospel message that transforms lives."[13] The campaign's use of religious language to make sense of efforts to address racial equity reflects an important wider pattern in faith-based community organizing; a recent national study shows that prayer practices and other religious forms are used as "cultural bridging practices" to unite groups across divides of race and class. That is, as internal racial/ethnic *or* socioeconomic diversity rise in these local coalitions, they engage more extensively in prayer and other religious practices.[14]

The "tool kit" included a media kit, sample materials for constructing a Facebook presence on local dimensions of racial equity, and a sample opinion editorial for local media.[15] But its central focus fell on ideas for praying, preaching, and acting to foster awareness, dialogue, and political change. Worship leaders were urged to "shape your pulpit messages around scriptures that allow congregants to understand better the theological implications for the injustice that pervades our community and what God is doing about it. Give a call for action that is grounded in a desire to please God and fulfill God's plan for a just world." One idea generated from this was a "hoodie worship service" at which congregants wore "hoodies" in solidarity with the fashion choices of young urban men.

This local innovation in organizing practice spread nationally as "hoodie holy days." In a further innovation, in some settings boys and men wore hoodies while girls and women wore headscarves, thus extending the message of solidarity to Muslims in America as well. In such ways, the federated structure and the technological capacity linked to it allowed the Lifelines campaign to take advantage of both strategic ideas generated centrally (like media tool kits) and local cultural innovations perceived as effective (like hoodie holy days), and quickly extend them to like-minded activists nationally.

Two other organizing resources offered via the federated structure focused on religious leaders, especially with regard to how they approach preaching and prayer. First, religious leaders were encouraged to "preach with young people in mind. Preach about what their faith teaches regarding life and living in accordance to the tenets of their beliefs. Preach hope; let them know that God loves them, believes in them and is preparing a world that will celebrate them."[16]

Note here the future-oriented tone and content of the message, and recall the context of the days leading up to the Trayvon Martin verdict: national fears that an acquittal would generate the kinds of massive rioting that followed previous verdicts highlighting racial inequity in the American justice system. When the acquittal was announced, the Lifelines campaign did not exploit the verdict to incite racial or class hatred and the acting out of rage devoid of any constructive political agenda, but neither did it ask people to suppress their outrage. Instead, the campaign focused precisely on using these energies for an agenda that strove to build an alternative future. Thus, second, religious leaders were also encouraged to link prayer and action. Note that among these religious activists committed to social change, public prayer is considered a *potent form of action*, not an escape from action:

> Lead your congregation in prayer for our young people, their safety and the blessings of God's grace and mercy for them, their families and their community. . . . Center your prayers on God's call that we act in support of the values central to our faiths—the values of love, life, and community wholeness. Start a prayer chain in your congregation and in the wider community that can unite congregations across faith, denominational, race and place lines. . . . Pray for God's abundant love and peace for our communities and that that love be richly shared on our youth. Pray for law enforcement and legal community that they hold in their hearts God's command to always be just and prudent in their dealings with our young people and the communities where they reside.

But Lifelines also encouraged more directly political action, including public marches and "nightwalks" that would "take the message of hope to the streets and build a deeper concern for our youth and the sanctity of life" and thus "move beyond the sanctuary."

How might we understand the relationship of "sanctuary" and "street" in this work? In the terms of democratic social theory introduced in chapter 1, the sanctuary as the central worship space of the congregation is held sacred, partially separate from the realm of political action with its divisive and conflictive dynamics. But the worship space is not wholly divorced from such dynamics; worship strives to gather the worshippers' lived experience—their whole lives including their political selves—and offer that experience up to God. We can thus understand the sanctuary and the street as two dimensions of a broad public sphere that includes but also transcends partisan politics. The public sphere understood in this sense lies at the heart of democratic life; it is the space in which the future is shaped via debate, dialogue, and conflict regarding what values and priorities should drive public decisions. The public sphere thus represents the sacred core of democratic life. Here, what Wood has previously termed "buffering the sacred core of worship" from politics should not be understood as privatizing religion.[17] The "sacred core" of faith communities in worship life is held partially separate from politics, but not privatized. Rather, the public arena overlaps and transcends the sanctuary and the street; the congregation even in its sacred moments of worship holds a public dimension. The sacred core of religion in worship and the sacred core of politics in public dialogue thus overlap in an understanding of public life as an arena transcending both; when held in creative tension, both are made more dynamic and meaningful because neither is held as a separate sphere devoid of the passions of the other.

The linking of religious witness and public protest was even starker during the events a year later in Ferguson, Missouri, following the police killing of African American teenager Michael Brown on August 9, 2014. PICO national staff, clergy, and lay leaders were in Ferguson within two days and regularly posted eyewitness updates contradicting official reports.

As ongoing demonstrations developed in Ferguson in ensuing weeks and months, McBride, Alvin Herring (see chapter 2), and others were regularly in Ferguson to work with local clergy and youth on nonviolent protest strategies.

These were fraught days. As one Philadelphia organizer, Rev. Dwayne Royster, recounted the experience:

We were there for some of the most difficult and violent moments, times we were wondering who was coming back alive and who wasn't. I did not grow

Figure 5.2 "Mike Brown Is Our Son": Mother and child protest in Ferguson, Missouri (August 2014). (Photo by Heather Wilson)

Figure 5.3 Interfaith prayer at "Hands Up, Don't Shoot!" rally in Ferguson, Missouri (August 2014). (Photo by Heather Wilson)

Figure 5.4 Rev. Alvin Herring (PICO National Network) at "Hands Up, Don't Shoot!" rally in Ferguson, Missouri (August 2014). (Photo by Heather Wilson)

up in Palestine, never thought I'd see the day when other Americans would point M-16s at me with live ammunition. Or a tank fifteen feet away from me on American soil, trying to push me into a gutter filled with sewage. Or police officers dressed up for guerilla warfare, treating me like garbage not deserving of being treated as a human being. I have experienced nothing like being pinned between two rows of armored cars and police; coming from both ends, squeezing people into an area with no escape.

Ultimately, everyone "came back alive"—but marked by the experience. The PICO leaders communicated their experiences in Ferguson to their constituents around the country in real-time using PICO's multiple social media strategies; an October 2014 message from McBride captures some flavor of the campaign's effort to link witness and protest with both universalist and multiculturalist framing:

For the past 67 days, I joined with the people of Ferguson and across the country, demanding justice for the senseless assaults on the lives of our black and brown youth at the hands of those who are called to protect and serve. Our actions this past week were an act of repentance, resistance, and solidarity with our youth and families directly impacted by these egregious evils.

The arrests in Ferguson were examples of how activists, including prominent local faith leaders, members of local faith congregations, students and community leaders, are being falsely accused of inciting violence when the truth in plain site is that we are seeking justice. It is critical for the whole world to know that protesters in Ferguson are peacefully making their voices heard and showing the best of our democracy. While I am home today, the fight for justice, equality, and our humanity, continues here and in your local community.

In October 2014, Herring, McBride, Royster, and a variety of PICO clergy, staff, and leaders would participate in civil disobedience in Ferguson, along with Dr. Cornel West (Princeton University and Union Theological Seminary), Dr. Iva Carruthers (Samuel DeWitt Proctor Conference), Rev. Traci Blackmon (pastor, Christ the King Church UCC in Missouri), and Rabbi Susan Talve (Central Reform Congregation, Saint Louis). The photo at the start of chapter 6 shows that protest.

Likewise, during the "Let My People Vote" drive in California in 2014 (a national effort to register and engage voters and to end policies excluding ex-felons from voting), PICO publicly linked religious witness and public protest in an effort to mobilize ex-felon voter engagement. In an October 2014 clergy event launching the final push to the election, Rev. Alvin Bernstine of Bethlehem Missionary Baptist Church in Richmond, California (part of the local PICO affiliate) used the biblical story of Lazarus being raised from the dead to provide cultural framing to the voter mobilization effort:

We are like Lazarus, we have young men and women who literally represent the life and the future of our communities, who will only live if we remove the stones of incarceration and use our votes to loose them from the grave clothes of felonization and let them go. Our young men and women have been encoffined in jail cells for too long and we need them in our communities as living evidence of a community that knows something about being once dead but now alive.

Also, like Lazarus, we have churches and faith communities that need to be called from the graves of individualized faith, personal piety, private privilege, and selfish prosperity, to be the voice-by-vote that calls our incarcerated brothers and sisters to live again. For too long, the church has been buried in the grave of safe religion. For too long the grave clothes of maintenance religion have bound preachers and muffled our voices. . . . Like Lazarus, we have a choice. We can answer the call and be living evidence of the power of

God, or we can stay in the grave and give death another victory. I don't know about you, but I'm ready to join Lazarus and make trouble for the status quo. I'm ready to embrace the Lazarus movement and answer the call, come forth and live free, remove grave clothes and mobilize our people to vote.

Thus the call to hope and love did not replace a call to action; rather, participants were asked to engage in street demonstrations and voter mobilization drives infused at times with anger, but with that anger embedded within an ethic of solidarity, of common destiny in a shared society. Religious leaders were asked to endorse both sides of this complex political culture, in which legitimate anger could be used to mobilize vigorous civic engagement, but not allowed to undercut long-term constructive political work.

Together with the key role of network staff, African American clergy, and local organizers in fostering change in PICO (see the previous chapter), this focus on religious leaders suggests that structure and culture alone did not produce change in the network. Rather, taking advantage of structural and cultural opportunities for change requires the artistry of leaders that are sensitive to local context, fluent in locally meaningful vernaculars, and capable of linking faith and public life in dynamic ways.

Figure 5.5 Desmond Meade, grassroots leader and returning citizen, speaks at the "Let My People Vote" rally near office of the attorney general of Florida. (Photo by Heather Wilson)

Ultimately, when well handled, the symbiosis of structure, culture, and leadership allowed PICO's five national campaigns to complement rather than undermine one another. For example, its federated network structure and the "Let My People Vote" allowed Lifelines to mobilize the outrage and passion generated by the Trayvon Martin killing, the subsequent Zimmerman acquittal, and the Michael Brown police killing, and connect them to long-term organizing for civic engagement and political change. As McBride also noted: "[Lifelines to Healing] is a movement that must be connected to the larger issue of transforming our country. *Let My People Vote* is a campaign to get us involved in the political process."[18]

Change over Time: The Institutional, Strategic, and Cultural Origins of Commitment to Racial Equity

As depicted above via the work of the PICO National Network, some sectors of faith-based community organizing and other forms of citizen empowerment have adopted new ways of addressing racial/ethnic inequity within their overall work for economic justice in America. These shifts did not just happen "naturally," that is, as simple evolution of prior practices; witness the fact that the field existed for decades *without* ever adopting a racial equity lens, and the fact that some sectors continue to operate without an explicit articulation of racial equity. Moving in this direction required specific choices by particular organizational decision makers as urged by active change agents. What drove this change over time within the field? Three sets of factors appear to have been crucial.

Institutionally, as shown in chapters 2 and 3, the field can be seen as having been primed to address racial equity by its whole structural makeup: rooted in religious congregations in urban areas, each of which by itself offered little racial/ethnic diversity but which together constituted a high level of diversity for decades and certainly so by 1999 (at least, in comparison to most other national organizations in American civil society).[19] In addition, the strong presence of African American pastors brought voices steeped in the experience of the black communities of America and the prophetic strand of Christianity as well as (in some cases) the more racially centered analyses figures such as Malcolm X and Stokely Carmichael articulated.

Yet institutions cut both ways. While the above factors primed the faith-based organizing field to address racial inequity, the structural makeup of the field was simultaneously an obstacle to such a direction. The broader institutional base of the field (mostly Catholic and liberal Protestant in addition to historic black churches, but also synagogues and mosques, and a few evangelical churches) often resisted—and sometimes continues to contest—any explicit focus on race, preferring instead more "race neutral" and "color-blind" approaches to improving the quality of life in poor and middle-class communities. Note, too, that the organizing networks themselves had by the turn of the century become "institutions"—often with institutionalized assumptions and standard practices that militated *against* any explicit racial analysis. Such a stance is of course defensible in that the strategic benefit of incorporating a racial equity lens is not self-evident. Thus institutional factors did not unilaterally drive organizing toward racial equity; other factors mattered as well.

Strategically, the pressures of staff recruitment, foundation priorities, and new ideas all contributed to shift sectors of the field toward a more race-conscious stance. As self-awareness of community organizing *as a field* (rather than as isolated organizations and networks) spread in the late 1990s, it became increasingly clear to all that the staff structure nationally was predominantly white, especially in its upper echelons. As a result, key strategic leaders began to make recruiting organizers of color a priority, in part due to pressure from within and in part due to foundation staff raising this as an issue of concern.[20] As the networks and individual coalitions made this recruitment a priority, coalitions whose organizational culture did not "connect the dots" of race, economic inequality, and political organizing struggled to *retain* their minority professional staff. Some coalitions thus moved to change how they trained new staff organizers, incorporating for the first time a focus on how racialization and implicit bias may structure organizational cultures for all participants. Most of the networks also created new structures specifically targeted at retaining organizers of color.

Michael-Ray Mathews and Gina Martinez launched PICO's national "Organizers of Color" initiative to recruit, retain, and develop cohorts of organizers from African American, Latino, and other communities of color. Partly as a result of that initiative, the composition of PICO's local-level organizing staff diversified considerably between 2010 and 2014. African Americans increased from twenty-one to twenty-nine, Latinos/Latinas from twenty-nine to fifty-three, American Indians from zero to two, and organizers identifying as multiracial from one to five—while the number of organizers identifying as white held steady at forty-six.[21] Along with the changing demographics, the network found new ways of talking about race; Mathews noted:

> Veterans in this work, more veteran than I am, remember the days when the response to bringing race up in the conversation was, "organizing is about

people, and people are about values; that transcends race, and getting into it will be a muddy conversation, will make it harder to see others as people, see the values that are underneath this work." So we used organizing language, values language, to silence the conversation about race. We haven't always had language and frames that allowed us to really talk about race, really examine it. Our experience of race is so personal, so emotional, that it's hard for people to talk about it without feeling responsible or guilty or complicit in what's happened in our society. I'm talking especially about white folks, but also for black folks: we've so internalized racism and American culture that we feel like we have to take care of white folks, make it okay *not* to talk about race.

Mathews went on to talk about where this has led the network:

> We now have four racialized caucuses [within the PICO staff]: Asian, Latino, African American, and white [with a multiracial caucus in formation]. The white caucus is the most recent, will have to decide whether to be a guilt fest or to really engage with the power of whiteness in our own lives. White people have to realize they are not "White," as Dave Chappelle says, that they can be as angry as others. Whiteness was not designed for them, it's for somebody *else's* privilege [that is, the wealthy].[22] Been hard because we have not had the language to analyze whiteness, reflect on it, in a way that's safe, that does not make people feel guilty and complicit, yet also helps people— black and white—understand that we *are* complicit and need new and more healthy ways to live.

Ana Garcia-Ashley, the executive director of the Gamaliel Foundation organizing network, likewise spoke of the struggle the network experienced in incorporating greater consciousness of how race structures poverty and inequality in American life:

> We went through the process of discerning whether to have a racial equity study of our network, and look at the state of our network racially. . . . There were a lot of questions about whether this really was the right thing to do, whether it was going to blow up in our faces.

She also noted that the resulting tensions had contributed to the organization's struggles in recent years. Nevertheless, Gamaliel has forged ahead with making racial equity a central part of its organizing, has publicly distributed its self-critique of racial equity within the network, and now appears to be gradually recovering from its earlier period of instability.

A further factor in the adoption of racial equity as a central theme in the field may lie in the fact that as organizing expanded in the new century, it began to depend more on funding from national foundations that placed a higher premium on having staff that reflected the coalition's membership base than did the local sources of funding that had often supported organizing previously. Major secular foundations such as Ford, Mott, Kellogg, and Needmor—along with religious funders such as the Unitarian Universalist Veatch Program at Shelter Rock, the Presbyterian Church (USA), the Evangelical Lutheran Church in America, Jewish Funds for Justice, and others, all encouraged funding applicants to show diversity of leadership. This pressure, combined with the long-standing requirement of the Catholic Campaign for Human Development that organizations be rooted in poor communities (and encouragement from the increasingly diverse staffing structures within CCHD and its parent, the United States Conference of Catholic Bishops) contributed to new strategic incentives to diversify staffing.

Finally, we should not underestimate the strategic pressure created by new analyses of poverty in America and its intimate links to race and racism. That is, staff at the top levels of the network structures and the more analytically inclined directors and lead organizers of local organizing coalitions are often voracious readers and sophisticated organic intellectuals. They think hard about the world. They came to read john powell and the other scholars cited in the previous chapter via word of mouth, invitations from local collaborators, or more formal structures such as annual staff gatherings or the "institutes for public life" whereby the Southwest Industrial Areas Foundation enters into dialogue with leading intellectuals. As they encountered this research, key strategists were sometimes simply compelled to rethink their prior practice of eliding discussions of race.[23] The challenge that confronted PICO also reverberated through the rest of the field. If poverty, inequality, and race were inextricably bound up with one another in American society, how could organizing really address the first two issues if it remained silent on the third? Of course, "compelled" is too strong a term; most participants believe the field *was* implicitly addressing racial inequality all along via its antipoverty work, and could have continued doing so. But the themes of racialization and racial equity became harder to ignore under the pressure of their increasingly prominent profile in critical approaches to American culture, and their obvious impact on policy discussions.

These structural and strategic pressures opened the way for key strategic leaders and adept critical thinkers within the field to begin to question the reigning organizational cultures within coalitions and networks. Pressure for cultural and organizational change came from above and below. New communication technologies may have played a role here as well, as internal insurgents could link together to reinforce one another's perception of the need for cultural change inside the organizing field. Not only the PICO National Network but also Gamaliel as a network and some sectors within other networks launched significant coordinated efforts to address racial equity more explicitly.

Culturally, the shift of some sectors toward incorporating a racial equity lens required the timely intersection of several factors. First, as in any organization, changing institutionalized habits and practices required agents of change actively arguing for new approaches.[24] Second, because change involved incorporating a new set of ideas at odds with existing assumptions in the field, it required a significant level of intellectual culture—an inclination to take ideas seriously and engage with them strategically in thinking about the future direction of organizing. Third, change appears to occur most substantially where the organizational culture of a network fosters significant autonomy within its local affiliate coalitions, yet balances that autonomy by vesting significant authority within the central network. We consider each factor in turn.

While chapter 4 rightly suggests that the key agents for change in the PICO National Network were African American clergy and organizers, it is important to reiterate that the group of change agents was also broader than that. Once concerns about racial equity had been raised, a broader dialogue—and sometimes conflict—emerged within the network, in which African American, white, Latino, and other voices all engaged on different sides of the question of whether racial equity belonged as a central theme in PICO's organizational culture. Thus African Americans were at the leading edge of the struggle for racial equity as an orienting frame, but they gained allies from other groups. Furthermore, Latinos in particular were active in pushing for a way of talking about equity that reflected the experiences of both native-born and immigrant Hispanics in America, including the sometimes-fraught relations between urban Latino and African American communities.[25] Advocacy for change was not isolated in one group, but broke out of such isolation to become a broad multiracial dialogue within the network.

But a racial equity analysis has not taken hold everywhere that local change agents articulated and struggled for one. Nationally, some networks, regional coordinating bodies, and local organizing efforts have embraced such an analysis, while others have not. Even within the PICO

National Network and Gamaliel, the adoption of racial equity as a key analytic frame remains uneven from one local coalition to another—varying partly but not only with local demographics. And we should not forget that while the particular language of "racial equity" is relatively new (at least in common organizing parlance), the claims of African Americans and others to a particular analytic point of view extends back decades, both within and beyond the world of organizing. So a second cultural factor explaining the adoption of the racial equity framework concerns what we will call "intellectual culture"; a racial equity framework has tended to take hold as a cornerstone of organizing culture where a culture of disciplined engagement with ideas has existed, such that the intellectual and political claims of racial equity could gain traction to actually pull organizations in a new direction. In the absence of such an intellectual culture, where new ideas that question reigning organizational assumptions are rarely welcome, new ideas about racial equity might never be articulated openly, or might be articulated and then dropped or suppressed, but in neither case could they gain much traction to actually produce organizational change.

Yet again, the existence of an "intellectual culture" does not prejudge the question of the best way forward on any given idea—indeed, a serious intellectual culture means new ideas are debated and may be rejected. For example, one regional network that pioneered more systematic intellectual work in organizing and retains one of the more active and disciplined intellectual cultures in the field has done important work addressing the situation of African American communities in several states, but it has not adopted a racial equity lens as an explicit set of ideas within its organizing culture.[26] Rather, it has incorporated such thinking within what is best characterized as a continuation of long-standing commitment to avoid anything that is likely to divide their organizing base. We do not suggest that a racial equity framework represents the "right" ideological framework for democratic organizing. Our analysis suggests racial equity offers one politically empowering framework, which also offers an ethically grounded response to the long specter of racialization in American politics. Having an organizational culture of intellectual debate appears to have *fostered* the adoption of a racial equity lens, but nothing predetermined that outcome.

Thus a third cultural factor in explaining the adoption of an explicit racial equity framework has been the relationship between networks and their affiliates. All the coalitions in this field share organizational DNA, both via their shared antecedents in the work of Saul Alinsky and in their mutual adoption of new organizing practices that any one of them discovers to be effective. But the networks were never clones of one another, and they are no longer full organizational siblings. Rather, they are something like organizational first cousins, as in recent years they have begun to diverge around an axis of differing forms of innovation, openness to collaboration, centralized or decentralized network structures, and the priority given to higher-level organizing. Furthermore, not all local organizing coalitions belong to a network. For all these reasons, if a local coalition adopts an innovative framework, it might or might not spread. One reason innovations do *not* spread is location in a weak network structure. An example of this is the PICO National Network two or three decades ago, when it was widely recognized for imposing less consistency on its affiliates (sometimes described as allowing greater freedom and local initiative to its affiliates, sometimes described as failing to systematically foster excellent organizing practices). During this period (when Wood first did fieldwork in several of its affiliates beginning in 1991), the network simply did not have the kind of organizational culture that could have fostered a shared analytic lens across its diverse and far-flung affiliates.

On the other hand, very strong network structures and more hierarchical organizational cultures can suppress innovation, in the name of a reigning orthodoxy about what constitutes best organizing practices. Doran Schrantz, a prominent figure in a younger generation of organizers that is shaping organizing nationally today, critiques this aspect of standard models of organizing:

> [Part of the origins of organizing orthodoxy] was a reaction to particular political excesses of the Left in the late '60s and '70s around identity politics and ideology. In the [later] 1970s, people started saying, "we need bread and butter organizations that are focused on the middle class and the working class and the everyday person, to actually meet their needs. We can't bother ourselves with all this ideology crap, because it's killing political and civic life." So they created a certain model of organizing, which is based on self-interest, based on "what is it you see in your neighborhood?" . . . Then what happened, I think, is that the organizing model that was created during that time, which made some sense, kind of got codified or "dogmafied." The symptoms of that insularity included all the fighting [between founders of the networks]. But it's the very infrastructure and paradigm of organizing orthodoxy that set everybody up for those internal dysfunctions. So internal cultural dysfunctions evolved inside these networks. They have their own particular strengths and capacities, but each one has their own little flavor of dysfunction. . . . The real problem is the lack of oxygen, the lack of account-

ability and transparency. That [accountability and transparency] will only get created when you're really relating to the [organizing] field *as a field*.

Note that Schrantz criticizes the old orthodoxy without caricaturing it. She sees orthodox organizing as an outgrowth of good choices made for one time and situation but believes that it eventually led the field astray. In the last decade, significant sectors of the organizing field have dropped the "dogmas" against collaboration and started relating to the whole field. Some sectors have dropped the dogmas against engaging racial identity and started addressing racial equity. In these and similar initiatives, the field has found a little "oxygen" that has breathed new life into strategic innovation in the field.

Organizing frameworks that explicitly address racial equity—one kind of strategic innovation—have taken hold most deeply in sites that fall on neither end of the spectrum from being completely decentralized to being highly hierarchical, but rather reflect a particular kind of middle ground between them: On one hand fostering significant levels of organizational autonomy, innovation of organizing practice, and creative thinking within their local affiliates; while on the other hand simultaneously embedding that autonomy, innovation, and creativity within a strong network structure capable of discerning and disseminating the best local innovations. Peter Evans—analyzing very different social challenges in very different contexts—has identified a parallel organizational strategy and termed it "embedded autonomy."[27] Innovative approaches to incorporating racial equity as an orienting framework have taken deepest hold where such *embedded autonomy* characterizes the network-affiliate relationship—and where change agents have won the internal intellectual debate. Examples of this include the PICO National Network in the last ten or fifteen years, as it has developed stronger national and state-level structures; the innovative work of National People's Action and (at the state level) the work of the Ohio Organizing Collaborative and ISAIAH in Minnesota;[28] and the emergent work within Gamaliel, DART, and the IAF as they currently undergo national leadership transitions (which are still developing and thus difficult to analyze).[29]

Doran Schrantz went on to note the bottom-up quality needed for innovation:

I think that a lot of the stuff that's really interesting and changing and powerfully happening in organizations, in states, or in communities—that those things sometimes trickle up, so to speak. They end up in the networks, but the national network is not *creating* those innovations. The national network is lifting it up, making it more public, trying to get that group to teach other groups how to do it. . . . I think the networks that are emerging [in prominence] are networks that have some clarity about this dynamic, and that have some humility, and some sense of evolving democracy and transparency in their own configuration. It's the networks that allow leadership and innovation to emerge, and allow it to actually be taught. The networks that can't do those things well, for whatever reason, are not doing well [overall].

Thus a combination of institutional, strategic, and cultural dynamics created pressure for the field to adopt a racial equity lens into its self-understanding and political work. That change has taken hold within some sectors of the faith-based organizing world and not in others. The presence of internal agents of change, an intellectual culture, and embedded autonomy appear to be the key conditions under which racial equity emerged as a cornerstone of new thinking. Where these did not characterize the field—in individual organizations or in regional groupings of them—innovative organizing explicitly framed as racial equity work either never got started, was tried and rejected for conscious reasons, or was still-born. In such cases, previously institutionalized patterns of "race neutral" thinking continued to hold sway.

Institutionalizing Commitment to Racial Equity

Gamaliel and PICO have moved to make racial equity a long-term commitment within their organizing cultures. Both have pursued top-to-bottom reviews of how they recruit and retain organizers of color and how they can sustain excellence and diversity within their staffing structures. Both efforts have produced some turbulence within the organization. Staff have wrestled with tensions regarding unconscious bias, white privilege, and the relative priority of addressing racial, ethnic, or gender diversity; with "black-white" and "black-brown" conflict regarding who would emerge in new leadership positions at the local, state, and national levels as well as on particular issues such as immigration and voting rights; and with the status of smaller racial/ethnic groups and multiracial identities within diversity initiatives.

Perhaps the sharpest tensions have arisen around two axes. First, when the analysis of racialized worldviews and implicit bias has led to defensiveness among white participants unaccustomed to reflecting on white privilege and how it has shaped their own experience. In faith-based organizing, as perhaps in most settings where white Americans are asked to understand the microdynamics of racism that play out unconsciously for many, defensiveness has arisen regularly. Here, john powell's analytic tools, outside consultants with expertise on racial dynamics, and role-playing and other experiential training tools have played important roles in getting beyond knee-jerk reactions and enabling a frank dialogue about race. While detailed presentations of those conflicts are beyond our purposes here (and would risk violating confidentiality and anonymity promises), some sense of the flavor of these interactions can be gained from Michael-Ray Mathews's description:

> Many of our national events now open with a training session on the dominant [American cultural] narrative and race, and how we are countering that hegemonic narrative. We do some analysis on race, drawing on jo[h]n powell and others. Then we do a pyramid exercise. People create a [horizontal] pyramid with chairs and sit in the seat that society has designed for them. White folks up front, blacks in back, others in the middle. Some folks intentionally transgress that, and then we get into a long hour and a half conversation. We do that early on, rather than doing the traditional content and then trying to "slip in race." Now we have race from the beginning on the table, and an ongoing conversation on race then informs all our work. . . . Engaging people at that level, intellectual and emotional, really tears down some walls, lets people . . . [pause] . . . lets us be honest with each other in a safe way about race.

A second sharp axis of tension has revolved around the relationship of gender equity, racial equity, ethnic stereotypes, and sometimes sexual preference as these play out within organizing—and how the networks can balance building excellent work on the complex terrain of organizing while simultaneously dealing with the "intersectionality" of all those axes of difference. That is, the time and energy needed to negotiate racial/ethnic and other differences, and their intersectionality, regularly run up against the sheer complexity of the tasks these organizations face as they strive to spur American institutions to overcome policy paralysis and address recrudescent inequality. That recurring tension between simultaneous commitment to equity and organizing excellence is a regular, perhaps inevitable, feature of the field today—but one at least some participants are determined to address as a creative and necessary tension. Indeed, it is a sine qua non of continuing involvement for many.

In that spirit, the PICO National Network has adopted specific "dashboard" metrics to assess each affiliate coalition's development, including progress it has made in institutionalizing racial equity and racial justice within its internal organizational life and external political work. As part of the network's overall effort to build high-quality work within every affiliate coalition, each PICO federation (local coalition) is now regularly rated by an external assessor across eleven different areas, including its work on racial equity. The racial equity metrics in the Network Health Dashboard include whether the organization has diverse staff, board, and leadership; has a "theory of change" statement in which a racial analysis is evident; conducts ongoing racial justice training; evaluates its director using criteria incorporating diversity and inclusion benchmarks; and has human resources policies and practices that reflect commitment to diversity and inclusion.

Network personnel perform these assessments, so we do not cite them as objective measures. But they appear to be taken seriously. In the most recent dashboard evaluations of forty-two PICO affiliates, scores on these racial equity metrics ranged from 0% to 100%, with a median score of 54% and a mean score of 67%. PICO's attention to institutionalizing racial equity within the formal organizational practices of the network—along with the "softer" institutionalization through the cultural dynamics discussed throughout these chapters—provides evidence of the network's commitment on this terrain.

Michael-Ray Mathews assessed the situation as of 2014 in this way:

We are still trying to grow, still struggling with all these things [regarding racial equity]. We're still figuring out how to do all this really well. But PICO will now never be able to unring the bell that says "PICO is a racial justice organization." We have outed ourselves; there really is no going back. It would take a *lot* to undo what we've done in the last six or ten years. When I came on board, lots of people were thinking this might be a one-off effort. But that's just clearly not true. . . . This struggle is lifelong. We have had to commit ourselves to one day at a time, seeking the kind of serenity, courage, and wisdom to lean into this, to try on new things to take on the way that suppression of difference has tainted our lives. We are not just getting our stuff together in organizations and institutions, we are focused on having an impact on the whole culture. That's a lifelong journey: the arc is indeed long. This thing is a beast, and our silence only feeds the beast. We have to continually dismantle the beast called racism, racial oppression.

Yet already one can discern significant accomplishments flowing from these initiatives. The transformation of organizational culture traced above surely must count as one such accomplishment. But more concretely, PICO identifies various outcomes of this work:[30]

- Following intense work by many PICO federations to highlight job discrimination against "returning citizens"—California took action last summer to forbid many employers from asking about criminal histories on job applications.
- After PICO's affiliate in Louisiana led an intensive campaign to promote the efficacy of pretrial services, the New Orleans City Council approved a significant increase in funding for a program that allows low-risk individuals to be released without posting bail; the program has reduced the average pretrial jail population by three hundred per day.
- PICO "is playing a lead role in the implementation of the Ceasefire violence reduction program in cities across California as well as in Louisiana, [helping] to change policing practices and city policies within the Ceasefire framework." PICO cites that fatal shootings are down 60 percent in Richmond; 55 percent in Stockton; 33 percent in Baton Rouge; and 30 percent in Oakland.

Other accomplishments claimed by the Lifelines to Healing/LiveFree campaign are more process oriented:[31]

- In 2013, PICO published op-ed articles in the *Washington Post, Huffington Post, New York Times, San Francisco Chronicle, Sojourners,* and other influential publications, and was featured on CNN, MSNBC, Clear Channel Radio, and other broadcast outlets.
- Hundreds of PICO congregations participated in "gun violence prevention Sabbaths," during which family members displayed photos of loved ones lost to gun violence while congregants prayed and committed to public expressions of support for programs and policies to reduce gun violence.
- In New Orleans, more than one thousand people participated in a "Just for All, Not Just for Some" campaign focused on incarceration and violence in that city.
- PICO staff and clergy were invited to serve as core participants on the task force convened by Vice President Joe Biden to discuss gun policy reform; PICO helped shape executive actions taken by the Obama Administration to reduce urban violence and participated in White House meetings that

helped shape the Administration's My Brother's Keeper Initiative (launched
March 2014) to increase opportunity for young men of color.

· Lifelines recruited five hundred new clergy and reached two thousand
potential new volunteer leaders through a series of church conventions,
focusing on congregations that have not previously worked with PICO and
are located in cities where PICO does not have a local organization.

· Since the beginning of 2014, PICO claims its training events in five states
have equipped 2,036 clergy, returning citizens, and family members to act
as leaders in strategic advocacy and communications work; and that it has
trained more than ten thousand leaders in race equity analysis.

· In March 2014, PICO organized a "Live Free Sabbath" featuring sermons,
prayer, and public events that drew participation from more than sixty-four
congregations including a dozen "mega-churches" with several thousand
members each.

While our research cannot verify these claims, the broad pattern suggests
that the substance of some coalitions' work indeed reflects the kind of priorities discussed here. At the same time, these accomplishments *built on* and
learned from early efforts launched within local coalitions. To offer just one
example among many: In 2011, PICO's federation in Kansas City, Communities Creating Opportunity (CCO), launched a three-pronged agenda
focused on economic dignity, health access, and "lifelines to hope and healing" with a thousand people in attendance (see photo at start of chapter 3).

Conclusion: Risks and Rewards of Ambitious Organizing

> Big changes are occurring in organizing. We are thinking more about worldview,
> the battle of big ideas in the country. I do not think enough progress has been
> made, but this level of wrestling with the question of scale is a big change. Orga-
> nizations that were founded by white leaders now have a much sharper racial jus-
> tice lens in their work. Organizing has an increased focus on corporate account-
> ability versus what has been only a government accountability approach. The
> emergence of new networks and new configurations inside and across networks is
> another exciting thing.
>
> —George Goehl, *National People's Action*[32]

This chapter has described some of the major changes that have occurred
in a broad sector of community organizing, and it has analyzed the thinking and organizational dynamics behind those changes. While the shift to

explicitly engaging ideas about racial equity and economic justice has occurred rather broadly across much of the faith-based community organizing sector, the extent of that shift (and how assertively groups have pursued it in practice) has varied significantly depending on particular local realities and organizational contexts. That, too, is part of the embedded autonomy behind the most successful organizing. Networks can foster (or fail to foster) the spread of innovative thinking and innovative organizing practices and help judge which innovations are most valuable, but in the final analysis how deeply such changes are embraced "on the ground" depends on local leaders and organizers.

The emergence of a discourse and practice of racial equity work in the faith-based community organizing sector does *not*, in our analysis, represent a fundamental shift to organizing on the basis of racial identity. In Wood's 2002 book *Faith in Action: Religion, Race, and Democratic Organizing in America*, he argues that although race-based organizing clearly has a place in American political culture, ultimately it faces obstacles *inherent* in the cultural dynamics of race in America. We believe that analysis remains accurate but requires more careful nuance. That is, what we portray here is a cultural and institutional shift within an overarching set of organizing practices fundamentally rooted in a universalist democratic creed and an appeal to religious faith as the cultural bases for mobilization.[33]

Thus the move to centrally highlight racial equity as part of the organizational cultures analyzed above represents not a turn to race-based organizing, but rather a new emphasis within what remains faith-based community organizing. But the shift appears to involve a change of emphasis *within* the worldview of universalist models of democratic life. The turn to racial equity represents a kind of targeted universalism writ large, to the level of an entire coalition and sometimes an entire network, rather than particular policy arenas. The shift thus is not a reversal but rather a continuation of the legacy of progressive movements that have insisted on deepening and extending universal democratic ideals, here insisting on their concretization via social policies and organizational practices designed to roll back the pernicious effects of racialization.

This shift has not occurred easily, but was forged gradually based on four kinds of organizational learning by strategic leaders in faith-based organizing coalitions and networks: their experience of the limits of democratic power based solely on abstract universalism and religious commitment; their analysis of the mutual constitution of economic inequality and racial inequality in America; their having repeatedly witnessed the strategic manipulation of white racial identity to eviscerate political struggles against inequality; and their determination not to allow those dynamics to continue to checkmate innovative social policy to address rising inequality.

Before returning to those themes, in the following unconventional chapter we hear more of the discourse and practice of the universalist and multiculturalist strands of democratic life as these are mobilized to fight economic inequality, racial injustice, and policy paralysis. But those strands will be interwoven via the voice of one person, committed to economic justice, racial equity, and democratic life *and* to living a life of faith—in his case, in a vein of Pentecostal Christianity that has not always connected those commitments.

Figure 6.1 Michael McBride (PICO) being arrested in Ferguson, Missouri, along with Jim Wallis (Sojourners), Cornel West (Union Theological Seminary), and faith-based leaders from around the United States (October 2014). (Photo by Wiley Price / St. Louis American)

SIX

Challenge to America:
An Interview with Rev. Michael McBride,
Lifelines to Healing LiveFree Campaign,
PICO National Network)

Since 2012, Rev. Michael McBride has served as the PICO National Network's director of urban strategies and of the network's Lifelines to Healing campaign to address the root causes of urban violence (subsequently called the LiveFree campaign). Whereas in the rest of this book the authors interpret and analytically frame interviewees' perspectives on the challenges and opportunities facing American society and the faith-based organizing sector, here we offer McBride's testimony in his own voice during Wood's 2013 interview of him. This approach seems fitting given the authors' position in a society within which voices emerging from democratic movements and communities of color are often supplanted by white voices from academe. McBride places racial equity work in historic, cultural, and political context as seen from the vantage point of an African American pastor in the Pentecostal Christian tradition, and of a leader of racial equity work in one national organizing project.

RLW: I have been struck by both the moral passion and the careful wording reflected in Lifeline's social media reaction to the George Zimmerman acquittal. Can you tell me about how Lifelines went about formulating its response? What did you want to accomplish?

MCBRIDE: It's important first to understand the verdict as a continuation of a long-term pattern of dehumanizing black and brown folks broadly. Our response was attempting to really tie the feelings of the verdict to a larger moral framework, the things that are tearing the fabric of our country apart.

And we wanted to ground our outrage in a set of principles, to lift up the inhumanity and the values that make that kind of verdict possible. So our re-action came out of our grounding in our long-term work . . . trying to restore the humanity of many kinds of people in our country. Too often our un-conscious bias—or sometimes our *conscious* bias—together create the condi-tions for a verdict like the Zimmerman trial, and for the degrading of young people of color in particular.

These communities are impoverished, they lack opportunities, they have drugs proliferating. There's this sense [in America] that they just got that way on their own, that this is the way things are just going to be. To the extent there's any outrage, it's most often around "neglect" of these communities, instead of around the responsibility that we think is *shared* . . . instead of outrage about how things have been allowed to get this way. It's not just the black or poor, it's a national thing that has allowed children to grow up in war zones . . . a disowning of black America and of poor people, a sense that we don't need to take care of each other, [a sense that] these communi-ties are on their own. I believe there's an important conversation there—we think one of the central things that needs to happen is the *values* conversation around who is our neighbor, around these American ideals. We do not want to live in a country where poor people and African Americans are seen as outside the community.

RLW: You spoke of the values in play in all of this, and talked about that in terms of civic values. In your writing I've seen you discuss faith values as well. Could you speak about that part of it?

MCBRIDE: I'm a fifth-generation African American Pentecostal kid. I have been grounded and nurtured in a spiritual formation that takes seriously the ac-tive and ongoing presence of the spirit of God to make all things new. . . . When really lived, this creates an active and forward vision. No matter how bad things are now, God's spirit is at work to redeem our lives. Coming out of that kind of foundation in the soil, I believe the kind of faith we bring to these conversation, when deeply interrogated, can bring lots of resources and tools to bring people to a way of thinking, to initiate a great healing of all these wounds. In a purely secular society, there is no real foundation in ideals; it turns into idolatry. . . . There needs to be a deeper critique of how we define, understand, and appropriate our language. So the faith language that comes out of our traditions—Christians, Catholics, Muslims, Jews, Uni-tarians, Buddhists, Hindus, others—we mine it for the kind of prophetic lan-guage that can redeem the soul of our country, a country that's been deeply soiled by racism, commodification, and a damning obsession with the mate-rial and with power. . . . Of course, in our faith traditions we are not immune from being seduced by those things, but we do have powerful resources to resist that, to help recenter us, to call us back to a more faithful application of our faith values and our human and civic and national values.

RLW: How long have you been involved in PICO? Were you involved in the early stages of PICO beginning to wrestle with a racial equity analysis? Please tell me about that process: what were the internal struggles involved? What were the fault lines? How did PICO manage to move forward?

MCBRIDE: I've been involved in local PICO work in the Bay Area [of California] since 2005, when I planted my church in Berkeley. . . . I was not very involved in national work until 2009, when I got involved as executive director of our local chapter. So I was exposed to the broader trajectory of our work, our theory of change and thinking about racial equity, only in last few years. That's a great challenge in a group like PICO, with a white middle-centric kind of ethos.[1] Race conversations were often mediated [by white people] and either mitigated or catapulted forward based on the comfort and courage of white people. Everybody else was forced to acquiesce or get comfortable in that kind of context. When I came in, this [more frank] conversation was just getting started. For African Americans and Latinos, the sharpest point of tension was in how PICO organized in response to Katrina and the emergent immigration fight. Because there was not much ability to answer those fights with some really constructive energy, some deep fissures emerged. So that launched a big conversation about how we can respond more powerfully to race and other differences in our network. And we began to engage deeply with the work of john powell. That provided a framework that was not condemnatory, but offered some deep learning and education and reflection that unleashed lots of good will and willingness to have those hard conversations.

RLW: Could you tell me about the current status of the racial equity work in PICO?

MCBRIDE: If I could use a biblical metaphor, I'd say we've left Egypt. Like the Israelites, we felt we were in bondage, in a place of challenge and difficulty in starting the conversation around race. We are not in the Promised Land now, but we're on the wilderness journey, and in PICO we share a deep commitment to what it means to do our work as faith-based organizers that embrace a race-based framework, and strive for honesty about our diminished humanity. Who gets to lead? Who gets to inform our best thinking? We're going deep in a different kind of way, and I'm very excited about it. We have some gaps in the speed people are willing to implement these new ways of thinking, but we're moving forward, and I'm deeply hopeful about it.

RLW: Who have been the key people and key partnerships in this effort?

MCBRIDE: Internally, I'd say people like Dr. George Cummings, Michael-Ray Mathews, Jennifer Jones-Bridgett, folks who've been around a little longer than I have. Scott Reed and Gordon Whitman have been champions of this kind of conversation, even as they were learning how to navigate these waters themselves. Some people from the past, like Joe Givens. Some key partners, like Bob Ross of the California Endowment through the "boys of color" work they have led nationally. Also Maya Harris-West at the Ford Foundation, and Heather McGhee from Dēmos [regarding work] around economic dignity. The most instructive and agitational voice was Michelle Alexander, a long-time mentor to me. She launched our Lifelines campaign in New Orleans, gave concrete expression to what it means if we do not start to take seriously the racial justice implications of this moment in America. She's been an accelerating force on addressing race, not in the abstract but in the concrete. Also Manuel Pastor and Dr. Iva Carruthers.[2]

RLW: One theme in our book is the relationship of "issue campaigns" to "federated structure"—that is, how does PICO's local-state-national structure make running a major campaign like Lifelines easier or harder (as compared to one big centralized movement *or* a bunch of autonomous local groups). Can you talk a bit about your experience?

MCBRIDE: Well, I'd say the PICO structure has made it easier *and* harder. I love our network, because we are not a network of contrived constituencies—we don't claim to represent folks and then fail to engage with them, fail to bring them into conversation about our priorities, our direction. We represent real leaders, real clergy, real congregations and neighborhoods. We can take you to a particular place at any given moment and show you local work that reflects their priorities. It [the relationship between state- and national-level PICO staff and local leaders and staff] is also not a transactional relationship, not locals just following an agenda set somewhere else. Local groups are involved in setting that agenda, refining it, and the constituency is real, concrete, it is not manufactured.

So because ownership of the Lifelines campaign is deeply local, it can create sometimes a set of competing narratives or interests—still around the shared issues, but with real challenges around aligning different views of [those issues]. In Lifelines, some folks imagine the tip of the spear being to reduce lives lost to gun violence. Other folks say "our work needs to be about ending mass incarceration, ending the school-to prison pipelines," say, or "our work needs to be about the transition back to society after being in jail"; other folks just want to do a jobs campaign focused on economic dignity—they say that's the way to bring some dignity to African American and Latino people. Those competing agendas can create some, well, some kind of "cycling" [i.e., moving from approach to approach in discussions, without making forward progress]. That's the role of us as national staff—to help move that conversation forward, see the best work being done and the best opportunities to expand it, so that all these individual parts can add up to greater work. It's a challenge but also a blessing. It keeps us up in the air.

RLW: Another theme we are working with is the relationship of "racial equity" work to PICO's broader issue agenda. Can you speak to that? How do you see racial equity fitting into the overall challenges facing this country that PICO is trying to address?

MCBRIDE: I want to believe that the way we understand race and opportunity, the dignity and humanity of everyone in our country, will not be "siloed" into one campaign. It will continue to be infused into everything we do as a network. We have a commitment as a multiracial, multicultural network with a translocal projection and impact. We will bring to bear the best thinking and organizing and our best selves to make sure that race and opportunity and justice and faith and dignity and humanity are . . . [pause] well, that those things will just be who we are, what people will say about us. We hope that by being that to our best ability, we can transform the country, build a better dialogue about the kind of work we are called to do. Not just be part of the status quo, but actually be a powerful transformative agent, a catalyst if you will, to move the racial justice and equity conversation forward.

I find it a deep challenge that I want to embrace. Dr. King said so many powerful things that we do not read carefully enough. His "Two Americas" speech is very descriptive of where we are today: folks being judged by the content of their character, not the color of their skin; he talked about "America wrote a check [to black Americans] that came back marked 'insufficient funds'" . . . We are still living with that, with the idea that there are 'insufficient funds' to right what's wrong in America. . . . What does it mean to invest enough capital—in every sense of that word—so that these checks will never come back insufficient again? That's what I hope and pray we can move the football forward on. If we can, our world and country will be better for it. I see all this as a continuing part of my ministry and my calling. I don't bifurcate my call into ministry and organizing; I pray many more will answer that call.

RLW: What other tensions or struggles have come up in leading Lifelines? What kinds of internal or external tensions around Latino and African American leaders' priorities?

MCBRIDE: I think much of the tension may have its origin more in staff than in leaders. Most of the leaders are in communities where young people, sometimes their own family members, are moving in and out of jail—either because of their immigration status or the urban crime context they face. This is not grounded in research, but my working assumption is that the brown-black divide in organizing is rooted more in organizers than it is in the communities themselves. It's a lack of *organizer* imagination [for how to bring that agenda together], not so much in the young people themselves. So we [organizers] need to expand our social networks, engage our imaginations, to see how these things can dovetail. The tension only exists in the sense of "how can we have enough capacity and resources to move both of these agendas." I experience no tension at all around finding a shared analysis on building a more just society for everybody. It's really about how organizing is staffed, how we all own the responsibility to create a framework for leaders to live into it fully, not choose one part of it to embrace.

One of the great challenges of this work is the philanthropic community: A month or two ago, Bob Ross and the Association of Black Foundation Executives announced a powerful commitment to leverage their resources to fund black men and boys. I think the funding community has mostly walked away from racial justice, at least in the last five years. People feel like this problem has a level of intractability that makes it hard to deliver the kind of immediate results that funders want to see. We need to figure out how to avoid walking away from communities with entrenched racial inequities, not think that

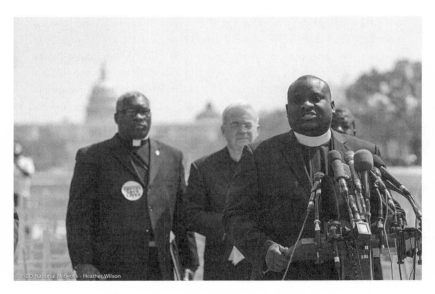

Figure 6.2 Rev. Michael McBride (PICO Lifelines to Healing/LiveFree) with Jim Wallis (Sojourners) and Rev. James Booker (Harriett Tubman Center, Detroit) in Washington, DC. (Photo by Heather Wilson)

even ten or fifteen years of funding is going to undo 400 years of inequalities and the building up of particular cultures. The funding community needs to reimagine that, and also be able to recognize the role of churches in meeting these [challenges]—funders tend to see faith communities as part of the problem, not as part of the solution. Philanthropy is more likely to fund white-led racial justice work, rather than people-of-color-led racial justice work. That needs to be interrogated. There tends to be a real assumption about the capacity and ingenuity and competency of folks of color to lead our own efforts for liberation. I want to challenge that from the White House all the way down to our house: if we're given the resources and opportunities, we can contribute to liberation for ourselves *and* others on the margins.

RLW: What has been most exciting or satisfying about your work with Lifelines?

MCBRIDE: Being able to go from city to city, from denomination to denomination, from congregation to congregation, and see everybody ready for this revolution, ready for this fight. There's a false narrative that people are apathetic, not passionate about changing this reality. There are hundreds of people everywhere we go, willing to walk neighborhoods and engage in organizing to interrupt violence. There's great promise. I get to wake up every day to try to imagine how to harness that energy to create real change. Along with preaching in my church every Sunday morning, that's the most exciting thing going on in my life.

Figure 7.1 "... and Justice for All": Universal democratic sentiment amid the demonstrations in Ferguson, Missouri (August 2014). (Photo by Heather Wilson)

SEVEN

Strategic Innovation and Democratic Theory

The previous chapter's interview of a key national leader of faith-based work for racial equity drew together many of the themes running through this book. This chapter recapitulates those themes and links them to larger questions of social theory and strategic innovation in democratic social movements.

Today, the disempowerment of entire communities—their loss of voice in society and loss of control over the future—affects not only poor communities but also once-comfortable communities of the American middle class. Faith-based community organizing exists in order to address issues of disempowerment and economic inequality in American life, and does so in two ways: by challenging communities to overcome their disempowerment and by challenging politicians and political institutions to overcome the policy paralysis that undercuts government credibility. In fighting for equality and against policy paralysis, faith-based organizing battles against two of the demons facing American society today.

But we have shown how some sectors of faith-based organizing have recently begun to explicitly do battle against a third demon of American political culture. Since before the founding of our nation, racial bias and its expression in the implicit racialization of nearly all facets of American culture have bedeviled American society. The dynamics of economic inequality are deeply and increasingly intertwined with racialization and ethnic bias—despite the reality of continuing poverty in some white communities and the fact that no sector has fallen further in recent decades than the (disproportionately white) working class in unionized or formerly unionized industries.[1] Today, racial and ethnic bias are manipulated by elite politicians to advance partisan interests and paralyze public policy on immigration, criminal justice, and other issues—one dimension of an apparent strategy to justify contempt for government and thus eviscerate government's ability to address issues ranging from inequality to environmental destruction. As a result of this imbrication of economic inequality, policy paralysis, and racial injustice, some sectors of faith-based organizing have decided they simply cannot fight the first two without explicitly challenging the third. They have done so by shifting their approach, now directly addressing racial inequity and implicit bias within their own organizing structures and advocating for policies based on "targeted universalism" in the wider society.

We obtained our closest look at that transition via the work of the PICO National Network in chapters 4–6. By mid-2014, the network's national staff was working to assure that organizing for economic and racial justice would not exist in isolation from one another, but rather would be intertwined in the network's overall organizational culture and understanding of power. As Michael-Ray Mathews noted regarding the Lifelines to Healing (now LiveFree) campaign analyzed in chapter 5:

> We have worked to liberate Lifelines to Healing from being the sole vessel that PICO uses to express its commitment to racial justice. Lifelines was the effort that forced PICO's work on race out of our internal space and into a public space. Because mass incarceration so impacts black and brown people, there was just no way to talk about that issue without talking about race . . . PICO had to have its own narrative about race, more deeply integrated and internalized, so that it shows up in all of our work: economic dignity, access to health care, immigration. That's the really big development, it's still underway, still happening, but our commitment to it is becoming much more deeply owned.

In the chapter 6 interview, Michael McBride connected that point to the network's broader ambitions:

> I want to believe that the way we understand race and opportunity, the dignity and humanity of everyone in our country, will not be "siloed" into one campaign. It will continue to be infused into everything we do as a network. We have a commitment as a multiracial, multicultural network with a translocal projection and impact. We will bring to bear the best thinking and organizing and our best selves to make sure that race and opportunity and justice and faith and dignity and humanity are . . . [pause] well, that those things will just be who we are, what people will say about us. We hope that by being that to our best ability, we can transform the country.

Thus one key analytic theme has been the way addressing economic inequality and policy paralysis—newly undergirded in some sectors by explicit attention to racial equity—forms the strategic core of the faith-based community organizing field.

McBride's interview captures a second analytic theme woven throughout this book: faith-based organizing's approach to addressing the tension between universalist and multiculturalist democratic commitments. He speaks in a multiculturalist vein of the "degrading of young people of color in particular" and of "a disowning of black America and of poor people, a sense that we don't need to take care of each other, [a sense that] these communities are on their own." Yet he also explicitly invokes "a larger moral framework" and the need to "restore the humanity of many kinds of people in this country." McBride locates PICO's commitment to minority children within such a larger framework as he notes, "it's not just the black or poor, it's a national thing that has allowed children to grow up in war zones," and emphasizes, "we think one of the central things that needs to happen is the *values* conversation around who is our neighbor, around these American ideals. We do not want to live in a country where poor people and African Americans are seen as outside the community." Thus the multiculturalist commitments that drive McBride's passion—like those of the faith-based community organizing we have analyzed throughout this book—are embedded within overarching universalist commitments. As we have seen, McBride has channeled his passion and outrage into PICO's advocacy of domestic policies shaped by "targeted universalism." Those passions are driven by how current domestic policy undercuts racialized minorities' opportunity to experience the universalist promises of American democracy, rather than by any special pleading in the name of multiculturalism. But his passion and outrage, like that of the wider field, are also rooted in and fueled by a very different realm: religious faith.

The Fire of Faith in Organizing

This book's focus on work for racial and economic justice, along with the fact that Wood's previous work analyzed the contributions of religious culture to faith-based organizing, mean we have paid less attention to a third theme running as an undercurrent throughout this book: the role of religious faith and spirituality in sustaining activists' commitment to the uphill struggle for economic equality, racial equity, and an effective role for government policy.[2] In so doing, we risk creating the illusion that faith and spirituality are somehow separate from the personal commitment or

© Heather Wilson

Figure 7.2 "Stop Killing Us" and "2 Timothy 1:7": Scripture amid protest, Ferguson, Missouri (August 2014): "For God did not give us a spirit of timidity but a spirit of power and love and self-control." (Photo by Heather Wilson)

public work of these organizations. That would be an illusion indeed. It is certainly the case that secular organizations actively engage as institutional members of faith-based organizing coalitions (recall from chapter 3 that almost a fifth of member institutions are not congregations or other faith-based groups). It is also the case that some local coalitions and some networks center their organizational cultures less around religious practices than do others; the meetings of those coalitions and networks thus have a less faith-based or spiritual ethos, while retaining an orientation toward ethical democracy. Despite these caveats, however, religious faith and spirituality run deeply through much of the field, in ways both apparent and hidden.

The more apparent way religion sustains commitment to economic and racial justice in this field is through the collective and personal rituals drawn from what popular culture pejoratively calls "institutionalized religion." What that really means is that faith-based organizing often draws on the religious experience and shared emotional "flow" that are constructed via the worship practices of communities of faith. That is, leaders often buttress the sense of meaning within the hard work of changing society by pulling elements of worship practices into settings in which people are being asked to fight economic inequality, policy paralysis, and racial injustice. Such cultural elements may be worship styles, specific prayers, symbols, scripture readings, songs, spiritual poetry, or even simply the shared understanding of a God who calls human beings beyond themselves and their own narrow concerns. Those elements often come from institutionalized religions; indeed, a large part of what makes such cultural elements meaningful and powerful in evoking commitment is precisely their quality as legitimate and accepted—"institutionalized"—practices.

The more hidden way religion undergirds commitment in this field is through what might be termed a *spirituality* of democratic struggle. By "spirituality" we mean an ethos carried internally and interpersonally rather than via commitment to a particular faith community (or often *along with* such commitment). We hear such a spirituality in Michael Mc-Bride's interview:

> I'm a fifth-generation African American Pentecostal kid. I have been grounded and nurtured in a spiritual formation that takes seriously the active and on-going presence of the Spirit of God to make all things new. . . . When really lived, this creates an active and forward vision. No matter how bad things are now, God's Spirit is at work to redeem our lives. Coming out of that kind of foundation in the soul, I believe the kind of faith we bring to these

Figure 7.3 Interfaith prayer in Washington, DC: Religious dimensions of the struggle for ethical democracy. (Photo by Heather Wilson)

conversations, when deeply interrogated, offer lots of resources and tools to bring people to a new way of thinking, to initiate a great healing of all these wounds.

Although McBride remains rooted in a specific institutionalized faith tradition (he is trained and serves part-time as a Pentecostal pastor), he does not accept his tradition "as is." Rather, he speaks of "deeply interrogating" his faith. When asked what he meant by that, McBride responded:

> There needs to be a deeper critique of how we define, understand, and appropriate our language. So the faith language that comes out of our traditions—Christians, Catholics, Muslims, Jews, Unitarians, Buddhists, Hindus, others—we mine it for the kind of prophetic language that can redeem the soul of our country, a country that's been deeply soiled by racism, commodification, and a damning obsession with the material and with power.

Part of that "interrogation" includes McBride's recognition that Christians and other believers are subject to those same negative cultural trends, but he argues that faith communities help ground their members in other commitments:

Of course, in our faith traditions we are not immune from being seduced by those things, but we do have powerful resources to resist that, to help recenter us, to call us back to a more faithful application of our faith values and our human, civic, and national values.

These quotes from McBride, like our interviews with Scott Reed, Ana Garcia-Ashley, Alvin Herring, Judy Donovan, Michael-Ray Mathews, George Goehl, Gordon Whiteman, Doran Schrantz, Stephanie Gut, and others that readers have met in this book, evoke this spirituality of democratic struggle. One cannot really understand their work's vigor or the field's dynamism without understanding the way this spirituality draws on multiple sources of meaning, including secular democratic commitment, the worship communities of institutionalized religion, and the wellsprings of spiritual formation in individual lives. For the hard work of building ethical democracy to thrive and succeed, it will need to draw on all that and more.

We certainly do not mean to suggest that all or even most participants in faith-based organizing—lay leaders, professional staff, or clergy—bring this level of reflection and critical insight to bear in their work. But neither are such capacities rare within the field. Time and again in our years of ethnographic participation, interviewing, and other professional relationships in the field, we have witnessed such spiritually, religiously, and intellectually grounded capacities for reflexivity and deliberation at work across a variety of coalitions and networks. These capacities constitute part of the artistry of community organizing at its best. Such reflexivity allows key strategists to bridge the tension between universalist and multiculturalist commitments and turn it into a creative tension driving the dynamism of their work. Surely not coincidentally, that reflexivity seems generally more common within the most developed local coalitions, statewide or regional organizing efforts, and national networks. We have seen it widely enough to consider it one of the primary resources for potential growth in the field. We have also seen the costs to organizations lacking a capacity for reflexivity, such that we consider its broader cultivation—whether from secular or religious sources—one of the key challenges facing the field's key strategic leaders.[3]

But democratic movements always face challenges, and faith-based community organizing has faced its share. Such challenges drove the organizers and religious leaders profiled throughout this book toward strategic innovation. The creative work ahead of building ethical democracy will require a similar spirit of innovation and daring within a variety of movements. In the hope that the daring spirit of innovative organizers and leaders may spread more widely, we next consider how some of them have adopted new ideas and new models of organizing in response to specific problems facing the field.

Creativity: Strategic Innovation in Faith-Based Organizing

As the scale and ambition of faith-based organizing expanded over the last decade, the field innovated to meet new challenges. This strategic innovation arose in parallel with—and partly as a result of—the rise in diversity we documented in part I.[4] Whereas fifteen years ago the senior leadership in the field was heavily composed of white men whose careers had been rooted in the field of faith-based organizing for decades, today that profile has diversified dramatically. As shown in chapter 2, the upper echelon of leadership now includes broad diversity across racial and ethnic groups, and women now regularly provide leadership at all levels.[5] Immigrants are strongly represented among organizers, and the national staff members of the organizing networks now appear to be recruited from a broader array of career sectors.[6] We briefly characterize some of the new thinking that has recently emerged, drawing on in-depth interviews with thirteen of the key strategic thinkers in the national and regional networks plus strategic funders of the field.[7] This is a story of strategic but unevenly distributed innovation, whose unevenness has produced some of the variation in strategic capacity across the field. The field's future contributions to ethical democracy in America depends greatly on whether the spirit of innovation characterized here spreads more broadly.

Although the origins of the recent wave of innovative organizing go back well before the Obama administration (at least to the experiences of the Texas IAF and PICO in California two decades ago and more), that innovation has accelerated since 2008. Organizers trained a cadre of campaign volunteers who were central to the election of Barack Obama as president, and his presidency slowed down the acceleration of inequality in America and even rolled back some of its worst effects (especially regarding access to health care). But on political terrain defined by distrust of public institutions generally and government particularly, even an administration as sympathetic and self-identified with organizing as Obama's could hardly begin to address inequality rooted in three decades of bipartisan pandering to economic elites. As California IAF lead organizer Judy Donovan said:

A lot of folks saw Obama as the great hope. [But] even the best of candidates, if there's not an organized constituency out there to hold them accountable and to put the pressure on them . . . [pause] . . . well, all kings will fail. So I think that despair is probably compounded by the fact that a lot of folks, whether they're willing to admit it or not, thought that these last years would have just been in the bag. And then found themselves in a really painful way.

That pain provided the anvil on which was forged some openness to innovation, fired by spreading recognition of the field's strategic failures even amid some tactical gains. As one anonymous national staff person put it in 2011, "We've been doing some good organizing in particular places for years, but inequality in America has only gotten worse. We've been getting our butts kicked in the places that matter most." As executive director George Goehl of National People's Action phrased it, only "big ideas" were going to challenge the field to greater efficacy. No one set of "big ideas" underlay recent changes, but driving most of them were two broad sets of insights, one concerning organizers' external diagnosis of the problems of American society and one regarding their diagnosis of internal shortcoming in organizing.

We have seen some of the key external diagnoses throughout this book, and thus summarize them here only briefly. First, that economic inequality was giving such dominant power and voice to economic elites that organizing had to more directly take on issues of economic justice. Second, that any effort to take on inequality had to address race, ethnicity, and the racialization of society much more centrally than had been done historically in this organizing tradition. Third, that organizing simply had to "get to scale"—that is, both replicate itself far more broadly and project influence into higher-level political venues than had ever been done before. Finally, organizers came to recognize that although the struggle against anti-majoritarian social and economic policies was "the right fight," allowing that fight to occur on the terrain of political culture defined by antigovernment assumptions held little promise. Rather, organizing had to begin to redefine the cultural terrain itself, the way a certain brand of antigovernment conservatives had done between 1964 and 1980.[8] Key strategic innovations throughout the foregoing chapters emerged partly in response to those insights.

Other strategic innovations arose in response to new insights about internal shortcomings or outdated assumptions within the field. For example, some organizers came to believe that community organizing's highly pragmatic and nonideological stance inherited from the Alinsky tradition no longer represented a strength but had become a real limitation of this model—particularly when it undercut the long-term vision and deep analytic work needed to motivate and sustain more ambitious political work. One key strategic innovation was to draw heavily from the resources for ethical critique and social vision carried in religious traditions, what Gordon Whitman termed "doubling down on religion." The informal national network of clergy affiliated with PICO encouraged its members to write a "prophetic vision statement" about the current moment in American life and how it falls short of God's desire for justice in human society, then to articulate that vision publicly and preach about it in worship services. As a result, many local coalitions and some national networks developed "prophetic voice" or similar statements that sought to articulate a religiously grounded vision of a more just and compassionate American society. Doran Schrantz, an innovative organizer with the then-independent coalition ISAIAH in Minnesota, noted:

> ISAIAH is partnering with PICO on this idea that they get clergy, our greatest asset, to actually move a coordinated strategy on a prophetic voice. I think the reason so many people are talking about [this prophetic voice effort] is that there is this roving anxiety and fear. And if that anxiety is not redirected or meaning made out of it that would support the kinds of things that we think should be in place, [then America is in trouble]. I mean basically a social contract that cares for the most vulnerable, provides retirement security, higher education, the basic policies that produce a middle class, all those public investments that need to be in place for communities to be healthy. If we don't re-grab that primary narrative, that's all going. It's going away. It's actually going away right before our eyes.

Scott Reed, whom we met in chapter 4, articulated a similar insight:

> We have not co-created, or helped nurture, a strong moral and prophetic voice that really competes for the hearts as well as the values. . . . An uncompassionate narrative now lives in a lot of the American public domain. It lives there because there hasn't been a strong counternarrative competing against it.

Such a "strong counternarrative" represents an effort to redefine the cultural terrain on which political struggles occur, as discussed above.

Alongside these initiatives, strategic thought leaders strove to embed more sophisticated analytic thinking within the culture of organizing. Pioneers in this regard included the Southwest Industrial Areas Foundation through their Institutes for Public Life, the PICO California Project, the Kirwan Institute under john powell, other Gamaliel initiatives on "regional equity" with Myron Orfield and David Rusk, and various grassroots think tanks such as the Grassroots Policy Project under Richard Healey. The analyses of economic inequality, racialization, and implicit racial/ethnic bias heard throughout this book arose from such efforts to advance the analytic dimension of professional organizing, albeit analytic work animated by concrete struggles of diverse communities.

A third form of internal innovation was to push the Alinsky-descended organizing model—which had become a fairly rigid orthodoxy focused on "building a power organization" via particular organizing techniques—in the direction of greater flexibility and collaboration. This included supplementing one-to-one organizing with the kind of sophisticated social media campaigns seen in the Lifelines to Healing/LiveFree campaign (chapter 5), which would previously have been anathema in the Alinsky-derived organizing tradition. It has also included supplementing Alinsky's focus on building a long-term power organization with short-term "campaigns" on particular issues, using the organization as a platform for generating a higher public profile and political influence on emergent issues.[9] Particularly widespread are voter registration and get-out-the-vote efforts, typically termed "civic engagement" campaigns. One national leader noted:

> We are moving our whole network into a much more robust and rigorous voter engagement mode, [focused on] civic engagement work. We really want to make that a core part of our work. It's the notion of, "if you are a citizen, what does that really mean?" Not just "are you naturalized"? But really, what is the *discipline* of citizenship?

In turn, those efforts opened up some sectors of the field to collaborating with other organizations at a strategic level, anathema in an older era in which Alinsky's "no permanent enemies, no permanent friends" held sway. As we saw in chapter 1, such collaborative efforts have become commonplace in the field—to such an extent that Scott Reed could say in 2011:

> I would imagine that we could be on the brink of doing some common infrastructure together. By "on the brink," I mean over the next five or six years. We could discover that the future of really strong organizing is not necessarily going to be just one mega-network emerging, but that there will be

multiple networks with their own unique voice in the landscape. Then there might be some common infrastructure built to develop talent, recruit that talent, and create a sense of really strong leader development.

While beyond our purposes here, such collaborative relationships have developed at the local level among coalitions around the country and at the state and national level in some networks.[10] These collaborations are often motivated by the urgency of the battle against the three demons that have been the focus of our analysis, and the sense that local influence is insufficient to fight them. In Schrantz's words, "The forces that we're up against are so huge. And they are not local. They're not local: We are not going to win a new social contract in St. Paul, Minnesota. And yet the forces that are unfolding in St. Paul are just crushing people."

In contrast, longtime IAF lead organizer Arne Graf emphasizes a different approach. He notes approvingly the new flexibility and willingness to collaborate that have entered the field, and his own coalitions have done extensive collaborative work with labor unions. But rather than building the kind of federated local-state-national structures emphasized here, Graf emphasizes a focus on strengthening local "mediating institutions," what he calls "going to the ground":

> We will create new and vibrant mediating institutions that will come out of what we do, or out of the ideas that people pick up of a more vibrant civil society . . . [speaks of various innovative metropolitan-level initiatives built by the IAF] . . . I just think out of that ferment, I hope would come movement towards a more just, equitable society. I think about the civil rights movement [and the possibility that such a movement might emerge again]. It might be a rationalization, but the way I like to think about all of our work, collectively, is that we are preparing for that moment.

Graf's emphasis on reinvigorating local mediating institutions represents an important countercurrent to the push for influence in higher-level political venues. As an anonymous national figure put it:

> Just emphasize the need to build strong local organizations. If you don't have that, I don't know how you authentically keep it grounded in a significant portion of the community, how you keep integrity to it. It worries me if there's less focus on that, if there's a move away from building local organizations.

Such concerns are not to be dismissed. In keeping with our focus on the need for higher-level power in order to fight economic inequality, policy paralysis, and racial injustice in American life, our analysis has emphasized the strategic importance of federated structures linking local, state, and national organizing. Previous scholars have identified the potential symbiosis of such structures, but have also shown the trade-offs inherent in them and the ways that—if not managed well, with the kind of organizing artistry we have seen—those trade-offs can undercut local organizing work.[11]

This combination of greater openness to collaboration, "doubling down on religion," striving for a prophetic critique of existing American culture, and the ambition to make a difference in the electoral dynamics that shape social priorities has driven strategic priorities in some sectors of the field. Thus sophisticated local organizers such as Kirk Noden and Rev. Troy Jackson of the Ohio Organizing Collaborative have forged strategic relationships with several networks to build a sophisticated voter engagement operation tied to their more traditional community organizing agenda.[12] That work includes substantial involvement from the usual core of faith-based organizing congregations from the historic African American, liberal Protestant, and Catholic traditions, but also substantial involvement from secular labor unions, Jewish synagogues, Unitarian churches, mosques, and evangelical churches. The first and last may be most crucial: unions due to their financial resources and ability to turn out volunteers, evangelicals due to their sheer demographic size and influence in American life—and the fact they have historically been so absent from the field of organizing.

The combination of ambitious political imagination and strategic innovation is reflected in thoughts from two anonymous strategic leaders:

> The evangelical voters in Ohio, where are they likely to be on any of the issues that we care about? How do we compete for *them*? How do we bring a voice that creates a value conflict that they have to struggle with? Frankly, that's kind of new territory for us. It's not about how do we speak to those who are already committed, but rather how do we create the internal conflict around values? Because values inherently have tension with each other, or often do. How do we expose that tension in ways that create more thoughtful decisions?
>
> Ohio is the best example of [some of these national trends]. With Kirk [Noden] and the Ohio Organizing collaborative, you can't understand it without understanding the relationships that have been built. And it's great: There you've got an organizer who was trained in NPA, IAF, and Gamaliel,

and is now essentially working with PICO on the faith-based organizing. . . . So in some ways you could see Ohio as a little bit of an example of all kinds of different trends in practice.

These kinds of ambitious political imagination and strategic innovation have undergirded the efforts of those sectors of faith-based organizing that have chosen to address economic inequality, policy paralysis, and racial injustice. They have also helped those sectors of the field effectively coordinate their resulting universalist and multiculturalist democratic commitments. As a result, faith-based organizing offers some real-world insight into the theoretical tensions posed by universalist and multiculturalist ideas of democracy. We now return to those ideas.

Reprise: The Theoretical Stakes behind Real-World Democratic Struggles

The introduction identified ways in which universalist and multiculturalist versions of democratic theory pull in divergent directions. Intervening chapters have shown how adroit work by democratic activists and grassroots intellectuals can manage universalist-multiculturalist tensions. However, we do not want to underplay those tensions; they represent an ongoing facet of the struggle to deepen democracy in a diverse society. We therefore now pause to connect what we have seen in faith-based organizing back to that theoretical debate.

Strong multiculturalists, including Iris Marion Young, Nancy Fraser in some aspects of her work, and others, have argued against any position that implies any one "truth" or universal standard of legitimacy. Their argument appears motivated by a fear that any such universal criteria will be used by those with power to marginalize newly identified "others," or to resubjugate those who have successfully struggled for societal recognition. This is more than a theoretical fear, of course. False "universal" standards have indeed been used throughout history to define the culture of dominant groups as universal and to exclude the less privileged.

Fraser's version of the multiculturalist position is best understood as a critique of Jürgen Habermas's ideal of the democratic public realm (presented in the introduction). Recall that Habermas posits a relatively unified public arena to which all in principle have access, and wherein a society-wide democratic dialogue shapes the future. In Fraser's formulation, this universalist ideal gives way to a vision of multiple communities of identity coexisting within a procedural republic.[13] Such a republic would include diverse "subaltern counterpublics," that is, public spheres *within* marginalized communities. These counterpublic spheres might be constituted around racial, ethnic, or gender identities, traditional or new religions, newly emergent political movements, or other subaltern groups. Fraser's emphasis on counterpublics prevents sheer domination of elites over all others or domination of majoritarian values over minority identities and communities. Thus the aspiration to universal democratic standards applicable to all gives way to insistence on democratic tolerance and willingness to embrace other cultures on their own autonomous and self-defined terms.

Fraser's multiculturalist position makes real sense. Communities whose interests, identities, aspirations, and sometimes very lives have been suppressed by dominant sectors of society—sometimes subtly, sometimes viciously—justifiably place priority on assuring themselves protection from such domination. The risk lies in how that priority may undercut commitment to internal democratic norms or to wider public life. Our analysis throughout this book sympathizes with the multiculturalist view, but we believe that universal standards can still play a democratic role. So before fully embracing a hard multiculturalism, with its rejection of universal democratic norms applicable to all in favor of a narrow emphasis on mutual toleration of difference, let us consider the potential costs of such an embrace.

Seyla Benhabib, Charles Taylor, and others adopt a more universalist position—albeit a kind of cautious universalism.[14] They affirm the need to foster identities and communities of interest not recognized as legitimate within dominant society or within the public sphere as constituted at any one moment in the history of a society. But they worry about at least two unintended consequences of the kind of hard multiculturalism described above. First, by embracing strong boundaries between the alternative public spaces of subaltern communities, might not counterpublics gradually erode the bonds of society that sustain functioning democratic life? Second, might those same strong boundaries also shelter subaltern communities from appropriate democratic critique (say, of the abuse of power by power holders within the subaltern community), or foster rejection of the very democratic institutions that allow multicultural diversity to thrive? These are not idle questions. In a world in which fundamentalist religionists (one kind of subaltern community) and secular anarchists (another kind of subaltern community) can both wall themselves off from critical debate of their ideas, such questions matter.

On these and other grounds, Seyla Benhabib argues for a *certain kind* of moral and political universalism. In order to protect the permanent ideal of ongoing democratization in society, she affirms the necessity for all communities to be exposed to the public dialogue through which democratic values are asserted, argued over, defended, and brought to bear on actual social worlds in their multicultural complexity. Benhabib recognizes that the sheltering of subaltern identities and communities might at any given historical moment be made necessary by the inadequacies of democratic life. But she insists on preserving the democratic hope that society might one day embrace currently marginalized communities, and that the latter might in turn embrace the wider democratic project. Such acceptance of course benefits the once-marginalized group. But it also benefits democratic society and the democratic vision, for most societal reform occurs via the initiative of previously subaltern groups (along with their allies in other groups).

Achieving such acceptance requires change in the dominant society and the embrace of democratic norms by the subaltern community. The power of the public sphere lies in its ability to advance both via democratic dialogue and process, through which previously incommensurable views may come to recognize one another as at least potentially capable of providing enlightenment. Such dialogue, however, can only occur on the basis of some shared commitments, which Benhabib locates in universal norms of democratic life. This is the moral and political universalism for which she argues, that is, a kind of soft universalism.

As suggested by the complexity of these theoretical tensions, they will not be resolved by conceptual debate, nor will they be resolved permanently. Rather, this book has sought concrete insight in the emerging efforts of particular democratic activists who walk the line between universalist and multiculturalist commitments, linking both to an ambitious project of political change. We have labeled that project a struggle for "ethical democracy."

Preserving a commitment to soft universalism becomes crucial for sustaining democratic possibility. We believe it necessary for sustaining the project of ethical democracy in particular, for the complex tensions between universalism and multiculturalism partly define the analytic terrain on which political actors must operate if they strive to deepen democracy in a multicultural world. In our analysis of faith-based organizing, we have seen such soft universalism linked to multiculturalist commitments; the most effective organizers, clergy, and leaders in the field operate on that terrain with artistry and insight.

Conclusion

This chapter has sought to recapitulate the key insights from our analysis of faith-based organizing for economic equality, racial equity, and effective public policy formulation. We have documented how strategic innovation has led some sectors of faith-based organizing toward linking those three priorities; we have argued that broadening such innovation will be required in any effective movement for ethical democracy; and we have teased out the theoretical implications of our analysis. In the concluding chapter, we look toward the challenging road ahead if ethical democracy is to thrive.

Figure C.1 Gloria Cooper, grassroots leader with the San Diego Organizing Project, speaks in Washington: Public sphere dimensions of the struggle for ethical democracy. (Photo by Sam Kittner—PICO National Network)

Conclusion: A Shared Future—Ethical Democracy, Racial Equity, and Power

> We are returning constantly to what it means to build power. We are striving to be clear about our interests and our orientation to power. We are bringing race into that lens, and being sure that faith-based work uses race as a critical lens for building power, so we contest the dominant narrative around economic and racial inclusion in the United States.
>
> —Anonymous national faith-based organizing leader

In the introduction, we suggested that a complex tension exists between universalist and multiculturalist democratic commitments in American life. Part I argued that faith-based community organizing has developed the strategic infrastructure, internal diversity, and democratic ambition to serve as a case study for understanding how that tension plays out within a significant national social movement. The introduction to part II introduced the "ethical democracy" framework, and part II analyzed the experience of a national faith-based organizing network in light of that framework—a network that effectively combines local- and state-level infrastructure, commitment to racial equity, and the political ambition to influence the highest levels of domestic policy formulation in the United States. More broadly, throughout the book we argued that the faith-based organizing field offers important insight regarding the three key domestic struggles facing American society: the struggles against economic inequality, policy paralysis, and racial injustice. Finally, in chapter 7 we reflected on the theoretical insights emerging from our analysis of the field's recent evolution and analyzed the strategic innovation that has driven its partial transformation.

Throughout, we have conceptualized the work of faith-based organizing as part of a broader effort to construct ethical democracy in America. In this concluding essay, we step back from the foregoing analysis to reflect on that broader effort.

Building Ethical Democracy by Reanchoring Democratic Life in Society

What might it look like to *succeed* at building ethical democracy? In asking this question, we mean "success" in the contingent sense of all things human: building something sufficiently closer to the idealized image of ethical democracy such that in the future we might reasonably say that American society has progressed from where it is today.

In thinking about success, we draw once again on the work of Jürgen Habermas and his interpreters among democratic theorists.[1] Habermas's insights are not new, but contemporary realities of American society make them relevant in new ways, offering a window into our shared challenges. We hope readers will bear with the abstract quality of what follows (and make it more concrete by linking it to their own struggles and experience of the contemporary world).

Habermas's approach to thinking about society divides the world up analytically into two kinds of settings: the Lifeworld and the Systems. The Lifeworld constitutes all facets of society still centered on human communication in search of mutual understanding—that is, all settings in which communicative action still guides human action. For the sake of simplicity, we can think of the Lifeworld as largely coterminous with what people mean when they speak of "community"; for our purposes, this approximates Habermas's meaning. The Systems are constituted anywhere that power or money guide human action—that is, anywhere that power and money substitute for human communication. The two primary Systems are Politics, constituted around power as a medium of exchange, and the Economy, constituted around markets of various kinds, wherein money serves as the medium of exchange.

Habermas's conceptualization provides a heuristic for dividing up and understanding the world analytically; however, the world itself is not cleanly divided this way, for two reasons: first, the Lifeworld and the Systems of Politics and the Economy interpenetrate constantly, since communities do not exist independently of power or money. Second, neither Politics nor the Economy exist independently of human communication; people inhabit the Systems and thus may refuse to let power and money substitute entirely for communicative action. But the Lifeworld/Systems distinction matters, for it allows us to see the overarching dynamics of contemporary society more clearly, as long as we understand it as a heuristic device useful for analyzing and diagnosing this historical moment.

Note, too, that we do not portray the Systems as inherently negative or evil. Far from it. The development of political systems has enabled human beings to coordinate large-scale action to solve societal challenges, and the development of a market economy has enabled human society to free itself from bare subsistence. The contemporary world—in all its cultural and technological glory—is partly a product of the Systems, impossible without them and indeed unimaginable prior to the emergence of power and money as media of exchange. But products of the Systems also include the dismaying inequality, violence, injustice, and environmental destruction of our contemporary world. Thus since political power and economic abundance can underwrite either good or evil, Politics and the Economy are ethically neutral. As Systems, they must be guided to the good via human choice and communicative action.[2]

In an ideal world as conceptualized under this view, the Systems of Politics and the Economy would serve to support a thriving Lifeworld, coordinating collective action to address urgent challenges facing society and providing the resources to do so effectively. Likewise, other social institutions that are still substantially centered on communicative action (and therefore not Systems), would also serve to enrich a thriving Lifeworld. Such institutions revolve around culture, education, the law, moral and ethical traditions whether religious or secular, the family, and science. We might visualize the ideal relationship of the Systems and these other institutional spheres to the Lifeworld as depicted in figure C.2: as a table where Lifeworld dialogue occurs (and meals with wine are shared!), standing on "legs" provided by the multiple institutions of social life.

But such is not the reality we live in. In Habermas's diagnosis, we live in a society in which the Lifeworld is "colonized" by the Systems. Politics and the Economy have become so powerful and autonomous from human communities of discourse that they now tower over the Lifeworld. Rather than supporting the Lifeworld dynamics necessary for society to thrive— the raising of children, the shaping of personality, the generation of meaning in people's lives, and the flow of social solidarity—the Systems distort these dynamics. They do so by subjecting Lifeworld dynamics to the logic of power and money unguided by communal interests or ethical commitments. Figure C.3 depicts this distorted relationship of the Systems to the Lifeworld.

Among the results of such colonization of the Lifeworld by the dynam-

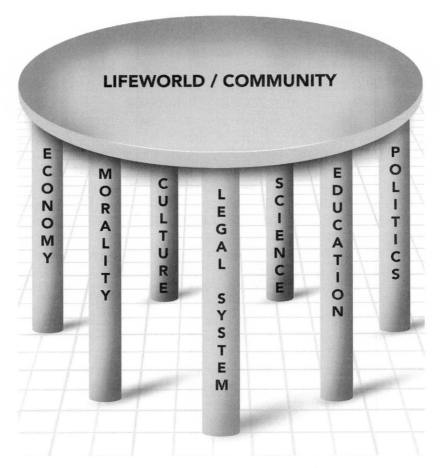

Figure C.2 Ideal relationship of the Lifeworld to the Systems and other institutional spheres.

ics of power and money are the three demons at the heart of our analysis. Economic inequality grows extreme as powerful economic elites strive to control social decisions in service of their own wealth. Racial injustice recrudesces as some political elites strive to manipulate it in service of their own partisan interests. Policy formulation stagnates as crosscutting partisan priorities trump the common good, with antigovernment ideology and accusations of "class warfare" and "racial hatred" invoked to checkmate any attempt to actually govern, much less to use government policy in pursuit of economic justice or racial equity. The net result is a silencing of real democratic voice. Such is our historic moment.

What, then, is to be done? As shown in figure C.5, democratic theorists

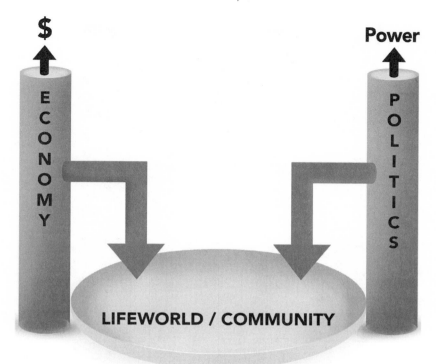

Figure C.3 Colonization of the Lifeworld by the Systems.

typically see social movements and their appeal to the politicians and the courts as the primary channel for social reform, providing leverage to move policy and the law toward reform. We might call this a "bootstrapping" operation, an effort to use the political influence and moral framing provided by social movements to convince politicians and judges to enforce justice in society and hold the Systems accountable to the common good—that is, in this way democracy "pulls itself up by its bootstraps."

Social movements, politicians, and the courts have sometimes played just such a role. The classic example came during the 1950s and 1960s when the civil rights movement, the US Supreme Court under Chief Justice Earl Warren, and the administration of President Lyndon Johnson forced the end of the "Jim Crow" era and passed landmark civil rights laws.[3] But in the twenty-first century, we must ask: Are social movements capable of playing such a role today? Are not social movements distorted by the same colonization dynamics as the rest of society, that is, distorted by the logic of power and money? Are not social movement activists likely to be at least

Figure C.4 Rev. Dawn Riley Duval, lead organizer of PICO's "Let My People Vote" campaign: Protest dimensions of the struggle for ethical democracy. (Photo by Heather Wilson)

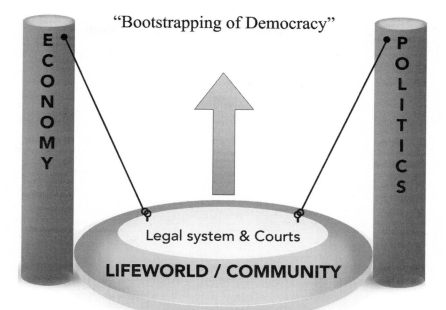

Figure C.5 The assumed role of social movements in social reform.

partly the products of cultural dynamics oriented to power and money, and thus focused on consumption (whether of things, of people, or of experiences)? Likewise, are not politicians and justices—who are elected, how they can govern, who is nominated and confirmed, and how they think about society and the law—distorted under the logic of the Systems?

Those are sobering questions for anyone committed to social reform in the direction of ethical democracy. But we do not think these realities completely undercut the possibility of bootstrapping democracy toward better serving human ends. Rather, they suggest a need for better bootstrapping: sophisticated social movements well-grounded in the Lifeworlds of real human communities and able to exert powerful leverage on the Systems— for the Systems' own good as well as that of society.

Here our diagnosis benefits from two insights. First, recent work in the study of social movements makes clear that movements do not change society by themselves, but rather they draw their strength from being rooted in social institutions and moral/ethical traditions that construct meaning within people's lives and communities.[4] Second, stepping back from the sharp analytic distinction between Lifeworld and Systems reminds us that in the real world, human communities, politics, and markets interpenetrate all the time. In particular, good people of good democratic will occupy important roles and powerful positions within both Politics and the Economy. Most of the large-scale policy gains of faith-based community organizing have been won via dialogue, collaboration, and negotiation with such people. Such allies can be invaluable in interpreting political and economic realities, forging effective policy, gaining public support, and (not least) actually passing new legislation and implementing new public policy. Similarly, while social institutions and moral/ethical traditions are not immune to distortion by power and money, they nonetheless remain firmly dependent on processes of human dialogue. That is to say they are anchored in the Lifeworld. If internally strong and not seduced entirely by the distorting dynamics of power and money, such institutions and traditions offer firm anchoring to the movements associated with them. Likewise, people working within the Systems may be socialized toward strong democratic commitments by Lifeworld institutions and moral/ethical traditions; such people are among the potential allies in the bootstrapping operation.

Strong societal institutions, moral/ethical traditions, and allies in the Systems all provide additional resources for the bootstrapping of democracy. Figure C.6 helps to visualize what that kind of more robust bootstrapping can look like.

This way of diagnosing the ills of contemporary society and how they might be addressed offers some analytic view into why faith-based community organizing has achieved the level of influence it has. The crucial societal institutions that anchor human lives, families, and communities in systems of meaning include religious congregations and faith communities across many traditions as well as schools, unions, and neighborhoods. The crucial moral/ethical traditions that foster meaning-making out of people's experience include religious teachings and processes of spiritual formation as well as secular democratic traditions. Key allies in Politics and the Economy include many who are deeply shaped by the religious institutions and spiritual traditions of the Lifeworld. When faith-based organizing coalitions go seeking potential leaders within congregations, schools, unions, and neighborhoods, they are scouring the Lifeworld for talent and commitment—and they find in these institutions both grassroots community leaders and relatively more elite System allies. When they hold local political actions that advocate for better schools in poor neighborhoods, living wages for working-class employees, or more effective and

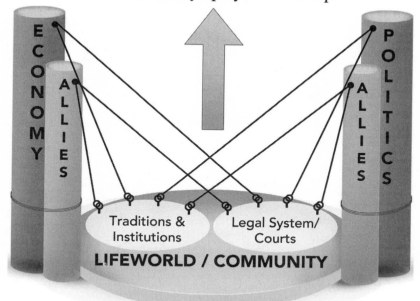

Social movements and their allies haul democracy up by its bootstraps

Figure C.6 A better view of how social movements advance social reform.

community-friendly policing in minority communities, they are engaging in some level of bootstrapping democracy. And when faith-based organizing networks collaborate with other advocacy groups to gain health care for uninsured kids, reform financial institutions, or protect immigrant rights at the state or federal level, they surely are doing likewise. All these faith-based efforts rely heavily on religious institutions as anchors for reformist politics and on religious traditions to provide ethical direction to their movements. Thus we might visualize the work of faith-based organizing as an institutionally and ethically grounded bootstrapping of democracy, in collaboration with allies within the Systems, as depicted in figure C.7.

Real-World Work for Ethical Democracy: Insights for Democratic Movements

This Lifeworld/System framework offers further insight into the struggles for racial equity, economic justice, and effective public policy—and into

Ethically & institutionally grounded
bootstrapping of democracy

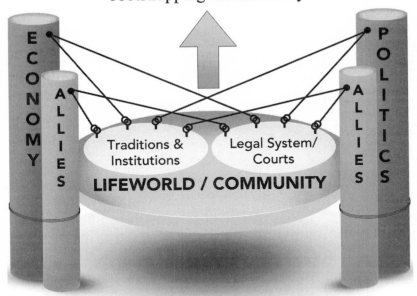

Key ethical sources for reform: Religious & democratic traditions
Key anchor institutions for reform: Religious & civic institutions
Allies in the Systems are key: but allies shaped by moral traditions
and accountable to Lifeworld institutions

Figure C.7 Bootstrapping of democracy by institutions and
traditions anchored in the Lifeworld.

the long struggle ahead for ethical democracy. Several points come immediately into focus.

First, these movements must not rely solely on the political system or
the courts to achieve economic or racial justice. The Lifeworld—and thus
the cultural terrain on which all politics occur and within which the legal
process unfolds—has been too fully colonized by the logics of money and
power, including racialized assumptions that buttress existing political and
economic interests. As a result, any such narrow strategy would be doomed
to failure. Doomed because such a strategy would operate under terms of
battle defined by economic and political elites, which undercut the very

strengths of democratic organizing in shared dialogue and participation. By seeking change solely via the political system and the courts, these movements might occasionally win, but any such victories will be gradually eviscerated. The mid-twentieth-century empowerment of labor, the great civil rights gains of the 1960s, and perhaps the current effort to extend health coverage to all Americans illustrate this dynamic. Instead, these movements must attend equally to both: (1) influencing public policy and legal decision making; and (2) shaping and defending the Lifeworld communities, institutions, and traditions (religious and secular) that preserve practices of human care, democratic voice, and social solidarity. If they do so with respect for values and practices that prioritize democratic voice and broad participation, these movements can help the Lifeworld strengthen and defend itself against colonization by the Systems—and thus shape a future terrain of political struggle and public dialogue more consonant with democratic values.

Second, these movements must also be vigilant against voices from *within* the Lifeworld that undermine democratic voice and equality. We must not romanticize the Lifeworld. As democratic critics and scholars of gender, race and ethnicity, sexuality, religion, and nationalism have shown, the Lifeworld can harbor deeply antidemocratic assumptions and antihuman practices. For example, as john powell and others have shown, implicit racial bias and racism dwell and are reproduced within Lifeworld dynamics, even when they have their origins in economic exploitation and political manipulation. So even as democratic movements must find firm anchoring within the Lifeworld, they also must be conscious agents of reform within that home terrain.

Third, these movements will continue to vociferously criticize privileged elites who are unaccountable to the wider society and the common good. But to the extent these movements aspire to succeed not just as moral witnesses to a good society but also as agents for actually reforming society, they must cultivate strategic alliances within the Systems—especially with potential allies who hold democratic values and are willing to be held publicly accountable for them. Potential allies sometimes include members of the political and economic elite, and forging alliances with them will often require compromises that raise the risk of being accused of "selling out." So democratic movements must simultaneously build such alliances and preserve sufficient autonomy to raise critical questions and press for deeper reform.

Fourth, such elites-as-potential-allies are more likely to hold democratic values to the extent they are personally embedded within Lifeworld traditions and institutions that carry such values. Organizing within such traditions and institutions can facilitate identifying potential allies and forging alliances that carry real accountability to Lifeworld priorities.

Fifth, none of the above is overly idealistic. As we have seen in these pages, though challenging, it is possible simultaneously to: (1) work for immediate public policy that reins in economic inequality, racial injustice, and other social ills; and (2) work to reshape the cultural and institutional terrain of politics—in other words, to strengthen and reform the Lifeworld. Faith-based community organizing coalitions seek to do precisely that when they reshape the dominant narratives of public life, fight implicit bias in society or in their own work, strengthen their member institutions, or invigorate a "prophetic voice" that applies religious or secular social ethics to contemporary problems.

Sixth, all this demands sophisticated analysis and principled engagement from leaders in democratic movements. The Systems contain—in their fundamental logics of money and power and often in their leaders—the very dynamics of colonization against which these movements must fight if ethical democracy is to thrive. So in seeking allies in the Systems, movement leaders must be willing to recognize and "push back" against colonization, even when it comes from sympathetic allies. Such push back may be especially important vis-à-vis allies, for the unintended consequences and unexamined dynamics of alliances may be the most pernicious route through which colonization occurs. Democratic leaders' analytic clarity about Lifeworld-System relations and their personal embeddedness in Lifeworld traditions will best enable them to build organizations that reject such colonization.

No one should hold any illusion that the bootstrapping of democracy as envisioned here will be easy. It will be a struggle of many years—thus the urgency of constantly strengthening and reforming the Lifeworld, so that the democratic struggle can be sustained for the long term. In the permanent struggle for democratic life, this book strives to help us see clearly our own historical moment and thus live up to the deep challenges and democratic promise of that moment.

In all of the above, we by no means want to imply that such bootstrapping has proceeded very far. If anything, this diagnosis highlights the profound challenges facing faith-based organizing and other reformist efforts—indeed, facing American society as a whole. Our focus on recalcitrant economic inequality, racial injustice, and the continuing political machinations and gerrymandering that have paralyzed policy development at the federal level undermine any easy optimism about reversing the colonization of our communities and lives. If "bootstrapping" democracy is to succeed, it still has a long way to go in pulling the Lifeworld up into a position to guide political and economic decision making toward more human ends. Yet we cannot help but find cause for hope in the strongest examples of faith-based organizing we have studied in the course of this research. Those efforts—multiplied across new settings; linked together in "federated" structures at local, state, and national levels; attentive to the potential risks of competing for influence in higher political arenas; yet ambitious to shape key decisions in those arenas—may in time allow American society to rest more firmly on political and economic foundations that support rather than colonize our many and diverse Lifeworlds. In that case society might indeed look more as it is depicted in figure C.2 above.

This diagnosis also suggests why democratic political institutions remain crucial in the struggle to construct a shared future of ethical democracy. Whereas the power of money as a medium of exchange means that economic transactions can occur in the near absence of human communication, the exertion of political power usually involves political communication. Thus, whereas money can substitute relatively fully for communicative action, all democratic power depends at least partially on communicative action. Politics is a system in the sense that communicative action is regularly short-circuited in favor of action guided by the flow of power, but ultimately Politics (at least in a democracy) remains relatively more rooted in the communicative dynamics of the Lifeworld than does the Economy. Thus government ever remains a potential ally in the project of ethical democracy.

Finally, note that the colonization of the Lifeworld by the systems of Politics and the Economy finds its expression not only in the issues on which we have focused but also in issues well beyond that, from the rampant disregard of privacy by the National Security Agency to the ongoing degradation of the Earth's ecosystem. We believe that diagnosing the overarching challenge of Systemic colonization offers analytic leverage against colonization. Movements cannot fight what they cannot see. We hope that diagnosis also lends itself more to indignation than to despair. In the times in which we live, only anger tempered by hope can sustain the long-term movements needed to build ethical democracy. The emotional and political vacuum generated by despair will ultimately only empower further colonization.

Conclusion

The racial and ethnic diversity we have documented among faith-based community organizing's professional staff, leaders, and board members has never been the field's goal in and of itself. Rather, faith-based organizing has from its origins focused on improving the quality of life of poor, working-class, and middle-class families. Because the field draws its participants from those sectors, and because the lower half of the income distribution is skewed toward "communities of color," its participant base has always carried impressive racial and ethnic diversity (at least in the aggregate, though not always in the case of any given local coalition).

New political realities and new ethical commitments among strategic decision makers in the field have deepened that diversity in ways documented in these chapters. Today, the leaders in faith-based organizing "look like America" in terms of race, ethnicity, and immigration status. That diversity—including the field's strong inclusion of whites committed to equality in America—represents a crucial strategic asset for the long struggle ahead.

If the evolution of faith-based organizing we have documented in these pages continues, that struggle will focus on fighting against the demons of contemporary American life: rising economic inequality, the racial injustice that is bound up with economic inequality, and the policy paralysis that prevents significant government action to advance economic and racial equity. Our analysis offers no easy and swift way to exorcise those demons from the American body politic. Casting out those demons will be a long struggle. But what better civic struggle might Americans commit themselves to than the battle for their communities and for the soul of their country? If successful, that effort will advance the building of ethical democracy in America, or at least the pursuit of that ideal. Our analysis offers not easy optimism but rather democratic hope and meaningful work. Hope grounded in the experience of real people who are dedicating their best selves to the public work of democracy.[5]

In time, the term *ethical democracy* may become more than a utopian construct used to pull our vision forward and upward. But for now that role is ambitious enough. We will never arrive at a fully ethical democracy, but surely we can and must do better at constructing a future shared by all.

ACKNOWLEDGMENTS

We thank all those who made this study possible, contributed their insight, and supported us throughout the years:

Our colleagues at Interfaith Funders were true research collaborators— executive director Kathy Partridge and board members Ned Wight, Cris Doby, Sue Engh, Randy Keesler, Mary Sobecki, Charlie Bernstein, Kevin Ryan, and Rachel Feldman, along with Seamus Finn, Molly Schulz Hafid, Sean Wendlinder, Ralph McCloud, and Katie DiSalvo. We learned from them in many ways, benefited from their insight, and greatly enjoyed the democratic dialogue around the Interfaith Funders table. May that dialogue continue via the forum provided by the Interfaith Organizing Initiative.

Primary funding for the National Study of Community Organizing Coalitions was provided by the institutional members of Interfaith Funders: The Unitarian Universalist Veatch Program at Shelter Rock, the Catholic Campaign for Human Development, the C. S. Mott Foundation, the Needmor Fund, the Evangelical Lutheran Church in America, the New York Foundation, the Missionary Oblates of Mary Immaculate, and the Presbyterian Church–USA. We hereby gratefully acknowledge their funding support.

The story we tell is brought to life by the artistry of photographers Heather Wilson, Stacey Schmitz, Jonathan Bell, Wiley Price, Sam Kittner, and anonymous photographers with the Gamaliel Foundation and the Indianapolis Congregation Action Network. Gordon Mayer at Gamaliel and Alia Zaki at PICO facilitated access to photos and photo permissions with remarkable grace and efficiency. Heather Wilson performed digital miracles to produce the figures in the final chapter. We are thankful to all for their generosity in allowing our use of their work.

We credit a large portion of the success of the National Study of Community Organizing Coalitions, both in its response rate and data quality, to the lead organizers and directors of the community organizing coalitions who participated in the study and to the leaders of the organizing networks who endorsed and promoted it. We benefited greatly from interviews with organizers, national staff, observers, and thought leaders from the faith-based organizing field, quoted at various points in *A Shared Future*.

At the University of Chicago Press, Doug Mitchell has been for many years an intellectual colleague and champion of theoretically driven sociology grounded in the real world; he is also a talented jazz drummer. In both roles, he contributes to making the world a culturally richer place. His colleagues Michael Koplow, Ashley Pierce, Kyle Wagner, and Timothy McGovern shepherded this book through the editing process with professionalism and grace. Copyeditor Dawn Hall sharpened our prose and perfected our grammar. We also thank two anonymous outside reviewers and reader Ella Wood, whose insight and criticism made this a stronger book.

Elements of the research reported here were presented by Wood and/or Fulton at the following venues: Yale University's Colloquium on Religion and Politics; Harvard University's Kennedy School of Government; the University of Southern California's Center on Religion and Civic Culture; annual meetings of the American Sociological Association, Society for the Scientific Study of Religion, Association for Research on Nonprofit Organizations and Voluntary Associations, and the Academy of Management; New York University's Wagner Graduate School of Public Service; Indiana University Lilly Family School of Philanthropy; the Haas Institute for a Fair and Inclusive Society at the University of California–Berkeley; the Catholic Campaign for Human Development of the United States Conference of Catholic Bishops; the University of Southern California's Center for Philanthropy and Public Policy and Price School of Public Policy; the Duke Network Analysis Center; Indiana University–Purdue University Indianapolis' School of Public and Environmental Affairs; Cornell University's School of Industrial and Labor Relations; the University of Chicago's School of Social Service Administration; and at briefings of funders, organizers, and clergy convened by Interfaith Funders, the Neighborhood Funders Group, and the Interfaith Organizing Initiative. Colleagues in all these settings sharpened our analysis and our view of the democratic terrain.

From Brad Fulton

I am thankful to the people who believed in me, supported me, and entrusted me with conducting the National Study of Community Organizing Coalitions and embarking on this ambitious project.

At Duke University, Mark Chaves provided excellent guidance and advice at critical points throughout the project. Lisa Keister, Nan Lin, and James Moody were always available to offer timely and helpful feedback. Charlie Clotfelter, Angie O'Rand, and Ken Spenner played a central role in helping me to secure seed money to implement the national study. Gary Thompson provided crucial assistance with data management, and my undergraduate research assistants Tian Chen, Tiphany Jackson, Kristin Lee, and Michael Habashi skillfully executed several important tasks related to the study.

The leaders of Interfaith Funders provided the perfect balance of oversight and freedom when they commissioned me to conduct the national study. Moreover, they were a joy to work with and became close friends in the process. I am also grateful for the additional funding that was provided by the Hearst Foundation, Society for the Scientific Study of Religion, William K. Kellogg Foundation, Religious Research Association, RGK Center for Philanthropy and Community Service, Association for Research on Nonprofit Organizations and Voluntary Associations, Center for the Study of Philanthropy and Voluntarism, and Duke University's Graduate School and Department of Sociology.

In the course of this project, Rich Wood has become a valued mentor, colleague, and friend. He has been a gracious collaborator who has provided iron-sharpening feedback, full confidence, wise counsel, and enthusiastic support.

My parents, Jim and Bonnie, my brothers, Scott and Brent, and my ever-expanding extended family instill the vision and confidence I need to wholeheartedly pursue my passions. And throughout this project, my immediate family provided daily relief and recreation that reenergized me each day to carry out this important work. Carla's strong presence, deep commitment, and critical engagement, along with Josh, Katie, and Emily's unbridled enthusiasm for life, sharpen and sustain me more than I realize. Thank you and I love you.

From Richard Wood

Colleagues at the University of New Mexico provided the stimulating intellectual environment, collegial support, and healthy challenge underlying this book. Together, may we keep moving toward the goal: excellence in the academic mission while truly being a flagship research university at the service of the emerging American majority.

Early funding that helped lead to this study was provided by the Lilly

Endowment via the Louisville Institute. The flexibility of assignment that made intense writing possible was provided by the University of New Mexico's Department of Sociology, College of Arts and Sciences, and Office of the Provost.

Brad Fulton was quietly brilliant in designing the online survey instrument and collecting and analyzing the data for the National Study of Community Organizing Coalitions—all with scholarly insight and remarkable professionalism. He was always a delightful collaborator, became a valued colleague and friend, and will contribute enormously to his future academic department.

Not everyone—and perhaps no one—in the field of faith-based community organizing will like this analysis of their work. But I have learned greatly from that work and its more thoughtful practitioners, strive here to capture and reflect on its importance to the American future, and hereby take responsibility for any inadequacies in the analysis. I hope this book offers grist and insight for ongoing critical dialogue, both within the field and in the wider American society.

My extended family—my sister Elisabeth, my brothers John and Bernard, and their spouses along with all my nieces and nephews—provide the rich fabric of a wider life. Friends too numerous to list (you know who you are) offer all that friendship should be; a few simply must be named: Javier Aceves, Yemane Asmerom, Cheryl Gooding, Jim Keddy.

Nothing will lead one to reflect on the future like the raising of the next generation. In this man's life, Ella DeEsta Wood and Adam Reavis Wood have offered the deepest of joys and the healthiest of challenges—and will no doubt continue to do so. My generation will hand on to theirs and their children's generations a society and a world permanently crying out for reform in the service of greater justice. We hope in you.

My wife Dana Bell continues ever to be rock, tender caress, intellectual colleague, challenging voice, and support in this journey.

Finally, in memory of those who have died in these years: William W. and Betty Jean (King) Wood, William Gerard Wood, Erin Valerie Wood, John Kemper, Bill Spohn, Gerardo Thijssen, Robert N. Bellah, Donald Gelpi SJ, and Sor Dolores Diez de Sollano. All were beloved.

ABBREVIATIONS

DART	Direct Action and Research Training Center
Gamaliel	Gamaliel Foundation
IAF	Industrial Areas Foundation
IVP	InterValley Project
NPA	National People's Action
PICO	PICO National Network (a.k.a. People Improving Communities through Organizing, and formerly the Pacific Institute for Community Organization)
RCNO	Regional Congregations and Neighborhood Organizations (defunct as of 2014)

NOTES

1. The most obvious example of this policy paralysis was the GOP decision, before Barack Obama took office in early 2009, to refuse any outreach across the congressional aisle in order to deny the president any claim to bipartisanship or policy gains; see Michael Grunwald, "The Party of No," *Time Magazine*, September 3, 2012, http://content.time.com/time/magazine/article/0,9171,2122776,00.html, and Grunwald, *The New New Deal: The Hidden Story of Change in the Obama Era* (New York: Simon and Schuster, 2012). The Senate minority subsequently erected obstacles at every step of the way in major policy arenas, essentially eschewing governance in favor of strategic polarization from above in the hope of gaining legislative power and eventually the White House. The initial success of this strategy in the 2010 midterm elections for the House of Representatives emboldened those advocating this approach; the strategy's failure to deny Obama a second presidential term in 2012 has hardly dented the GOP's enthusiasm for this approach.

2. In this book we use the terms *racial injustice* and *racial inequity* interchangeably, selecting the one best suited to a particular context.

3. Important recent work analyzes the origins of political polarization and the resulting policy paralysis in the United States. Doug McAdam and Karina Kloos, in *Deeply Divided: Racial Politics and Social Movements in Post-War America* (New York: Oxford University Press, 2014), trace the origins of political polarization to the social movements of the 1960s and 1970s, including the civil rights movement and especially the conservative backlash against black empowerment. In contrast, in *Godless Democrats and Pious Republicans* (New York: Cambridge University Press, 2015), Ryan L. Claassen argues that current polarization accurately reflects cultural and attitudinal chasms within the American electorate. The two arguments may be reconcilable. We return to this debate in the conclusion.

4. See chapter 1 for a full introduction to faith-based community organizing. Although practices differ somewhat across different organizing coalitions, all models strive to work through *institutions* (primarily religious congregations, but also sometimes labor unions, public schools, community organizations, and others) to identify potential leaders from low- to middle-income communities, train them in community organizing skills, and build an organization that can advance the interests of poor communities.

5. For a selection of national coverage reflecting the influence of faith-based organizing, see Bernie Becker, "Obama Casts Health Effort in Moral Terms," *New York Times*, August 19, 2009; Lesli A. Maxwell, "Community Organizing Seen as Help to Schools," *Education Week*, published online April 10, 2008, see http://www.piconetwork.org/news-media/coverage/image/0442.pdf; Christi Parsons, "Obama Plan Would Curb Health Insurers on Rate Hikes," *Los Angeles Times*, February 22, 2010; Robert Pear, "Obama Signs Children's Health Insurance Program Bill," *New York Times*, February 4, 2009; Cyrus Sanati, "Protests Planned for Banks' Shareholder Meetings," *New York Times*, April 8, 2010; and David Waters, "Immigration Reform Advocates to Pray, Rally and March in Washington," *Washington Post*, March 19 2010.

6. Wood 2013 interview with George Goehl.

7. The term *subaltern* derives from the work of Antonio Gramsci and is essentially synonymous with *marginalized*, but more precisely denotes those sectors that exist outside the economic, political, and cultural hegemony of a particular social formation.

8. In this book, we use the term *racial equity* to note work that seeks to assure equal opportunity and equal treatment for all, regardless of racial or ethnic identity. Occasionally (especially in part II) we will distinguish between racial equity work internal to an organization and racial justice work in the wider society, but in general *racial equity* will refer to both.

9. The discussion throughout this section draws from Seyla Benhabib, *The Claims of Culture* (Princeton, NJ: Princeton University Press, 2002). See also the subsequent discussion of her book in the journal *Constellations*, especially Max Pensky, "Comments on Seyla Benhabib, *The Claims of Culture*," *Constellations* 11 (2004): 258–65.

10. See especially Jürgen Habermas, *The Theory of Communicative Action* (Boston: Beacon Press, 1984); Habermas, "Religion in the Public Sphere," *European Journal of Philosophy* 14, no. 1 (2006); and Habermas, *The Structural Transformation of the Public Sphere: An Inquiry into a Category of Bourgeois Society* (London: Polity Press, 1989). See also Craig J. Calhoun, ed., *Habermas and the Public Sphere*, Studies in Contemporary German Social Thought (Cambridge, MA: MIT Press, 1992); John S. Dryzek, "Political Inclusion and the Dynamics of Democratization," *American Political Science Review* 90, no. 3 (1996): 475–87; Jeffrey C. Alexander, *The Civil Sphere* (New York: Oxford University Press, 2006); and Jean L. Cohen and Andrew Arato, *Civil Society and Political Theory* (Cambridge, MA: MIT Press, 1992).

11. This necessarily brief overview of the notion of the democratic public sphere can only offer a rather sketchy glimpse of a wide and important literature. Over the last quarter century, Habermas's work has provided one of the central axes of thought within theories of democratic life, and no concept has been more central than this one.

12. See Seyla Benhabib, "Models of Public Space: Hannah Arendt, the Liberal Tradition, and Jürgen Habermas," pp. 73–98 in Calhoun, *Habermas and the Public Sphere*; and Nancy Fraser, "Rethinking the Public Sphere: A Contribution to the Critique of Actually Existing Democracy," pp. 109–142 in Calhoun, *Habermas and the Public Sphere*.

13. A similar intuition, predating Fraser's theoretical work on this terrain, drives the analysis in Sara M. Evans and Harry C. Boyte, *Free Spaces: The Sources of Democratic Change in America* (New York: Harper and Row, 1986).

14. Nancy Fraser, *Justice Interruptus: Critical Reflections on the "Postsocialist" Condition*

(New York: Routledge, 1997); and Nancy Fraser and Axel Honneth, *Redistribution or Recognition? A Political-Philosophical Exchange* (New York: Verso, 2003).

15. Seyla Benhabib, "The Liberal Imagination and the Four Dogmas of Multiculturalism," *Yale Journal of Criticism* 12 (1999): 401–13, especially 405ff.

16. Ibid., 407.

17. Benhabib, "Models of Public Space: Hannah Arendt, the Liberal Tradition, and Jürgen Habermas," 76.

18. Benhabib, *Claims of Culture*, 70.

19. Iris Marion Young, "Ruling Norms and the Politics of Difference: A Comment on Seyla Benhabib," *Yale Journal of Criticism* 12 (1999): 415–21.

20. Ibid., 415.

21. Ibid., 417.

22. Wood used the term "ethical democracy" in *Faith in Action: Religion, Race, and Democratic Organizing in America* (Chicago: University of Chicago Press, 2002) in the same sense as used here. Wes Markofski uses the concept insightfully in his forthcoming book *Evangelical Christianity and American Democracy*; the authors hereby acknowledge Markofski's helpful framing there of the concept of ethical democracy within the work of Jane Addams and John Dewey.

23. See john powell, *Racing to Justice: Transforming Our Conceptions of Self and Other to Build an Inclusive Society* (Bloomington: Indiana University Press, 2012) as well as chapter 2 here. The term and analysis derive also from Theda Skocpol, "Targeting within Universalism: Politically Viable Policies to Combat Poverty in the United States," in *The Urban Underclass*, ed. C. Jencks and P. E. Peterson (Washington, DC: Brookings Institution, 1991), 411–36.

24. Good accounts of the early decades of this kind of organizing can be found in Luke Bretherton, *Resurrecting Democracy: Faith, Citizenship, and the Politics of a Common Life* (Cambridge and New York: Cambridge University Press, 2015); Edward T. Chambers and Michael A. Cowan, *Roots for Radicals: Organizing for Power, Action, and Justice* (New York: Continuum, 2003); Stephen Hart, *Cultural Dilemmas of Progressive Politics: Styles of Engagement among Grassroots Activists* (Chicago: University of Chicago Press, 2001); Mary Beth Rogers, *Cold Anger: A Story of Faith and Power Politics* (Denton: University of North Texas Press, 1990); and Mark Warren, *Dry Bones Rattling* (Princeton, NJ: Princeton University Press, 2001). Note that this model is one among a variety of approaches to community organizing that emerged from overlapping roots. On this wider community organizing tradition, see http://www .trincoll.edu/depts/tcn/valocchi.htm, and Robert Fisher and Joseph M. Kling, "Leading the People: Two Approaches to the Role of Ideology in Community Organizing," *Radical America* (Spring 1988). The pioneering work of Saul Alinsky in drawing earlier strands together and launching the model that became a reference point for most later community organizing is described in Saul David Alinsky, *Rules for Radicals: A Practical Primer for Realistic Radicals* (New York: Random House, 1971) and *Reveille for Radicals* (New York: Vintage Books, 1969).

25. This characterization of the field as focused on recruiting institutions as members remains accurate, but is beginning to change. In response to the decline of the institutions that once at least tenuously anchored low-income communities in the United States (urban congregations, ethnic and immigrant associations, labor union locals, etc.), some networks created mechanisms for individuals to become active outside of institutions or launched efforts to establish institutions in these settings.

26. The Alliance of Community Organizations for Reform Now (ACORN) was also a leading practitioner of an individual-membership model of community before its 2010 demise in the face of external attacks and internal failures. Some of its more effective regional branches continue to organize under other structures, including the Alliance of Californians for Empowerment, New York Communities for Change, and the Affordable Housing Centers of America.

27. Data come from a new national census of all community organizing coalitions that practice the "institution-based" model, including what is termed here "faith-based community organizing." For fuller description and methodology underlying the study, see chapter 1 as well as "Interfaith Organizing Based in Institutions: State of the Field and Emerging Challenges" by Brad R. Fulton and Richard L. Wood in the *International Journal of Public Theology* (2012) and Richard L. Wood, Brad R. Fulton, and Kathy Partridge, "Building Bridges, Building Power: Developments in Institution-Based Community Organizing," available at http://hdl.handle .net/1928/21413 (Boulder, CO: Interfaith Funders, 2012). The national data on all American congregations come from the National Congregations Study led by Mark Chaves.

28. On religious "nones," see http://www.pewforum.org/2012/10/09/nones-on-the -rise/.

29. In the interests of scholarly transparency, perhaps of the unpopular kind. In contrast to a great deal of recent writing on this field, which too often treats one network as the only—or the only important—case to study, we believe that the only sound scholarly position lies in treating the various networks as variations on a core model of organizing. Using PICO's national work as an exemplar reflects our scholarly judgment that it most strongly represents those in the field who seek to project political power beyond the local level and has also advanced furthest in adroitly walking the universalist-multiculturalist boundary; in doing so, we do not assert (nor believe) that each local PICO coalition/federation does better work than do affiliates of other networks. Rather, the picture varies significantly depending on location and organizing talent. We also recognize that not all networks (or even all coalitions within networks that *are* committed to it) aspire to translocal influence. All typically embrace the centrality of the "all politics are local" mantra usually associated with former Speaker of the US House Tip O'Neill—and some assert an *exclusive* primacy to local work.

    Full disclosure: Wood has studied and/or advised nearly all of the faith-based organizing networks over the last fifteen years, in a variety of capacities. As of late 2014, he serves as a pro bono member of the advisory board of the PICO National Network.

30. For previous work on the PICO National Network, see Paul W. Speer et al., "The Intentional Exercise of Power: Community Organizing in Camden, New Jersey," *Journal of Community and Applied Social Psychology* 13 (2003): 399–408; Heidi Swarts, *Organizing Urban America: Secular and Faith-Based Progressive Movements* (Minneapolis: University of Minnesota Press, 2008); Gordon Whitman, "Beyond Advocacy: The History and Vision of the PICO Network," *Social Policy* (2007): 50–59; and Wood, *Faith in Action*.

31. On the SCHIP reauthorization, see Pear, "Obama Signs Children's Health Insurance Bill," *New York Times*, February 4, 2009, accessed September 7, 2013, http:// www.nytimes.com/2009/02/05/us/politics/05health.html. On the importance of the SCHIP debate in the early Obama administration, see Jeffrey Young, "Baucus In-

troduces SCHIP Bill as House Readies Votes," *New York Times*, January 14, 2009, 15. On the role of religious voices in the national health care reform more broadly, see "Faith Leaders Emerge as Key to Health Care Outreach," *Legal Monitor Worldwide*, August 12, 2013.

32. On the significant influence at the statewide level pioneered by the Texas Industrial Areas Foundation, especially on public education and workforce training policy in the 1980s and early 1990s, see the accounts in Paul Osterman, *Gathering Power: The Future of Progressive Politics in America* (Boston: Beacon Press, 2003); and Warren, *Dry Bones Rattling*. But statewide influence in Texas floundered with the Democratic Party implosion and GOP takeover of state politics in the 1990s and 2000s. The most prominent state-level work since then has been done by PICO in California (especially) and Colorado, and more recently by an important coalition of groups brought together as the Ohio Organizing Collaborative. For early assessments of the political capacity of such efforts and the challenges they face, see Richard L. Wood, "Higher Power: Strategic Capacity for State and National Organizing," in *Transforming the City: Community Organizing and the Challenge of Political Change*, ed. Marion Orr (Lawrence: University Press of Kansas, 2007), 164–92; and Richard L. Wood and Mark R. Warren, "A Different Face of Faith-Based Politics: Social Capital and Community Organizing in the Public Arena," *International Journal of Sociology and Social Policy* 22 (2002): 6–54.

33. On the latter as a crucial shortcoming of progressive policy advocates in the United States, see especially Hart, *Cultural Dilemmas of Progressive Politics*. On how marginalization of religious voices from the public sphere disempowers nonelite communities, see Stephen L. Carter's *The Culture of Disbelief: How American Law and Politics Trivialize Religious Devotion* (New York: Basic Books, 1993).

34. The classic Christian articulation of the "ongoing discernment" view came from Cardinal John Henry Newman in the nineteenth century; for recent analyses of this tradition, see John Henry Newman and James Gaffney, *Conscience, Consensus, and the Development of Doctrine*, 1st ed. (New York: Image Books, 1992) and *Roman Catholic Writings on Doctrinal Development* (Kansas City, MO: Sheed and Ward, 1997). The "new revelation" approach has been repeatedly adopted by the Church of Jesus Christ of Latter-Day Saints, in its early embrace of plural marriage, its subsequent turn to systematic monogamy, and its recent acceptance of black members into the Mormon priesthood.

35. See Richard L. Wood, *Faith in Action* and *Faith and the Fire of Public Life: Congregational Development through Civic Engagement* (forthcoming); as well as Richard L. Wood and Mary Ann Flaherty, *Renewing Congregations* (New York: Interfaith Funders and the Ford Foundation, 2003).

36. See Habermas, "Religion in the Public Sphere."

37. Michele Dillon, *Catholic Identity: Balancing Reason, Faith, and Power* (Cambridge: Cambridge University Press, 1999).

38. Jerome Baggett, *Sense of the Faithful: How American Catholics Live Their Faith* (New York: Oxford University Press, 2009).

39. See Habermas, "Religion in the Public Sphere."

40. On this concept, see Kenneth M. Roberts, *Deepening Democracy? The Modern Left and Social Movements in Chile and Peru* (Palo Alto, CA: Stanford University Press, 1998).

41. For the outstanding analysis of the state of "voice" and "equality" within American democracy, see Sidney Verba, Kay Lehman Schlozman, and Henry E. Brady, *Voice and Equality: Civic Voluntarism in American Politics* (Cambridge, MA: Harvard Univer-

sity Press, 1995). On ethical democracy, see the discussion above plus Markofski, *Evangelical Christianity and American Democracy* (forthcoming) and Wood, *Faith in Action.*

CHAPTER ONE

1. For the best sources tracing the early decades, see note 16 in the introduction. For an insider account of organizing, see Mike Miller's *Community Organizing: A Brief Introduction* (Berkeley, CA: Euclid Avenue Press, 2012) and Miller, *A Community Organizer's Tale* (Berkeley, CA: Heyday Books, 2009).

2. The key initial publications were Hart, *Cultural Dilemmas*, on the Gamaliel network; Warren, *Dry Bones Rattling*, on the Texas IAF from 1980 into the late 1990s; and Wood, *Faith in Action*, on the PICO National Network. Osterman, *Gathering Power*, treats the Texas IAF's experience into the early century. On the PICO California project, see Wood, "Higher Power"; Paul W. Speer, "People Making Public Policy in California: The PICO California Project" (research report) (Knoxville, TN: Vanderbilt University, 2002); and Speer et al., "The Intentional Exercise of Power."

3. The explosion in scholarly and practitioner-oriented literature on this field since 2002 has been impressive. In addition to earlier cited works, key writings include Edward T. Walker and J. D. McCarthy, "Legitimacy, Strategy, and Resources in the Survival of Community-Based Organizations," *Social Problems* 57, no. 3 (2010): 315–40; Jim Keddy, "Human Dignity and Grassroots Leadership Development," in *Jossey-Bass Reader on Nonprofit and Public Leadership*, ed. James L. Perry (San Francisco: Jossey-Bass, 2010); Luke Bretherton, *Christianity and Contemporary Politics: The Conditions and Possibilities of Faithful Witness* (London: Wiley-Blackwell, 2010); Mark R. Warren, "Community Organizing in Britain: The Political Engagement of Faith-Based Social Capital," *City and Community* 8, no. 2 (2009); Stephen Noble Smith, *Stoking the Fire of Democracy: Our Generation's Introduction to Grassroots Organizing* (Skokie, IL: ACTA, 2009); Swarts, *Organizing Urban America*; Kavitha Mediratta et al., *Organized Communities, Stronger Schools: A Preview of Research Findings* (Providence, RI, and New York: Annenberg Institute for School Reform at Brown University, 2008); Gordon Whitman, "Beyond Advocacy: The History and Vision of the Pico Network," *Social Policy* 37, no. 2 (2007): 50–59; Robert Kleidman, "Public Sociology and Community Organizing," *Journal of Applied Sociology/Sociological Practice* 23, no. 1 (2006): 68–82; Kleidman, "Community Organizing and Regionalism," *City and Community* 3 (2004): 403–21; Richard L. Wood, "Religion, Faith-Based Community Organizing, and the Struggle for Justice," in *Cambridge Handbook of Sociology*, ed. Michele Dillon (Cambridge: Cambridge University Press, 2003); Dennis A. Jacobsen, *Doing Justice: Congregations and Community Organizing* (Minneapolis, MN: Fortress Press, 2001); Ross J. Gittell and Avis Vidal, *Community Organizing: Building Social Capital as a Development Strategy* (Thousand Oaks, CA: Sage Publications, 1998); Jonathan Sacks, *Faith in the Future: The Ecology of Hope and the Restoration of Family, Community, and Faith* (Macon, GA: Mercer University Press, 1997); Michael Gecan, *Going Public* (Boston: Beacon Press, 2002), and Gecan, *After America's Midlife Crisis* (Cambridge, MA: MIT Press, 2009); and Kendall Clark Baker, *When Faith Storms the Public Square: Mixing Religion and Politics through Community Organizing to Enhance Our Democracy* (Alresford, UK: Circle Books, 2011).

4. For further information on the National Study of Community Organizing Coalitions, see information archived at sircs.unm.edu.

5. Interfaith Funders was an "affinity group" collaboration of program officers from a

variety of religiously based and secular funders interested in the work of faith-based community organizing. See www.interfaithfunders.org. It was founded in 1996 and dissolved at least temporarily in 2014, in favor of supporting the ongoing work of the Interfaith Organizing Initiative.

6. For the 1999 study, see Richard L. Wood and Mark R. Warren, "Different Face of Faith-Based Politics: Social Capital and Community Organizing in the Public Arena," *International Journal of Sociology and Social Policy* 22 (2002): 6–54. http://hdl .handle.net/1928/22763. The coauthors were not responsible for the initial design or data collection for the study, but they did the data analysis and writing. In what follows, we draw on it for comparative purposes to highlight changes in the field since 1999, focusing on where we believe that data to be reliable and noting where it may not be comparable to the 2011 data reported here.

7. We use the term "Mainline Protestant" in deference to its wide usage to refer to those liberal and moderate Protestant denominations once considered the "main-line" of American religions. It includes those denominations of historic Protestant-ism usually listed as theologically liberal or moderate, including the Evangelical Lutheran Church in America, Presbyterian Church (USA), Episcopal Church, Ameri-can Baptist Churches, United Methodist Church, United Church of Christ, and the Disciples of Christ.

8. For an early analysis of higher-level organizing, see Wood, "Higher Power."

9. For an exception to the overall pattern of reliance of faith language and practices to construct meaning and publicly frame the organizing work, see Kristin Geraty's recent work on the absence of religion in organizing in neighborhoods of Chicago (forthcoming).

10. See Ruth Braunstein, Brad R. Fulton, and Richard Wood, "The Role of Bridging Cultural Practices in Racially and Socioeconomically Diverse Civic Organizations," *American Sociological Review* 79, no. 4 (2014): 705–25; see also further discussion in chapter 4 here. Note that we have elsewhere used the term "institution-based community organizing" in order to emphasize the field's diverse organizational membership.

11. Funding for the project was generously provided by Interfaith Funders and its mem-ber foundations. Key collaborators for Interfaith Funders included Ned Wight and Molly Schultz Hafid of the Unitarian Universalist Veatch Program at Shelter Rock Full, Randy Keesler at the Catholic Campaign for Human Development, Katherine Partridge of Interfaith Funders, Cris Doby then of the Charles Stewart Mott Foun-dation, Mary Sobecki of the Needmor Fund, Charles Bernstein of Maine Initiatives, Kevin Ryan of the New York Foundation, and Rachel Feldman of Bend the Arc: A Jewish Partnership for Justice. Survey instruments can be accessed via sircs.unm.edu.

12. Each director who completed the study received an honorarium that ranged be-tween $25 and $100 based on the size of their coalition (and thus the complexity and time commitment involved in responding to the survey).

13. Our assessment of the key characteristics of those faith-based community organiz-ing coalitions that did not respond to the survey suggests that no systematic pat-terns of nonresponses are likely to have produced a biased profile of the field. So when providing total numbers for the entire field, we multiply values by a factor that accounts for information not provided by the nonresponsive coalitions (i.e., we project figures from the 94% of respondents to the entire field).

14. However, in some instances data limitations in the 1999 study make fully rigorous comparison impossible; we flag such instances below.

15. For example, Paul Osterman's *Gathering Power* and Jeffrey Stout's *Blessed Are the Organized* (Princeton, NJ: Princeton University Press, 2010)—both outstanding otherwise—simply embrace without critical distance one organizing network's self-interested portrayal of the field.

16. Some of the "new" coalitions existed in 1999 but did not meet the criteria for being included in the 1999 study.

17. The exception is Tennessee, which had three active coalitions in 1999 but no longer had any active as of 2011; as of 2014 at least one coalition had reorganized and become active.

18. On mobilizing structures, see Aldon D. Morris, *The Origins of the Civil Rights Movement: Black Communities Organizing for Change* (New York: Free Press, 1984); Doug McAdam, John D. McCarthy, and Mayer N. Zald, *Comparative Perspectives on Social Movements: Political Opportunities, Mobilizing Structures, and Cultural Framings* (New York: Cambridge University Press, 1996), especially the chapter by Kim Voss, "The Collapse of a Social Movement: The Interplay of Mobilizing Structures, Framing, and Political Opportunities in the Knights of Labor," 227–60.

19. The 1999 data include one coalition that reported having 230 member institutions, by far the largest reported membership base (ten times larger than the median coalition). This coalition now has forty institutions. Because the 1999 study did not properly account for this outlier, it likely overestimated the total number of member institutions in the field. A more accurate estimate accounting for this outlier suggests that the field had approximately 3,900 member institutions in 1999, meaning the field has increased by 15% since then.

20. A wide variety of other community-based organizations make up the remaining 38%, including community and economic development corporations, immigrant associations, social service programs, civic organizations, and such.

21. See *Renewing Congregations* and the related fuller report *Faith and Public Life* (Interfaith Funders 2003, 2004; available at http://hdl.handle.net/1928/10678 and http://hdl.handle.net/1928/10664 respectively), as well as Wood's forthcoming book *Faith and the Fire of Public Life*. For more information on the Interfaith Organizing Initiative's work, see http://www.interfaithfunders.org/Inter -ReligiousOrganizingInitiative. Especially significant has been work within the Evangelical Lutheran Church in America, the Unitarian Universalist Association, and the Union for Reformed Judaism to strengthen congregations using tools from community organizing; see http://www.elca.org/Our-Faith-In-Action/Justice/Congregation -based-Organizing.aspx and http://urj.org/socialaction/training/justcongregations and www.uua.org. On related interfaith work based on the Jewish ethical tradition, see http://bendthearc.us, all accessed August 21, 2013.

22. On potential trade-offs to higher-level organizing, see Lara Rusch, "Rethinking Bridging: Risk and Trust in Multiracial Community Organizing," *Urban Affairs Review* 45 (2010): 483–506; and Rusch, "Going Regional: The Evolution of an Organizing Strategy in Detroit," *City and Community* 11, no. 1 (2012): 51–73. On the potential symbiosis between local and higher-level organizing, see Warren, *Dry Bones Rattling*, and Wood, "Higher Power." Some organizing networks eschew higher-level organizing, either due to inadequate organizing capacity or having calculated that its risks outweigh the benefits and potential impact; even within those networks who have moved to influence policy in higher-level arenas, some individual coalitions have chosen not to do so.

23. In the 1999 study, when coalition directors were asked to identify the critical needs

of the field, several mentioned the need to develop an ability to address issues and impact policy at levels beyond the city.

24. In addition, in 2011, 4% of faith-based community organizing coalitions reported addressing at least one issue at an international level. This claim is hard to interpret and may simply reflect a vague claim to involvement in international work by whichever network the coalition is affiliated with; several networks do some degree of work in particular international settings (the IAF in the United Kingdom, Germany, and Australia; PICO in El Salvador, Guatemala, Haiti, and Rwanda; Gamaliel in South Africa).

25. The authors worked with professional foundation staff to verify the claims reported here. Other researchers who have sought to substantiate similar claims have found them quite credible (though likely overestimating the financial impact attributable directly to funder and organizing initiatives). See especially Lisa Ranghelli, *Leveraging Limited Dollars: How Grantmakers Achieve Tangible Results by Funding Policy and Community Engagement* (Washington, DC: National Committee for Responsive Philanthropy, 2012).

26. Further analysis could assess how collaboration affects faith-based community organizing coalitions by comparing coalitions from the 1999 study that participated in multiorganizational coalitions and addressed issues at higher levels with those that did not. Further research is also needed on the emergent national issue work by the networks and the strategic alliances that have developed from that work.

27. The soft power / hard power distinction as used here is adapted from the international relations literature; see Robert O. Keohane and Joseph S. Nye, "Power and Interdependence in the Information Age," *Foreign Affairs* 77 (1998): 81–94.

28. Coalitions vary in the number of people they can mobilize for their events, and their capacity often corresponds with the number of member institutions they have. While the average number of member institutions per coalition has declined, the ability of member institutions to mobilize their constituents has remained the same. On average, each member institution tends to mobilize approximately thirty participants to public events. When considering a coalition's overall ability to mobilize participants, it can expect, on average, approximately sixty different people per member institution to attend at least one of their events per year. However, the mobilizing abilities of member institutions vary greatly and depend on several factors, including size and level of involvement with the coalition.

29. See the various ethnographic studies of organizing cited previously. Note that this reputation for constructive engagement with elected officials stands in contrast *both* to this field's previous reputation for negative "targeting" of politicians *and* to the antigovernment posturing common in the Tea Party movement (both of which were built on a narrow reading of the most antigovernment strands of Saul Alinsky's thought).

30. See Theda Skocpol, Marshall Ganz, and Ziad Munson, "A Nation of Organizers: The Institutional Origins of Civic Voluntarism in the United States," *American Political Science Review* 94, no. 3 (2000): 527–46. Note that in order to allow historical analysis to accurately capture cases of mass membership and societal influence, the authors analyze data from the nation's origins to 1940 (but argue convincingly that the analysis offers important insight to contemporary dynamics).

31. See Marshall Ganz, "Resources and Resourcefulness: Strategic Capacity in the Unionization of California Agriculture, 1959–1966," *American Journal of Sociology* 105, no. 4 (2000): 1003–63; and Ganz, *Why David Sometimes Wins: Leadership, Or-*

ganization, and Strategy in the California Farm Worker Movement (New York: Oxford University Press, 2009).

32. Ganz's insight on strategy represents a particularly good case of what Bent Flyvbjerg analyzes as the context dependence of social knowledge more generally. Bent Flyvbjerg, *Making Social Science Matter: Why Social Inquiry Fails and How It Can Succeed Again* (Cambridge: Cambridge University Press, 2001); Bent Flyvbjerg and Todd Landman Sanford Schram, eds., *Real Social Science: Applied Phronesis* (Cambridge: Cambridge University Press, 2011).

33. In 1999, $150,000 had the purchasing power equivalent of about $202,000 in 2011 (US Bureau of Labor Statistics); the change would thus be a 12% drop from 1999 to 2011 (the latter in the midst of recession, thus likely accounting for at least part of the decline). Note that the reported decline pertains only to local coalitions and does not reflect revenues to national-level organizing efforts, nor does it reflect what budgets may have been just prior to the 2008 recession.

34. The 1999 data do not allow us to separate out donations from corporations and donations from secular foundations.

35. Countering this trend, however, in 2013 the C. S. Mott Foundation—a longtime funder of community organizing in Michigan and nationally—announced it was withdrawing from those efforts in light of new priorities of the new leadership.

36. On the internal CCHD review, see http://www.usccb.org/about/catholic-campaign -for-human-development/Who-We-Are/review-and-renewal.cfm. Full disclosure: Wood serves as a pro bono advisor to the bishops' committee that oversees CCHD, including the internal review. For a critical view of that review and its impact, see John Gehring, *Be Not Afraid? Guilt by Association, Catholic McCarthyism, and Growing Threats to the U.S. Bishops' Anti-Poverty Mission* (Washington, DC: Faith in Public Life, 2013), available at http://www.faithinpubliclife.org/wp-content/uploads/2013/ 06/FPL-CCHD-report.pdf, and http://americamagazine.org/issue/new-report-urges -support-cchd. For an example of the sectarian Catholic critiques of CCHD and the Catholic bishops, see http://reformcchdnow.com/cchd-2011-2012-grants-report/, and the bishops' response at http://www.usccb.org/about/catholic-campaign-for -human-development/Who-We-Are/cchd-report-9-28-2011.cfm.

37. As this book goes to press, the PICO National Network is planning a major event to highlight the field during Pope Francis I's visit to Philadelphia in September 2015.

38. Anecdotal evidence since our 2011 data collection suggests that local coalitions have struggled to sustain their previous funding levels as the economy continued to stall into 2013, but we do not have systematic evidence in that regard, nor can we know what has occurred since the economy began to recover (albeit with almost no wage growth for low-income sectors).

39. See Sidney Tarrow, *Power in Movement: Social Movements, Collective Action, and Politics* (Cambridge: Cambridge University Press, 1994); Walker and McCarthy, "Legitimacy, Strategy, and Resources in the Survival of Community-Based Organizations"; Mayer N. Zald and John D. McCarthy, *Social Movements in an Organizational Society* (New Brunswick, NJ: Transaction, 1987).

40. On the cultural turn generally, and the role of culture in social movements, see Jeffrey C. Alexander, Bernhard Giesen, and Jason L. Mast, *Social Performance: Symbolic Action, Cultural Pragmatics, and Ritual* (New York: Cambridge University Press, 2006); Elizabeth A. Armstrong and Mary Bernstein, "Culture, Power, and Institutions: A Multi-Institutional Politics Approach to Social Movements," *Sociological Theory* 26, no. 1 (2008): 74–99; Nina Eliasoph, *Avoiding Politics: How Americans Produce Apathy*

in Everyday Life (Cambridge: Cambridge University Press, 1998); Mustafa Emirbayer and Jeff Goodwin, "Network Analysis, Culture, and the Problem of Agency," *American Journal of Sociology* 99, no. 6 (1994): 1411–54; Jeff Goodwin, James M. Jasper, and Francesca Polletta, *Passionate Politics: Emotions and Social Movements* (Chicago: University of Chicago Press, 2001); Hank Johnston and Bert Klandermans Johnston, eds., *Social Movements and Culture* (Minneapolis: University of Minnesota Press, 1995); Anne E. Kane, "Theorizing Meaning Construction in Social Movement," *Sociological Theory* 15, no. 3 (1997): 249–76; Michèle Lamont and Marcel Fournier, *Cultivating Differences: Symbolic Boundaries and the Making of Inequality* (Chicago: University of Chicago Press, 1992); Patricia M. Mische and Melissa Merkling, *Toward a Global Civilization? The Contribution of Religions* (New York: P. Lang, 2001); Francesca Polletta, *It Was Like a Fever: Storytelling in Protest and Politics* (Chicago: University of Chicago Press, 2006); Isaac Reed, Jeffrey C. Alexander, and Nina Eliasoph, *Culture, Society, and Democracy: The Interpretive Approach* (Boulder, CO: Paradigm Publishers, 2007); Michael Schudson, "How Culture Works: Perspectives from Media Studies on the Efficacy of Symbols," *Theory and Society* 18 (1989): 153–80; Margaret R. Somers, "Citizenship and the Place of the Public Sphere: Law, Community, and Political Culture in the Transition to Democracy," *American Sociological Review* 58 (1993): 587–620; Ann Swidler, "Culture in Action," *American Sociological Review* 51 (1996): 273–86; Lisa Wedeen, "Conceptualizing Culture: Possibilities for Political Science," *American Political Science Review* 96, no. 4 (2002): 713–28; Rhys H. Williams, "Politics, Religion, and the Analysis of Culture," *Theory and Society* 25, no. 6 (1996), and Williams, "From the 'Beloved Community' to 'Family Values': Religious Language, Symbolic Repertoires and Democratic Culture," in *Social Movements: Identity, Culture, and the State*, ed. Nancy Whittier, David S. Meyer, and Belinda Robnett (Oxford: Oxford University Press, 2002); Richard L. Wood, "Religious Culture and Political Action," *Sociological Theory* 17, no. 3 (1999): 307–32; Robert Wuthnow, James Davison Hunter, Albert Bergesen, and Edith Kurzweil, *Cultural Analysis: The Work of Peter L. Berger, Mary Douglas, Michel Foucault, and Jürgen Habermas* (Boston: Routledge and Kegan Paul, 1984); Lynne G. Zucker, "The Role of Institutionalization in Cultural Persistence," *American Sociological Review* 42 (1977): 726–43; and Sharon Erickson Nepstad, *Religion and War Resistance in the Plowshares Movement* (New York: Cambridge University Press, 2008).

41. Kleidman, "Community Organizing and Regionalism"; Osterman, *Gathering Power*; Heidi Swarts, "Setting the State's Agenda: Church-Based Community Organizations in American Urban Politics," in *States, Parties, and Social Movements: Protest and the Dynamics of Institutional Change*, ed. Jack Goldstone (Cambridge: Cambridge University Press, 2001), and Swarts, *Organizing Urban America*.

42. Stout, *Blessed Are the Organized*. On one-to-one "relational" meetings, see also Wood, *Faith in Action*.

CHAPTER TWO

1. Address at a PICO national gathering, October 2014, Philadelphia, Pennsylvania.

2. Although religious clergy and lay leaders often play rather distinct roles in the internal cultures of these coalitions, they routinely sit together on the governing boards. Thus for present purposes we combine their demographic profiles under the heading "board members."

3. On the aspiration and sometime reality of faith-based organizing's contributions to the organizational development of member institutions, especially religious con-

gregations, see Flaherty and Wood, *Faith and Public Life*; Wood, *Faith and the Fire of Public Life* (forthcoming); and Wood and Flaherty, *Renewing Congregations*.

4. In addition, most faith-based community organizing coalitions indicated that they also provide smaller training events throughout the year at which even more leaders are trained.

5. The 2010 comparison figures are from the US census; see http://www.census.gov/prod/2012pubs/acs-19.pdf.

6. See http://www.usccb.org/about/catholic-campaign-for-human-development/grants/, for CCHD's policies regarding low-income representation. This policy, in place for more than forty years, appears to have helped institutionalize low-income representation on boards in the field. The policy is somewhat more complicated; religious clergy serving on a governing board "count" as low income only if they live in a low-income neighborhood.

7. The key study of democratic "voice" in the United States remains Verba, Schlozman, and Brady, *Voice and Equality*. Note that the National Study of Community Organizing Coalitions did not include Interfaith Worker Justice or other community labor organizations, which represent a middle ground between faith-based community organizing model and the labor movement discussed next.

8. The best comparative data come from Swarts, *Organizing Urban America*, which compares the work of ACORN prior to its demise with that of Gamaliel and PICO. See also Wood's analysis of the work of the Center for Third World Organizing and PICO in *Faith in Action*.

9. On class-based cultural dynamics in social movement organizations, see especially the important new work by Betsy Leondar-Wright, *Missing Class: How Seeing Class Cultures Can Strengthen Social Movement Groups* (Ithaca, NY: Cornell University Press, 2014).

10. For instance, Gamaliel, the IAF organization in Arizona, PICO, and DART in Florida all report strong engagement from various immigrant sectors, as they have become strong advocates for immigrant rights. Likewise, as PICO has begun to systematically address mass incarceration and voting rights for ex-felons returning to society, they report that about a third of recent attendees at national leader trainings are either ex-prisoners themselves or have immediate family members in prison (September 2014 interview with Scott Reed).

11. Stout, *Blessed Are the Organized*.

12. US adult population data come from the 2010 General Social Survey. Data on all members of nonprofit boards come from Francine Ostrower, *Nonprofit Governance in the United States: Findings on Performance and Accountability from the First National Representative Study* (Washington, DC: Urban Institute Center on Nonprofits and Philanthropy, 2007).

13. We defined "large" member institutions as those with between one thousand and five thousand members, and "very large" member institutions as those with more than five thousand members. Twenty-seven percent of large member institutions and 31% of very large member institutions are Hispanic, more than double the proportion of Hispanic member institutions overall. Fifty-seven percent of large member institutions and 59% of very large member institutions are Catholic, again more than double the proportion of Catholic member institutions overall. Member institutions that are *both* Catholic and Hispanic make up nearly three times the proportion of large and very large members than in the field as a whole (23% and 27% respectively, compared to 8% of all member institutions).

14. Immigrants predominantly make up 25% of large member institutions and 27% of very large member institutions; three-quarters of those are predominantly Hispanic/ Latino. In addition, presumably some member institutions that are not *predominantly* immigrant do have significant numbers of immigrant attendees.

15. The most rigorous research on the impact of this form of organizing on participants' leadership skills and civic engagement has been done by Paul Speer at Vanderbilt University. See Speer, "People Making Public Policy" and Speer et al., "The Intentional Exercise of Power." Speer's key finding, not yet published but used here by permission: In a well-designed two-year longitudinal study comparing faith-based organizing participants to similar nonparticipant residents of similar socioeconomic status, those involved in this form of organizing showed a 13% gain in civic engagement versus a marginal decline in civic engagement for the comparison group (Speer, forthcoming).

16. Note that although we collected data on *all staff* of these coalitions, the data reported here include only the *organizing staff*, that is, those paid staff members (including lead organizers and directors) whose primary work was described as organizing rather than clerical, administrative, or other such categories. We believe this to be the crucial sector within the cultural and organizational dynamics of the field, and thus the right focus for analytic attention. The broader "all staff" profile actually represents *greater* racial and ethnic diversity. Also note that the 1999 figure for total organizing staff is an approximation due to uncertainty regarding the data collection in the earlier study.

17. The mean number of member institutions per organizer for the average faith-based community organizing coalition decreased from 15/1 in 1999 to 12/1 in 2011. This drop presumably allows for greater focus on strengthening member institutions, as well as more organizing time for projecting locally constructed organizational power up into higher-level political arenas. However, we do not know how the extra organizer hours are actually allocated between these and other demands.

18. On the discomfort of some organizers of color with the dominant Alinsky-derived tradition as of the 1980s and 1990s, see Francis Calpotura and Kim Fellner, "The Square Pegs Find Their Groove: Reshaping the Organizing Circle," http://comm -org.utoledo.edu/papers96/square.html; Gary Delgado, *Organizing the Movement: The Roots and Growth of Acorn* (Philadelphia: Temple University Press, 1986), and Delgado, *Beyond the Politics of Place: New Directions in Community Organizing in the 1990s* (Oakland, CA: Applied Research Center, 1994); Rinku Sen, *Stir It Up: Lessons in Community Organizing* (San Francisco: Jossey-Bass, 2003); and Susan Stall and Randy Stoecker, "Community Organizing or Organizing Community? Gender and the Crafts of Empowerment," *Gender and Society* 12 (1998): 729–56.

19. Although beyond our purposes here, the authors have done participant observation in many such settings both within the various networks and in funder-sponsored workshops and research colloquia.

20. *Visions* is a nonprofit consulting firm on issues of racial equity; see http://visions -inc.org.

CHAPTER THREE

1. A large literature documents the paucity of social capital bridging racial/ethnic divides of American life; the best entry point remains Robert C. Putnam, *Bowling Alone: The Collapse and Revival of American Community* (New York: Simon and Schuster, 2000).

2. See notes in chapter 1 for citations of this work. Some of those scholarly accounts—especially Swarts, *Organizing Urban America*; Warren, *Dry Bones Rattling*; and Wood, *Faith in Action*—focus on a sufficient number of cases to offer analytic leverage beyond purely local insight, and many of the practitioner accounts are written from broad experience and thus provide translocal insight, albeit from within the point of view of a particular network. The most important exceptions to this portrayal of the literature all draw on the 1999 Interfaith Funders study that provides the change-over-time data presented later in this chapter.

3. Since we relied on locally held knowledge for assessing the racial/ethnic profiles of member congregations, we treated racial and ethnic identity in keeping with grassroots practice in American civil society: as mutually exclusive categories. Thus a given director assessed each member institution as *either* majority white, majority African American, majority Hispanic, majority other, or multiracial (where "majority" meant greater than 50%). This procedure does not very fully capture the complexity of identity for individuals, in which a given individual may well be both Hispanic and black, for example, but does have the virtue of capturing tacit local knowledge of broad profiles of member institutions, our goal here.

4. Data on all US nonprofits come from Ostrower, *Nonprofit Governance*. Of the 14% of nonprofit board members who were not white, 7% were black and 3.5% were Hispanic/Latino. Note that nonprofits in the large urban areas defined as "metropolitan statistical areas" were somewhat more diverse—but even there 45% of nonprofit boards were composed *entirely* of white members.

5. On the tendency toward homogeneity ("homophily") in voluntary associations, see J. Miller McPherson and Lynn Smith-Lovin, "Homophily in Voluntary Organizations: Status Distance and the Composition of Face-to-Face Groups," *American Sociological Review* 52, no. 3 (1987): 370–79; Miller McPherson, Lynn Smith-Lovin, and James M. Cook, "Birds of a Feather: Homophily in Social Networks," *Annual Review of Sociology* 1, no. 27 (2001): 415–44; Martin Ruef, Howard E. Aldrich, and Nancy M. Carter, "The Structure of Founding Teams: Homophily, Strong Ties, and Isolation among U.S. Entrepreneurs," *American Sociological Review* 68, no. 2 (2003): 195–222.

6. Alternatively, the field might achieve meaningful diversity of interaction by pulling those local coalitions that embody little diversity into higher-level organizing where greater diversity exposes participants to more cross-cultural dynamics.

7. More formally, diversity $= 1 - \Sigma_k \rho_k^2$ where ρk is the proportion of member institutions in group k (this widely used measure is known as the Herfindahl index).

8. The effects of diversity can also be influenced if one particular racial/ethnic group has a dominating presence (i.e., represents more than 50% of the members). A coalition that is majority white but has the same "diversity index" as a majority black coalition is likely to operate quite differently.

9. The mean diversity score for public schools is based on the 2009–10 NCES Common Core of Data Public Elementary/Secondary School Universe Survey, the score for counties is based on the 2010 Census Demographic Profile, and the score for congregations is based on the 2006–7 National Congregations Study (all calculated using the Herfindahl index).

10. On the concept of "subaltern counterpublics," see the introduction of this book and especially Fraser, "Rethinking the Public Sphere."

11. On the continuing segregation of American religious congregations as well as important trends toward more multiracial congregations, see the important work of Michael O. Emerson and several collaborators: Brad Christerson, Korie L. Edwards,

and Michael O. Emerson, *Against All Odds : The Struggle for Racial Integration in Religious Organizations* (New York: New York University Press, 2005); Michael O. Emerson and Christian Smith, *Divided by Faith: Evangelical Religion and the Problem of Race in America* (New York: Oxford University Press, 2000); Michael O. Emerson and George A. Yancey, *Transcending Racial Barriers: Toward a Mutual Obligations Approach* (New York: Oxford University Press, 2011); Jason E. Shelton and Michael O. Emerson, *Blacks and Whites in Christian America: How Racial Discrimination Shapes Religious Convictions* (New York: New York University Press, 2012).

12. The phrase *"appears* to have declined" reflects the uncertainties embedded in the 1999 study that provides the only data available for anything like a rigorous longitudinal comparison of diversity in the field. There were significant problems in that study design, which led to some uncertainty in the following comparisons. But the trends that the comparative analysis allows us to see are important for thinking through changes in the field over the last ten to fifteen years, subject to the later caveat regarding more sophisticated measures of diversity.

13. The data reported in these figures for 1999 differ slightly from those reported at the time; during reanalysis we discovered an error in how that data was collected and analyzed.

14. However, see discussion above: The faith-based community organizing field remains substantially more diverse than its institutional equivalents. Member congregations represent greater diversity than the field of congregations in the United States, and the boards of directors of these coalitions represent greater diversity than the boards of the nonprofit sector. See Mark Chaves, Shawna L. Anderson, and Alison Eagle, *National Congregations Study: Cumulative Data File and Codebook* (Durham, NC: Duke University, Department of Sociology, 2014); and Ostrower, *Nonprofit Governance.* The field is also substantially more diverse than the US population as a whole. But the key question in the present discussion is the direction of racial/ethnic *change* in the field.

15. Of the fifty-three coalitions for which we have data from both 1999 and 2011, 60% became more diverse while 25% became less diverse.

16. Note that there has also been extensive outreach to white Evangelical churches (most systematically by Rev. Troy Jackson of the Ohio Organizing Collaborative and by Robert Linthicum, Helene Slessarev-Jamir, and the organization Christians Supporting Community Organizing) and Muslim mosques in the last ten years. See http://emergingvoicesproject.org/troy-jackson; http://www.cscoweb.org; Robert C. Linthicum, *Signs of Hope in the City*, Urban Ministry (Monrovia, CA: Marc, 1995), and Linthicum, *City of God, City of Satan: A Biblical Theology for the Urban Church* (Grand Rapids, MI: Zondervan, 1991); and H. Slessarev-Jamir, "Exploring the Attraction of Local Congregations to Community Organizing," *Nonprofit and Voluntary Sector Quarterly* 33, no. 4 (2004).

17. See D. Paul Sullins, "Institutional Selection for Conformity: The Case of U.S. Catholic Priests," *Sociology of Religion* 74, no. 1 (2013): 56–81.

18. We do not have data to show this effect. Although it seems plausible, it also begs the question of what happened post-2011 to regenerate vibrant Hispanic engagement in the immigration reform debate—a movement in which faith-based organizing networks and local coalitions were central actors.

19. On the work of Unitarian Universalist, Jewish, and (ELCA) Lutheran denominations on this terrain, see http://www.uua.org/action/cbco/, http://bendthearc.us, and http://www.elca.org/Our-Faith-In-Action/Justice/Congregation-based-Organizing

.aspx respectively, as well as Wood, *Faith and the Fire of Public Life* (forthcoming); Wood and Flaherty, *Renewing Congregations*.

20. Note that because such a large proportion of the Hispanic institutions involved in faith-based organizing are Catholic parishes, we cannot clearly disentangle the relative influence of Catholic dynamics (the shift in emphasis in authoritative teaching or the institutional crisis linked to the sexuality and authority scandals) from wider political dynamics (the anti-immigrant and anti-Hispanic tone of public discourse in the years leading up to the 2011 data collection).

21. Of the total of 133 faith-based organizing coalitions that were identified in 1999, the 101 that survived until 2011 (either on their own or as a result of mergers) had a mean diversity score of 0.46; the thirty-two coalitions that did not survive from 1999 to 2011 had a diversity score of 0.49 (calculated at the individual *coalition* level, where it is most relevant). But the nonsurviving coalitions had higher diversity by virtue of having both more black and more white member institutional members (41% of each group) than did those coalitions that did survive (which were 34% white and 33% black; note that this means that the mean diversity score calculated at the level of the overall *field* was higher for survivors). The attrition of coalitions between 1999 and 2011 thus generated a much higher loss of black and white member institutions (23% and 22% of member institutions lost to coalition attrition respectively) than for Hispanic and "other" member institutions (11% and 13% lost to coalition attrition respectively). However, given the large size of many Hispanic Catholic congregations, the latter loss may have represented significantly diminished presence of Hispanic *individuals* at public meetings.

22. We analyzed our data for the surviving versus nonsurviving coalitions, seeking patterns to explain attrition. On first pass, the important pattern appeared to be that the nonsurviving coalitions had larger numbers of both white and black member institutions, suggesting the hypothesis that black-white tensions might drive attrition. However, further analysis shows that this pattern only holds in the aggregate. At the level of individual coalitions—where whatever dynamics led to coalition attrition likely played out—no such pattern existed, that is, nonsurviving coalitions were no more likely to have high proportions of both white *and* black member institutions than were surviving coalitions; rather, they typically had *either* more black *or* white member institutions. Perhaps black institutional vulnerability to economic pressures drove part of the pattern, and unknown factors associated with white institutions separately drove others parts of the pattern—thus this is not a simple story, and remains to be explored.

23. The relevant data comes from those coalitions that existed in *both* 1999 and 2011 and for which we have data from both years (n = 53). For this "panel data," we can calculate how many predominantly white, black, Hispanic, or other institutions dropped out of membership. We cannot be sure, however, that they dropped out due to economic stresses. Thus we cannot be sure whether these data reflect economic stress during recent downturns or other reasons for dropping organizing. Note that to whatever extent this can be interpreted as a story of lack of wealth to support member institutions during economic downturns, that is a story grounded in the lack of black wealth in America. In the panel data, black member institutions were the most likely to depart organizing.

24. The data here must be interpreted with caution, as they reflect the memory of staff organizers in 2011 for how long different institutions have been members of the relevant coalition. That data suggest attrition rates for member institutions of differ-

ing predominant racial/ethnic makeups as follows: 68% for white, 79% for black, 73% for Hispanic, and 70% for institutions of mixed or predominantly other racial/ethnic makeups—it is just that many of these are subsequently replace by new institutions. Thus there is significant cyclic replacement of institutions across all racial/ethnic groups; it just occurs somewhat more frequently for predominantly black and Hispanic institutions.

25. Note that our data do not allow us to know the post-1999 coalitions' proportion of white member institutions or diversity scores *at the time of their founding*, but these data as of 2011 represent a reasonable proxy.

26. A contributing factor: Those coalitions established after 1999 in counties with a larger proportion of white people tended to have more member institutions in 2011 and (unsurprisingly) a larger proportion of predominantly white institutions than the average coalition. Note that we report all the figures in this paragraph comparing our 1999 data to 2000 US Census data, and comparing our 2011 data to 2010 US Census data.

27. This statement should not be misread as implying that faith-based organizing's power and influence comes only or even primarily as a direct result of public actions. Their influence is likely rooted at least as much in their role in *negotiating* policy priorities and policy development in smaller-scale venues. However, their ability to "get to the table" and exert this kind of negotiated influence derives very substantially from their ability to project power via public actions. Thus public actions and accountability sessions are indeed the central source of political influence.

28. Note that the total N in tables 3.1 and 3.2 includes only those member institutions for which we have size-of-membership, race/ethnicity, and religion data; thus smaller than total institutional membership in the field.

29. See Stout, *Blessed Are the Organized*; Swarts *Organizing Urban America*; Warren, *Dry Bones Rattling*; and Wood, *Faith in Action*.

30. The diversity score approach in the next paragraph better captures the complexity that this paragraph truncates, by taking into account *both* the number of racial/ethnic groups *and* the proportion of each group.

31. Scholarly works documenting extensive cross-racial and cross-ethnic political relationships within the field include Kleidman, "Community Organizing and Regionalism"; Osterman, *Gathering Power*; Rusch, "Rethinking Bridging"; Swarts, "Setting the State's Agenda" and *Organizing Urban America*; Stout, *Blessed Are the Organized*; Warren, *Dry Bones Rattling*; and Wood, *Faith in Action*.

32. Braunstein, Fulton, and Wood, "The Role of Bridging Cultural Practices." As documented there, all patterns discussed here hold even while controlling for a variety of other variables that plausibly might also drive the use of prayer vigils.

PART TWO INTRODUCTION

1. On "ethical democracy," see especially pp. 183–85 and passim in Wood, *Faith in Action*, and Markofski, *Evangelical Christianity and American Democracy* (forthcoming).

2. Other than the publications that emerged from the 1999 "state of the field" surveys and the 2011 *National Study of Community Organizing Coalitions*, none of the writing by practitioners *or* scholars has included a broad assessment across the various institution-based community organizing efforts. Several productively analyze one institution-based network with a different organizing model: Hart, *Cultural Dilemmas of Progressive Politics*, compares Gamaliel's faith-based work with Amnesty International's human rights work; Swarts, *Organizing Urban America*, includes both Ga-

maliel and PICO's faith-based work and compares it with ACORN's model; Donna Day-Lower, "Prelude to Struggle: African American Clergy and Community Organizing for Economic Development in the 1990s" (PhD diss., Temple University, 1996), compares faith-based organizing and community development initiatives; and Wood, *Faith in Action*, compares PICO's faith-based work with the race-based work of the Center for Third World Organizing. Others offer a rich internal portrait of this work by focusing solely on specific organizations or networks: Speer, "People Making Public Policy in California: The PICO California Project," and "The Intentional Exercise of Power," on PICO; Stout, *Blessed Are the Organized*; Bretherton, *Resurrecting Democracy*; Warren, *Dry Bones Rattling*; Osterman, *Gathering Power*, and earlier Rogers, *Cold Anger*, on the Industrial Areas Foundation; Kleidman "Community Organizing and Regionalism," on Gamaliel; and from the practitioners side Whitman, "Beyond Advocacy," and Baker, *When Faith Storms the Public Square*, on the PICO National Network; Ed Chambers, *Roots for Radicals*, and Gecan, *After America's Midlife Crisis*, on the IAF; Jacobsen, *Doing Justice*, on Gamaliel—but all without locating the work studied within the broader field of organizing.

3.   For those accounts, see references in previous note.

4.   See Wood, *Faith in Action*, 183–84. Note that Warren, *Dry Bones Rattling*, identifies the political-cultural dynamics within the Texas IAF, with its strong involvement of Catholic priests and African American pastors of historic black churches, as "participative hierarchy." This probably represents some combination of local variation in emphasis and systematic network differences of organizational culture; in any case, the rest of Warren's book as well as Stout's *Blessed Are the Organized* and Osterman's *Gathering Power* all make clear that the Texas IAF also includes heavy doses of participative democracy.

CHAPTER FOUR

1.   See http://www.educationvoterspa.org/index.php/site/issues/who-runs-the-school-district-of-philadelphia, accessed September 10, 2014.

2.   On the PICO California project, see a research report by Paul W. Speer, *People Making Public Policy*.

3.   Wood did participant-observation research periodically in PICO New Voices' work during this period. A fuller analysis of the PICO New Voices' early efforts can be found in Richard L. Wood, "Higher Power: Strategic Capacity for State and National Organizing," in *Transforming the City: Community Organizing and the Challenge of Political Change*, ed. Marion Orr (Lawrence: University Press of Kansas, 2007), 164–92. Sections of the following discussion follow this source, updated to reflect recent events. On the PICO network generally and its current geographical and political profile, see www.piconetwork.org.

4.   On the Bush vetoes, see Jonathan Weisman and Michael Abramowitz, "Bush Vetoes Health Measure; President Says He's Willing To Negotiate," *Washington Post*, October 4, 2007, A1; and Jeffrey H. Birnbaum, "A Look Back at the Year's Winners and Losers," *Washington Post*, January 1, 2008, A9. Through this same period, PICO New Voices and its Louisiana affiliates were also active in successful efforts to pass federal relief and reconstruction funds for the Gulf Coast, following Hurricane Katrina in 2005. See Miriam Axel-Lute, "Picking Up the Pieces," *Shelterforce Online* 145 (2006), accessed September 7, 2013, doi:www.nhi.org/online/issues/145/pickinguppieces.html. All accessed via LexisNexis, September 7, 2013.

5.   For an example of national media coverage of the PICO National Network's role

in the health care reform debate, see Jacqueline L. Salmon, "Pulling Together on Health Care," *Washington Post*, July 25, 2009, B02; see also by Rev. Rayfield Burns, LaCresia Hawkings, and Jeremy Kaercher, "Public Comments of PICO National Network before the Presidential Advisory Commission on Medicaid" (PICO National Network, 2005). For a sampling of national media coverage of the network's role in wider issues, see Michelle Boorstein, "At Cathedral, the Gospel of Activism," *Washington Post*, Metro, January 24, 2013, B2; Dennis Brady, "Federal Initiative Expands Mortgage Relief for Unemployed," *Washington Post*, July 8, 2011, A11; Hamil R. Harris, "Faith Groups Launch Effort Aimed at the Causes of Urban Violence," *Washington Post*, January 30, 2013, A6; Samuel Freedman, "Mortgage Crisis Inspires Churches to Send Lenten Season Message to Banks," *New York Times*, March 10, 2012, A16; Jacqueline L. Salmon, "Coming Together in a Crisis: Faith-Based Coalition Is Pushing for a Treasury Policy That Prevents More Foreclosures," *Washington Post*, November 29, 2008, B7; Jennifer Steinhauer, "Ire in Foreclosure Crisis Turns to a Home Builder," *New York Times*, April 3, 2009, A16; Philip Rucker and Peter Wallsten, "Gun Task Force Heard All Sides but Kept Goal in Sight," *Washington Post*, January 20, 2013, A3. All accessed via LexisNexis, September 7, 2013.

6. On the SCHIP reauthorization, see Jeffrey Young, "Baucus Introduces SCHIP Bill as House Readies Votes," January 14, 2009, 15; and Robert Pear, "Obama Signs Children's Health Insurance Bill," February 4, 2009.

7. On the burden of whites in the work of fighting racism, see Noel Ignatiev and John Garvey, *Race Traitor* (New York: Routledge, 1996); and Mark R. Warren. *Fire in the Heart: How White Activists Embrace Racial Justice* (New York: Oxford University Press, 2010).

8. The best study of governing boards in the nonprofit sector is Ostrower, *Nonprofit Governance*—which shows fully 86% of members of nonprofit governing boards being white.

9. All quotations in this section are from Scott Reed, "Remarks at Applegate, 2012" (opening speech at the annual retreat for all organizing staff of the PICO National Network, held at Applegate Retreat Center, California, June 18, 2012).

10. From *Agamemnon* 179–83. Note that this is actually a slight mistranslation commonly cited, apparently as a result of Robert F. Kennedy's usage of it immediately following the death of Dr. Martin Luther King Jr. The more accepted translation is: "even in our sleep pain that cannot forget / Falls drop by drop upon the heart / And in our own despite, against our will / Comes wisdom to us by the awful grace of God." See http://en.wikiquote.org/wiki/Aeschylus#Agamemnon.

11. On racialization, see the later discussion of john powell's work as well as Michael Omi and Howard Winant, *Racial Formation in the United States: From the 1960s to the 1990s* (New York: Routledge, 1994); and David O. Sears, Jim Sidanius, and Lawrence Bobo, eds., *Racialized Politics: The Debate about Racism in America*, Studies in Communication, Media, and Public Opinion (Chicago: University of Chicago Press, 2000). In our ethnographic observation, the concept of racialization appears to foster discussion of the realities of racism and its continuing impact in reproducing inequality without asserting that individual interlocutors are racist, which tends to shut down rather than open up dialogue.

12. In 2012, john powell (he does not capitalize his names) held the Williams Chair in Civil Rights and Civil Liberties and served as the executive director of the Kirwan Institute, both at the Ohio State University. He subsequently moved to a position at the University of California–Berkeley, where he holds the Robert D. Haas Chan-

cellor's Chair in Equity and Inclusion and directs the Haas Institute for a Fair and Inclusive Society.

13. Visions is a nonprofit organizational consulting firm that works with organizations nationally on issues of inclusion and racial equity. See http://visions-inc.org.

14. See William Julius Wilson, "Revisiting Race-Neutral Politics," *American Prospect* 22, no. 3 (2011): A7+. Wilson concludes that interview by summarizing as follows: "So, as you can see, my position has significantly changed since I wrote "Race-Neutral Politics and the Democratic Coalition" . . . I now see the need, in this atmosphere of 'reactionary colorblindness,' as you put it, to strongly emphasize both class-based and race-based programs, couched in a very strong and consistent message featuring a political framing that captures basic American values." His reference is to his classic earlier statement, "Race-Neutral Programs and the Democratic Coalition," *American Prospect* 1 (1990): 74–81.

15. On regional inequality and the geography of opportunity, see john powell, "Race, Place, and Opportunity," in *The American Prospect* online, September 21, 2008, accessed July 10, 2014, at http://prospect.org/article/race-place-and-opportunity; powell, "Race, Poverty, and Urban Sprawl: Access to Opportunities through Regional Strategies," in *Growing Smarter: Achieving Livable Communities, Environmental Justice, and Regional Equity*, ed. Robert Bullard (Cambridge, MA: MIT Press, 2007); and powell, "Structural Racism and Spatial Jim Crow," in *The Black Metropolis in the Twenty-First Century: Race, Power, and the Politics of Place*, ed. Robert Bullard (Lanham, MD: Rowman and Littlefield, 2007).

16. john powell has written and lectured extensively; my summary of his framework for thinking about racial equity is drawn primarily from *Racing to Justice: Transforming Our Conceptions of Self and Other to Build an Inclusive Society* (Bloomington: Indiana University Press, 2012) and a public presentation at the Boalt School of Law at UC–Berkeley, sponsored by Interfaith Funders in February 2013. Material from that version of powell's presentation, titled "Racial Justice and Racialized Structures," is used here by permission.

17. See Alexander, *The Civil Sphere.*

18. On the foundational research underlying the social psychology of implicit bias, see Jennifer L. Eberhardt, "Imaging Race," *American Psychologist* 60, no. 2 (2005): 181; Jennifer L. Eberhardt and Susan T. Fiske, "Affirmative Action in Theory and Practice: Issues of Power, Ambiguity, and Gender versus Race," *Basic and Applied Social Psychology* 15, no. 1–2 (1994): 201–20; Jennifer L. Eberhardt et al., "Seeing Black: Race, Crime, and Visual Processing," *Journal of Personality and Social Psychology* 87, no. 6 (2004): 876; and Aneeta Rattan and Jennifer L Eberhardt, "The Role of Social Meaning in Inattentional Blindness: When the Gorillas in Our Midst Do Not Go Unseen," *Journal of Experimental Social Psychology* 46, no. 6 (2010): 1085–88.

19. See Douglas Massey, *Categorically Unequal: The American Stratification System* (New York: Russell Sage Foundation, 2007), 8–14. For slightly different mappings using similar categories, see Amy J. C. Cuddy, Susan T. Fiske, and Peter Glick, "Interpersonal Relations and Group Processes—the Bias Map: Behaviors from Intergroup Affect and Stereotypes," *Journal of Personality and Social Psychology* 92, no. 4 (2007): 631+; Amy J. C. Cuddy et al., "Stereotype Content Model across Cultures: Towards Universal Similarities and Some Differences," *British Journal of Social Psychology* 48, no. 1 (2009): 1–33; and Susan T. Fiske, Amy J. C. Cuddy, and Peter Glick, "Universal Dimensions of Social Cognition: Warmth and Competence," *Trends in Cognitive Sciences* 11, no. 2 (2007): 77+.

20. For a rich discussion of targeted universalism, see powell's *Racing to Justice*, chapters 1 and 5.

21. Note that all these central figures in the early assertion of an explicit focus on racial equity in PICO and in America are African American; subsequently, that dialogue would be taken up by national staff (especially Scott Reed; Gordon Whitman, national deputy director and head of the Washington, DC, office; Stephanie Gut, national director for organizational development; and Gina Martinez, Mathews's partner in organizer recruitment and retention), state and local organizers including Ron Snyder and Jim Keddy, religious leaders, outside scholars, and some local leaders of a variety of racial/ethnic identities.

22. See above on john powell's writings; see also George Cummings and Dwight N. Hopkins, eds., *Cut Loose Your Stammering Tongue: Black Theology in the Slave Narratives* (Maryknoll, NY: Orbis Books, 1993); George Cummings, *A Common Journey: Black Theology (USA) and Latin American Liberation Theology* (1995; Maryknoll, NY: Orbis Books, 2003); James Cone, *Black Theology and Black Power* (New York: Seabury Press, 1969), and Cone, *Risks of Faith: The Emergence of a Black Theology of Liberation, 1968–1998* (Boston: Beacon Press, 1999); and Michelle Alexander, *The New Jim Crow: Mass Incarceration in the Age of Colorblindness* (New York: New Press, 2010).

23. The account here is drawn from Wood's ethnographic field notes at the November 2011 national clergy gathering, as well as subsequent interviews.

24. On overlapping and contrasting attitudes toward immigration among black and white Americans, see the periodic studies by the Pew Research Center for the People and the Press, especially "Attitudes Toward Immigration: In Black and White" (2006) and "Most Say Illegal Immigrants Should Be Allowed to Stay, But Citizenship Is More Divisive" (2013); both accessed August 2013, via http://www.pewresearch.org/2006/04/25/attitudes-toward-immigration-in-black-and-white and http://www.people-press .org/files/legacy-pdf/3-28-13%20Immigration%20Release.pdf. Note that although non-Hispanic black attitudes toward immigrants are generally far more positive than non-Hispanic white attitudes (in both 2006 and 2013), blacks *also* felt far more strongly that immigrants took jobs away from them.

25. For a full listing of sponsors of New Bottom Line and links to the full campaign, see http://www.newbottomline.com/about. The descriptions here summarize the core PICO national campaigns as of late 2013 (websites accessed September 30, 2013); by 2014, in light of the midterm elections and in anticipation of the 2016 presidential elections, the network had added emphases on civic engagement and voter access via the "Let My People Vote" initiative (http://www.piconetwork.org/issues/let-my-people-vote).

26. On community organizing and school reform, see especially Mark R. Warren, Karen L. Mapp, and the Community Organizing and School Reform Project, *A Match on Dry Grass: Community Organizing as a Catalyst for School Reform* (New York: Oxford University Press, 2011).

27. All these quotes come from the previously cited websites for each issue campaign.

CHAPTER FIVE

1. While encouraging local innovation, Lifelines also notes that "the national campaign provides technical assistance to communities who are interested in adopting the *Ceasefire* violence prevention model" and specifically encourages local PICO activists to read David Kennedy's *Don't Shoot* (New York: Bloomsbury USA, 2011);

on mass incarceration policy, it refers activists to Michelle Alexander, *New Jim Crow*; both at http://www.lifelinestohealing.org/resources.

2. On one hand, PICO, National People's Action, and Gamaliel (as well as RCNO before its demise) appear to have embraced such thinking systematically within their central national structures and have sought to infuse it into their local coalitions, and the InterValley Project, Industrial Areas Foundation, DART, and independent coalitions have done so to a less certain extent, typically driven by the priorities of local coalitions and regional organizers. Even where done systematically, adoption occurs unevenly. In 2014, a few years into the push toward racial equity analysis, one PICO insider estimated that about 60% of local coalitions have significantly embraced racial equity framing as an important part of their work. On the other hand, in our 2011 survey, coalitions reported "addressing racial justice"—a somewhat different construct, reported three years earlier—in patterns associated with networks that vary substantially from this characterization. We thus cannot reliably estimate extent of adoption.

3. Data come from the "Network Health Dashboard" compiled for purposes of internal evaluation with the PICO National Network; see further discussion later in this chapter. Access to this database was generously provided by PICO. The database includes information on forty-two local- or state-level PICO coalitions, and assessments were done by consulting directors from elsewhere in the network and in dialogue with network staff. The authors are not able to independently verify the full picture presented by this data.

4. On the federated model of national organizational structures, see especially Skocpol, Ganz, and Munson, "A Nation of Organizers." Note that, as discussed in chapter 1 above, none of the faith-based organizing networks has achieved a fully federated structure on a national scale; all lack either the fully national scope or the robust state-level structures inherent in the federated model. However, PICO's structure clearly comes closest to that full model today.

5. See http://www.lifelinestohealing.org/about/faq.

6. The nineteen states in which the PICO National Network has a formal organizational presence as of 2014 are Alabama, California, Colorado, Florida, Indiana, Kansas, Louisiana, Massachusetts, Michigan, Minnesota, Missouri, Nevada, New Jersey, New Mexico, New York, Ohio, Pennsylvania, Vermont, and Virginia. It is building its own organizing capacity or forming partnership agreements in several others, including Texas, Utah, and Arizona.

7. All these examples come from local-, state-, and national-level work outlined by faith-based organizing directors and lead organizers as part of the National Study of Community Organizing Coalitions.

8. Quotations in this paragraph can each be found in a variety of PICO organizational materials, where they reoccur regularly, and are most easily seen at the Lifelines website at http://www.piconetwork.org/lifelines.

9. The name of the campaign was subsequently (2014) changed to the "Live Free Campaign."

10. On the power of anger within political culture, but now seen from the perspective of how anger can be manipulated in order to invoke implicit bias against racial minorities, see important new work from Antoine J. Banks, *Anger and Racial Politics: The Emotional Foundation of Racial Attitudes in America* (New York: Cambridge University Press, 2014).

11. See www.piconetwork.org/this-is-the-movement; information entered there enters

a sophisticated social communications database through which the national PICO staff both communicate directly with participants and link them to more local-level efforts.

12. The movie trailer is available at http://www.piconetwork.org/campaign-folders/l2h/fruitvale-station, accessed July 10, 2014.

13. Quote from McBride's biographical sketch is posted at http://partnership forsafecommunities.org/who-we-are/founding-board-members.

14. The study draws ethnographic fieldwork, logistic regression models, and standard probability calculations to establish the national pattern and underlying dynamics that link rising racial/ethnic and class diversity to increased use of prayer. See Braunstein, Fulton, and Wood, "The Role of Bridging Cultural Practices."

15. See, for example, the editorial by Troy Jackson, a key white pastor who was an ally and leader in the effort, at http://sojo.net/blogs/2013/07/17/american-story.

16. Blog post July 17, 2013, on http://pastormikemcbride.com and shared nationally via the Lifelines to Healing website and Twitter feed.

17. Wood, *Faith in Action*, 142; the phrase parallels the key concept of "buffering the technological core" from the sociology of industrial firms; see James D. Thompson, *Organizations in Action: Social Science Bases of Administrative Behavior* (New York: McGraw-Hill, 1967). Via such buffering, firms shield their core production processes from distortion by other demands, emanating from the demands of political relations, legal liability, risk management, human resources, and such. Buffering of the sacred core of religion shields worship from buffeting by political conflict.

18. See the Let My People Vote website at http://www.lifelinestohealing.org/projects/let-my-people-vote. The campaign was driven by a coalition of clergy leaders, with heavy involvement by African American pastors around the state. Thanks to Professor Korie Edwards at the Ohio State University for her insight into efforts there.

19. On the picture of the field in 1999, see Warren and Wood, "Faith-Based Community Organizing"; and Wood and Warren, "A Different Face of Faith-Based Politics."

20. Full disclosure: In a limited way, Wood was part of that pressure from foundations, via public speaking and writing that emerged from the 1999 *State of the Field* study done in conjunction with Interfaith Funders (see previous note). Recruiting more organizers of color was one of several key "strategic challenges" we presented to the field in that work—a challenge that emerged partly from our analysis and that partly simply echoed arguments already being articulated by some organizers, clergy, and lay leaders in the field. In that sense, the various strategic sources of change discussed here served mostly to empower particular voices *already active* within and around faith-based organizing at the turn of the century, rather than presenting entirely new strategic challenges. For example, Wood heard critiques along these lines from more explicitly race-focused organizations in the early 1990s while doing research for an earlier book.

21. Internal data compiled by the PICO National Network in 2014. See the concluding chapter regarding later developments in the "Organizers of Color" initiative.

22. Mathews refers to a widely viewed routine in which the comedian Dave Chappelle discusses the way that whites, too, are victimized by whiteness in that few of them enjoy its economic privileges; rather, Chappelle portrays "whiteness" as used to divide and rule those not part of the economic elite.

23. The work of the late Eugene Williams (died 2012) at the RCNO (Regional Congregations and Neighborhood Organizations) Training Center and Los Angeles Metropolitan Churches, some of it done in collaboration with the Center on Religion

and Civic Culture at the University of Southern California, also focused substantially on racial identity and racial equity (see http://crcc.usc.edu/blog/news/eugene-williams/); it is unclear to what extent that work became influential beyond the Los Angeles area.

24. The literature on organizational change is massive and of uneven quality; among the more insightful works are Rosabeth Moss Kanter, *The Change Masters: Innovation for Productivity in the American Corporation* (New York: Simon and Schuster, 1983); Rosabeth Moss Kanter, Barry A. Stein, and Todd D. Jick, *The Challenge of Organizational Change* (New York: Free Press, 1992).

25. For the sake of brevity, the discussion here necessarily simplifies the complex dynamics that played out over years, involving the interplay of crosscutting identities within individuals and both collaboration and conflict among different groups constituted along racial/ethnic or ideological/analytic lines.

26. We do not identify the regional grouping here, to protect confidentiality of sources; Wood has interviewed and done limited participant-observation work in nearly all the national networks, including in this regional grouping.

27. On the concept of embedded autonomy in economic development strategies and the relationship between industrial firms and the state, see Peter B. Evans, *Embedded Autonomy: States and Industrial Transformation* (Princeton, NJ: Princeton University Press, 1995). Evans articulated this concept in analyzing the conditions of successful economic development in semiperipheral economies in relationship to the world system, in particular the relationship between firms and the state. While recognizing the differences of analytic context, we adopt the concept here for its usefulness as a heuristic device for understanding the parallel question of how local coalitions relate to their networks.

28. Note that although ISAIAH today is a PICO affiliate, its genesis is more complex and was independent at the time of this study's data collection. A longtime stalwart of the Gamaliel national network, it separated as an independent organization for several years (partly due to conflicts around racial equity) before negotiating to join the PICO National Network in 2012.

29. Nearly all the networks have undergone or will soon undergo significant transitions of national leadership, as the 1970s "founding generation" of those trained directly by Alinsky gives way to a younger generation of organizers. How different organizations handle these transitions also appears to be a significant variable, as the instability that comes with organizational change can facilitate innovation—but does not necessarily do so, itself a function of organizational leadership in both generations.

30. "LiveFree Overview 2014," internal document within the PICO National Network. Note that these are internal claims of the network, received just as this book was going to press; they have not been independently verified.

31. Note that this list of accomplishments was discovered by the authors just as this book went to press, and has not been verified.

32. Wood 2011 interview of NPA executive director George Goehl.

33. As noted in chapter 1, the various nomenclatures used in different organizing networks—faith-based, broad-based, congregation-based, and institution-based organizing—represent different mixtures of religious and secular democratic creeds in this work. We have used the term "faith-based community organizing" for the sake of simplicity, and due to the fact that all do appeal to religious commitment and religiously grounded social ethics in their work. Likewise, for the sake of sim-

plicity we do not introduce these nuances in the present paragraph, where the point is that organizing for racial equity is not the same as what Wood in 2002 termed "race-based organizing."

CHAPTER SIX

1. Note McBride's interesting locution "white middle-centric ethos," which may represent a melding of what he saw as the state of PICO's internal culture at the time he entered the work: white-centric and middle class (and perhaps middle of the road). The phrase is interesting in part because it may articulate something important about predominantly white middle-class organizations, as seen from the perspective of working-class people of color.

2. Michael-Ray Mathews is part of the national staff of the PICO National Network and at various times has led its national clergy development program and organizer recruitment efforts. Jennifer Jones-Bridgett is the director of PICO-Louisiana. Scott Reed is the executive director of the PICO National Network. Gordon Whitman leads PICO's office in Washington, DC. Joe Givens was the longtime director of PICO's affiliate in New Orleans. Mathews, Jones-Bridgett, and Givens are African American; Reed and Whitman are white. Bob Ross is president of the California Endowment. Maya Harris-West is vice president for democracy, rights, and justice at the Ford Foundation, and Heather McGhee is vice president for policy and outreach at Dēmos, a public advocacy group in Washington, DC. Legal scholar Michelle Alexander is the author of *The New Jim Crow: Mass Incarceration in the Age of Colorblindness* (New York: New Press, 2010). Manuel Pastor is the director of the Program for Environmental and Regional Equity and codirector of the Center for the Study of Immigrant Integration, both at the University of Southern California. Iva Carruthers served on the faculty at Northeastern Illinois University and is the president of the Urban Outreach Foundation. Other key elements in the development of PICO's work on racial equity and racial justice included Elder Joseph Forbes of the African Methodist Episcopal Church; Ron Snyder, formerly the director of Oakland Community Organization; Stephanie Gut, director of organizational development for the national network; and Sybil Morial, member of the PICO National Board from New Orleans. Forbes, Morial, and Cummings were particularly crucial in providing a generational bridge from the civil rights movement into PICO's twenty-first-century push onto racial equity terrain.

CHAPTER SEVEN

1. Massey, *Categorically Unequal.*

2. See especially Wood, "Religious Culture and Political Action"; "Religion, Faith-Based Community Organizing, and the Struggle for Justice"; and the second half of *Faith in Action.*

3. We hasten to add that we would say that same thing about academe, and about American culture as a whole—including our own roles within it. Of course, the cultivation of reflexivity might occur in either secularly or spiritually grounded ways.

4. On strategic capacity and its dependence on the diversity of leaders' backgrounds, see Ganz, "Resources and Resourcefulness," and Ganz, *Why David Sometimes Wins.* Ganz's analysis shows that the strategic capacity of a movement suffers if key leaders are drawn from a narrow range of social backgrounds and biographical experience and expands significantly as leaders' backgrounds diversify.

5. Fifty-five percent of professional organizers and 46% of the lead organizers/direc-

tors of local coalitions were women. Because the National Study of Community Organizing Coalitions focused on local coalitions, we do not have systematic data on the national staff of the networks, but certainly women are strongly represented at that level in DART, PICO, Gamaliel, and the Southwest IAF.

6. Our wording here is cautious: Lacking systematic data on the staffing of national networks, we cannot confidently characterize how general this pattern is. In keeping with Ganz's framework (see note 9 in this chapter), further research should consider whether the spread of higher strategic capacity in the field correlates with the spread of diverse staff backgrounds. Although Scott Reed, Gordon Whitman, Jim Keddy (earlier, in the PICO California Project), and Stephanie Gut (in less obvious ways) were key early architects of PICO's heightened strategic capacity, it was surely no coincident that this capacity developed simultaneously with the network's recruitment of more diverse staffing, including from career tracks in ministry, legacy organizations from the movement for black civil rights and black power, the immigrant rights movement, other social movement fields, academe, think tanks, philanthropy, and others.

7. Wood conducted these interviews by telephone, mostly during 2011. All quotations are drawn from his transcribed notes at the time of the interviews. These interviews were done as part of our collaboration with Interfaith Funders and the National Study of Community Organizing Coalitions.

8. On the conservative movement's long march through civil society institutions to national power, see David R. Farber, *The Rise and Fall of American Conservatism* (Princeton, NJ: Princeton University Press, 2010).

9. Marshall Ganz, a former organizer with the United Farm Workers in California and more recently a prominent scholar of organizing and trainer of organizers within Harvard University's Kennedy School of Government, was instrumental in the move toward a "campaign" dimension to organizing. See https://exed.hks.harvard.edu/programs/loa/overview.aspx, and http://www.hks.harvard.edu/about/faculty-staff-directory/marshall-ganz.

10. Emerging work by the authors in collaboration with Rebecca Sager at Loyola Marymount University considers the dynamics of secular-religious collaborations and alliances.

11. On the potential symbiosis of state and local level organizing, see Warren, *Dry Bones Rattling*. On the tensions and trade-offs in such aspirations—and the potential costs to the local work that represents the lifeblood of these organizations—see Rusch, "Rethinking Bridging" and "Going Regional."

12. Little academic writing has analyzed the relatively new Ohio Organizing Collaborative. Key collaborators include several major unions (as institutional members) and the Center for Community Change, National People's Action, and the PICO National Network. See http://www.ohorganizing.org.

13. See Nancy Fraser, "Rethinking the Public Sphere"; Fraser, "False Antitheses: A Response to Seyla Benhabib and Judith Butler," *Feminist Contentions: A Philosophical Exchange* 71 (1995): 26–28; Fraser, "Rethinking Recognition," *New Left Review* 3 (May/June 2000): 107–20.

14. See Charles Taylor, *Multiculturalism and "The Politics of Recognition"* (Princeton, NJ: Princeton University Press, 1991); and Benhabib, "Models of Public Space"; Benhabib, *Claims of Culture*; and Benhabib, *Another Cosmopolitanism* (New York: Oxford University Press, 2006).

CONCLUSION

1. See the introduction for more on this literature. We owe parts of our interpretation to Cohen and Arato, *Civil Society and Political Theory*. But ultimately this presentation of Habermas's diagnosis of contemporary society, its challenges, and how they can be met, is our own, drawing especially from Habermas's *Theory of Communicative Action*, volumes 1 and 2 (1984, 1987). The brief discussion here necessarily shortchanges the depth of analytic insight possible in the thick book-length treatments above and in the rich literature flowing from Habermas's work.

2. In the terms used here, we can understand the eons-long development of human society as originating in tribal settings throughout the globe, in which social life revolved almost entirely around communicative action in small group settings. With the rise of agriculture several millennia ago, hierarchical state-like structures began to gain power over these communities, gradually emerging into city-states and eventually empires and then nation-states. In the last millennium, true market economies based on money gained relative autonomy from control by nation-states and generated a dramatic new economic dynamism within human history. In recent centuries, as power and money increasingly substituted for interpersonally based and small group-based communicative flows, the Systems emerged as dominant realities of social life. Ironically, this only became truer with the modern rise of mass communications and information technologies and their use for political mobilization and consumer marketing.

    Democratic institutions arose as some sectors sought to hold the emerging system of politics accountable to societally defined goals and desires for justice. Meanwhile, due to the powerful capacity of money to substitute for communicative action, efforts to hold the economy systematically accountable to societally defined goals struggled for efficacy. At times, the legal system, reformist movements, unions, and ethical commitments of individual business leaders have served this purpose, but overall the economy has inexorably gained greater autonomy from societal coordination.

3. The best history of the civil rights era comes in Taylor Branch's three volumes, *Parting the Waters: America in the King Years, 1954–1963* (New York: Simon and Schuster, 1988); Branch, *Pillar of Fire: America in the King Years, 1963–65* (New York: Simon and Schuster, 1998); and Branch, *At Canaan's Edge: America in the King Years, 1965–68* (New York: Simon and Schuster, 2006).

4. The cultural turn in social movements research includes a broad literature; key sources include Anne E. Kane, "Theorizing Meaning Construction in Social Movement," *Sociological Theory* 15, no. 3 (1997): 249–76; Morris, *The Origins of the Civil Rights Movement*; Nepstad, *Religion and War Resistance in the Plowshares Movement*, and *Nonviolent Revolutions: Civil Resistance in the Late Twentieth Century* (New York: Oxford University Press, 2011); Francesca Polletta, *It Was Like a Fever: Storytelling in Protest and Politics* (Chicago: University of Chicago Press, 2006); Francesca Polletta and James M. Jasper, "Collective Identity and Social Movements," *Annual Review of Sociology* 27 (2001): 283–305; Christian Smith, *Resisting Reagan: The U.S. Central America Peace Movement* (Chicago: University of Chicago Press, 1996), and Smith, ed., *Disruptive Religion: The Force of Faith in Social-Movement Activism* (New York: Routledge, 1996); Rhys Williams, "From the 'Beloved Community' to 'Family Values': Religious Language, Symbolic Repertoires, and Democratic Culture," in *Social Movements: Identity, Culture, and the State*, ed. Nancy Whittier, David S. Meyer,

and Belinda Robnett (Oxford: Oxford University Press, 2002), and Williams, "Constructing the Public Good: Social Movements and Cultural Resources," *Social Problems* 42, no. 1 (1995): 124–44; and Elisabeth J. Wood, *Forging Democracy from Below: Insurgent Transitions in South Africa and El Salvador* (Cambridge: Cambridge University Press, 2000), and Wood, *Insurgent Collective Action and Civil War in El Salvador* (Cambridge: Cambridge University Press, 2003).

5. On "public work," see Harry Chatten Boyte and Nancy N. Kari, *Building America: The Democratic Promise of Public Work* (Philadelphia: Temple University Press, 1996).

BIBLIOGRAPHY

Alexander, Jeffrey C. *The Civil Sphere*. New York: Oxford University Press, 2006.
Alexander, Jeffrey C., Bernhard Giesen, and Jason L. Mast. *Social Performance: Symbolic Action, Cultural Pragmatics, and Ritual*. Cambridge Cultural Social Studies. New York: Cambridge University Press, 2006.
Alinsky, Saul David. *Reveille for Radicals*. New York: Vintage Books, 1969.
———. *Rules for Radicals: A Practical Primer for Realistic Radicals*. New York: Random House, 1971.
Armstrong, Elizabeth A., and Mary Bernstein. "Culture, Power, and Institutions: A Multi-Institutional Politics Approach to Social Movements." *Sociological Theory* 26 (2008): 74–99.
Baggett, Jerome. *Sense of the Faithful: How American Catholics Live Their Faith*. New York: Oxford University Press, 2009.
Baker, Kendall Clark. *When Faith Storms the Public Square: Mixing Religion and Politics through Community Organizing to Enhance Our Democracy*. Alresford, UK: Circle Books, 2011.
Banks, Antoine J. *Anger and Racial Politics: The Emotional Foundation of Racial Attitudes in America*. New York: Cambridge University Press, 2014.
Bellah, Robert N. *Religion in Human Evolution: From the Paleolithic to the Axial Age*. Cambridge, MA: Harvard University Press, 2011.
Benhabib, Seyla. *Another Cosmopolitanism*. Oxford: Oxford University Press, 2006.
———. *The Claims of Culture*. Princeton, NJ: Princeton University Press, 2002.
———. "Models of Public Space: Hannah Arendt, the Liberal Tradition, and Jürgen Habermas." In *Habermas and the Public Sphere*, edited by Craig Calhoun, 73–98. Cambridge, MA: MIT Press, 1992.
Boyte, Harry Chatten, and Nancy N. Kari. *Building America: The Democratic Promise of Public Work*. Philadelphia: Temple University Press, 1996.
Branch, Taylor. *At Canaan's Edge: America in the King Years, 1965–68*. New York: Simon and Schuster, 2006.
———. *Parting the Waters: America in the King Years, 1954–1963*. New York: Simon and Schuster, 1988.v
———. *Pillar of Fire: America in the King Years, 1963–65*. New York: Simon and Schuster, 1998.
Braunstein, Ruth Lauren. "Political Cultures of Accountability: Practicing Citizenship

across the Ideological Divide." Paper Presented at the Annual Meeting of the American Sociological Association, Denver, Colorado, August 2012.

Braunstein, Ruth, Brad R. Fulton, and Richard L. Wood. "The Role of Bridging Cultural Practices in Racially and Socioeconomically Diverse Civic Organizations." *American Sociological Review* 79, no. 4 (2014): 705–25.

Bretherton, Luke. *Christianity and Contemporary Politics: The Conditions and Possibilites of Faithful Witness*. London: Wiley-Blackwell, 2010.

———. *Resurrecting Democracy: Faith, Citizenship, and the Politics of a Common Life*. Cambridge Studies in Social Theory, Religion, and Politics, edited by Ken Wald, David Leege, and Richard L. Wood. Cambridge and New York: Cambridge University Press, 2015.

Calhoun, Craig J. *Habermas and the Public Sphere*. Studies in Contemporary German Social Thought. Cambridge, MA: MIT Press, 1992.

Calpotura, Francis, and Kim Fellner. "The Square Pegs Find Their Groove: Reshaping the Organizing Circle." 1996. Accessed January 9, 2015. http://comm-org.wisc.edu/papers96/square.html.

Chambers, Edward T., and Michael A. Cowan. *Roots for Radicals: Organizing for Power, Action, and Justice*. New York: Continuum, 2003.

Chaves, Mark, Shawna L. Anderson, and Alison Eagle. *National Congregations Study: Cumulative Data File and Codebook*. Durham, NC: Duke University, Department of Sociology, 2014.

Christerson, Brad, Korie L. Edwards, and Michael O. Emerson. *Against All Odds: The Struggle for Racial Integration in Religious Organizations*. New York: New York University Press, 2005.

Claassen, Ryan L. *Godless Democrats and Pious Republicans: Party Activists and the Mythical God Gulf*. New York: Cambridge University Press, 2015.

Cohen, Jean L., and Andrew Arato. *Civil Society and Political Theory*. Cambridge, MA: MIT Press, 1992.

Cummings, George. *A Common Journey: Black Theology (USA) and Latin American Liberation Theology*. 1995; Maryknoll, NY: Orbis Books, 2003.

Cummings, George, and Dwight N. Hopkins, eds. *Cut Loose Your Stammering Tongue: Black Theology in the Slave Narratives*. Maryknoll, NY: Orbis Books, 1993.

Day-Lower, Donna C. "Prelude to Struggle: African American Clergy and Community Organizing for Economic Development in the 1990's." PhD diss., Temple University, 1996.

Delgado, Gary. *Beyond the Politics of Place: New Directions in Community Organizing in the 1990s*. Oakland, CA: Applied Research Center, 1994.

———. *Organizing the Movement: The Roots and Growth of ACORN*. Philadelphia: Temple University Press, 1986.

Dillon, Michele. *Catholic Identity: Balancing Reason, Faith, and Power*. Cambridge: Cambridge University Press, 1999.

Dryzek, John S. "Political Inclusion and the Dynamics of Democratization." *American Political Science Review* 90 (1996): 475–87.

Eliasoph, Nina. *Avoiding Politics: How Americans Produce Apathy in Everyday Life*. Cambridge: Cambridge University Press, 1998.

Emerson, Michael O., and Christian Smith. *Divided by Faith: Evangelical Religion and the Problem of Race in America*. New York: Oxford University Press, 2000.

Emerson, Michael O., and George A. Yancey. *Transcending Racial Barriers: Toward a Mutual Obligations Approach*. New York: Oxford University Press, 2011.

Emirbayer, Mustafa, and Jeff Goodwin. "Network Analysis, Culture, and the Problem of Agency." *American Journal of Sociology* 99 (1994): 1411–54.

Evans, Peter B. *Embedded Autonomy: States and Industrial Transformation.* Princeton, NJ: Princeton University Press, 1995.

Evans, Sara M., and Harry C. Boyte. *Free Spaces: The Sources of Democratic Change in America.* New York: Harper and Row, 1986.

Farber, David R. *The Rise and Fall of American Conservatism.* Princeton, NJ: Princeton University Press, 2010.

Flaherty, Mary Ann, and Richard L. Wood. *Faith and Public Life: Faith-Based Community Organizing and the Development of Congregations.* New York: Interfaith Funders and the Ford Foundaiton, 2004.

Flyvbjerg, Bent. *Making Social Science Matter: Why Social Inquiry Fails and How It Can Succeed Again.* Cambridge: Cambridge University Press, 2001.

Flyvbjerg, Bent, Todd Landman, and Sanford Schram, eds. *Real Social Science: Applied Phronesis.* Cambridge: Cambridge University Press, 2011.

Fraser, Nancy. "False Antitheses: A Response to Seyla Benhabib and Judith Butler." *Feminist Contentions: A Philosophical Exchange* 71 (1995): 26–28.

———. "Rethinking Recognition." *New Left Review* 3 (May/June 2000): 107–20.

———. "Rethinking the Public Sphere: A Contribution to the Critique of Actually Existing Democracy." In *Habermas and the Public Sphere,* edited by Craig Calhoun, 109–42. Cambridge, MA: MIT Press, 1992.

Ganz, Marshall. "Resources and Resourcefulness: Strategic Capacity in the Unionization of California Agriculture, 1959–1966." *American Journal of Sociology* 105 (2000): 1003–63.

———. *Why David Sometimes Wins: Leadership, Organization, and Strategy in the California Farm Worker Movement.* New York: Oxford University Press, 2009.

Gecan, Michael. *After America's Midlife Crisis.* Cambridge, MA: MIT Press, 2009.

———. *Going Public.* Boston: Beacon Press, 2002.

Gittell, Ross J., and Avis Vidal. *Community Organizing: Building Social Capital as a Development Strategy.* Thousand Oaks, CA: Sage Publications, 1998.

Goodwin, Jeff, James M. Jasper, and Francesca Polletta. *Passionate Politics: Emotions and Social Movements.* Chicago: University of Chicago Press, 2001.

Habermas, Jürgen. "Religion in the Public Sphere." *European Journal of Philosophy* 14 (2006): 1–25.

———. *The Structural Transformation of the Public Sphere: An Inquiry into a Category of Bourgeois Society.* London: Polity Press, 1989.

———. *The Theory of Communicative Action,* vols. 1 and 2. 1984; Boston: Beacon Press, 1987.

Hart, Stephen. *Cultural Dilemmas of Progressive Politics: Styles of Engagement among Grassroots Activists.* Chicago: University of Chicago Press, 2001.

Jacobsen, Dennis A. *Doing Justice: Congregations and Community Organizing.* Minneapolis, MN: Fortress Press, 2001.

Johnston, Hank, and Bert Klandermans, eds. *Social Movements and Culture.* Minneapolis: University of Minnesota Press, 1995.

Kane, Anne E. "Theorizing Meaning Construction in Social Movements." *Sociological Theory* 15 (1997): 249–76.

Kanter, Rosabeth Moss. *The Change Masters: Innovation for Productivity in the American Corporation.* New York: Simon and Schuster, 1983.

Kanter, Rosabeth Moss, Barry A. Stein, amd Todd D. Jick. *The Challenge of Organizational Change.* New York: Free Press, 1992.

Keddy, Jim. "Human Dignity and Grassroots Leadership Development." In *Jossey-Bass Reader on Nonprofit and Public Leadership*, edited by James L. Perry, 108–15. San Francisco: Jossey-Bass, 2010.

Kleidman, Robert. "Community Organizing and Regionalism." *City and Community* 3 (2004): 403–21.

———. "Public Sociology and Community Organizing." *Journal of Applied Sociology/Sociological Practice* 23 (2006): 68–82.

Lamont, Michèle, and Marcel Fournier. *Cultivating Differences: Symbolic Boundaries and the Making of Inequality*. Chicago: University of Chicago Press, 1992.

Leondar-Wright, Betsy. *Missing Class: How Seeing Class Cultures Can Strengthen Social Movement Groups*. Ithaca, NY: Cornell University Press, 2014.

Lichterman, Paul. *Elusive Togetherness: Church Groups Trying to Bridge America's Divisions*. Princeton Studies in Cultural Sociology. Princeton, NJ: Princeton University Press, 2005.

———. *The Search for Political Community: American Activists Reinventing Commitment*. Cambridge: Cambridge University Press, 1996.

Linthicum, Robert C. *City of God, City of Satan: A Biblical Theology for the Urban Church*. Grand Rapids, MI: Zondervan, 1991.

———. *Signs of Hope in the City*. Monrovia, CA: Marc, 1995.

McAdam, Doug, and Karina Kloos. *Deeply Divided: Racial Politics and Social Movements in Post-War America*. New York: Oxford University Press, 2014.

McAdam, Doug, John D. McCarthy, and Mayer N. Zald. *Comparative Perspectives on Social Movements: Political Opportunities, Mobilizing Structures, and Cultural Framings*. Cambridge: Cambridge University Press, 1996.

McPherson, J. Miller, and Lynn Smith-Lovin. "Homophily in Voluntary Organizations: Status Distance and the Composition of Face-to-Face Groups." *American Sociological Review* 52 (1987): 370–79.

McPherson, Miller, Lynn Smith-Lovin, and James M. Cook. "Birds of a Feather: Homophily in Social Networks." *Annual Review of Sociology* 27 (2001): 415–44.

Mediratta, Kavitha, Sara McAlister, Seema Shah, Norm Fruchter, Christina Mokhtar, and Dana Lockwood. *Organized Communities, Stronger Schools: A Preview of Research Findings*. Providence, RI, and New York: Annenberg Institute for School Reform at Brown University, 2008.

Mische, Ann. "Cross-Talk in Movements: Reconceiving the Culture-Network Link." In *Social Movements and Networks: Relational Approaches to Collective Action*, edited by Mario Diani and Doug McAdam, 258–77. Oxford: Oxford University Press, 2003.

Morris, Aldon D. *The Origins of the Civil Rights Movement: Black Communities Organizing for Change*. New York: Free Press, 1984.

Nepstad, Sharon Erickson. *Nonviolent Revolutions: Civil Resistance in the Late Twentieth Century*. New York: Oxford University Press, 2011.

———. *Religion and War Resistance in the Plowshares Movement*. New York: Cambridge University Press, 2008.

Newman, John Henry, and James Gaffney. *Conscience, Consensus, and the Development of Doctrine*. 1st ed. New York: Image Books, 1992.

———. *Roman Catholic Writings on Doctrinal Development*. Kansas City, MO: Sheed and Ward, 1997.

Omi, Michael, and Howard Winant. *Racial Formation in the United States: From the 1960s to the 1990s*. New York: Routledge, 1994.

Osterman, Paul. *Gathering Power: The Future of Progressive Politics in America.* Boston: Beacon Press, 2003.

Ostrower, Francine. *Nonprofit Governance in the United States: Findings on Performance and Accountability from the First National Representative Study.* Washington, DC: Urban Institute Center on Nonprofits and Philanthropy, 2007.

Polletta, Francesca. *It Was Like a Fever: Storytelling in Protest and Politics.* Chicago: University of Chicago Press, 2006.

Polletta, Francesca, and James M. Jasper. "Collective Identity and Social Movements." *Annual Review of Sociology* 27 (2001): 283–305.

powell, john. "Race, Place, and Opportunity." In *The American Prospect* online, September 21, 2008. Accessed July 10, 2014, at http://prospect.org/article/race-place-and-opportunity.

———. "Race, Poverty, and Urban Sprawl: Access to Opportunities through Regional Strategies." In *Growing Smarter: Achieving Livable Communities, Environmental Justice and Regional Equity*, edited by Robert Bullard, 51–72. Cambridge, MA: MIT Press, 2007.

———. "Structural Racism and Spatial Jim Crow." In *The Black Metropolis in the Twenty-First Century: Race, Power, and the Politics of Place*, edited by Robert Bullard, 41–66. Lanham, MD: Rowman and Littlefield, 2007.

Putnam, Robert D. *Bowling Alone: The Collapse and Revival of American Community.* New York: Simon and Schuster, 2000.

Reed, Isaac, Jeffrey C. Alexander, and Nina Eliasoph. *Culture, Society, and Democracy: The Interpretive Approach.* Yale Cultural Sociology. Boulder, CO: Paradigm Publishers, 2007.

Rogers, Mary Beth. *Cold Anger: A Story of Faith and Power Politics.* Denton: University of North Texas Press, 1990.

Ruef, Martin, Howard E. Aldrich, and Nancy M. Carter. "The Structure of Founding Teams: Homophily, Strong Ties, and Isolation among U.S. Entrepreneurs." *American Sociological Review* 68 (2003): 195–222.

Rusch, Lara. "Going Regional: The Evolution of an Organizing Strategy in Detroit." *City and Community* 11, no. 1 (2012): 51–73.

———. "Rethinking Bridging: Risk and Trust in Multiracial Community Organizing." *Urban Affairs Review* 45 (2010): 483–506.

Sacks, Jonathan. *Faith in the Future: The Ecology of Hope and the Restoration of Family, Community, and Faith.* Macon, GA: Mercer University Press, 1997.

Schudson, Michael. "How Culture Works: Perspectives from Media Studies on the Efficacy of Symbols." *Theory and Society* 18 (1989): 153–80.

Sears, Davis O., Jim Sidanius, and Lawrence Bobo, eds. *Racialized Politics: The Debate about Racism in America.* Studies in Communication, Media, and Public Opinion. Chicago: University of Chicago Press, 2000.

Sen, Rinku. *Stir It Up: Lessons in Community Organizing*: San Francisco: Jossey-Bass, 2003.

Shelton, Jason E., and Michael O. Emerson. *Blacks and Whites in Christian America: How Racial Discrimination Shapes Religious Convictions.* Religion and Social Transformation. New York: New York University Press, 2012.

Skocpol, Theda, Marshall Ganz, and Ziad Munson. "A Nation of Organizers: The Institutional Origins of Civic Voluntarism in the United States." *American Political Science Review* 94 (2000): 527–46.

Slessarev-Jamir, H. "Exploring the Attraction of Local Congregations to Community Organizing." *Nonprofit and Voluntary Sector Quarterly* 33 (2004): 585–605.

Smith, Christian. *Resisting Reagan: The U.S. Central America Peace Movement*. Chicago: University of Chicago Press, 1996.

Smith, Christian, ed. *Disruptive Religion: The Force of Faith in Social-Movement Activism*. New York: Routledge, 1996.

Smith, Stephen Noble. *Stoking the Fire of Democracy: Our Generation's Introduction to Grassroots Organizing*. Skokie, IL: ACTA, 2009.

Somers, Margaret R. "Citizenship and the Place of the Public Sphere: Law, Community, and Political Culture in the Transition to Democracy." *American Sociological Review* 58 (1993): 587–620.

Speer, Paul W. "People Making Public Policy in California: The PICO California Project" (research report). Knoxville, TN: Vanderbilt University, 2002.

Speer, Paul W., Mark Ontkush, Brian Schmitt, Padmasini Raman, Courtney Jackson, Kristopher M. Rengert, and N. Andrew Peterson. "The Intentional Exercise of Power: Community Organizing in Camden, New Jersey." *Journal of Community and Applied Social Psychology* 13 (2003): 399–408.

Stall, Susan, and Randy Stoecker. "Community Organizing or Organizing Community? Gender and the Crafts of Empowerment." *Gender and Society* 12 (1998): 729–56.

Sullins, D. Paul. "Institutional Selection for Conformity: The Case of U.S. Catholic Priests." *Sociology of Religion* 74 (2013): 56–81.

Swarts, Heidi. *Organizing Urban America: Secular and Faith-Based Progressive Movements*. Minneapolis: University of Minnesota Press, 2008.

———. "Setting the State's Agenda: Church-Based Community Organizations in American Urban Politics." In *States, Parties, and Social Movements: Protest and the Dynamics of Institutional Change*, edited by Jack Goldstone, 78–106. Cambridge: Cambridge University Press, 2001.

Swidler, Ann. "Culture in Action." *American Sociological Review* 51 (1996): 273–86.

Tarrow, Sidney. *Power in Movement: Social Movements, Collective Action, and Politics*. Cambridge: Cambridge University Press, 1994.

Taylor, Charles. *Multiculturalism and "The Politics of Recognition."* Princeton, NJ: Princeton University Press, 1991.

Verba, Sidney, Kay Lehman Schlozman, and Henry E. Brady. *Voice and Equality: Civic Voluntarism in American Politics*. Cambridge, MA: Harvard University Press, 1995.

Voss, Kim. "The Collapse of a Social Movement: The Interplay of Mobilizing Structures, Framing, and Political Opportunities in the Knights of Labor." In *Comparative Perspectives on Social Movements: Political Opportunities, Mobilizing Structures, and Cultural Framings*, edited by Doug McAdam, Mayer N. Zald, and John D. McCarthy, 227–60. New York: Cambridge University Press, 1996.

Walker, E. T., and J. D. McCarthy. "Legitimacy, Strategy, and Resources in the Survival of Community-Based Organizations." *Social Problems* 57 (2010): 315–40.

Warren, Mark R. "Community Organizing in Britain: The Political Engagement of Faith-Based Social Capital." *City and Community* 8 (2009): 9–127.

———. *Dry Bones Rattling*. Princeton, NJ: Princeton University Press, 2001.

Warren, Mark R., Karen L. Mapp, and the Community Organizing and School Reform Project. *A Match on Dry Grass: Community Organizing as a Catalyst for School Reform*. Oxford: Oxford University Press, 2011.

Warren, Mark R., and Richard L. Wood. *Faith-Based Community Organizing: The State of the Field*. Jericho, NY: Interfaith Funders, 2001.

Wedeen, Lisa. "Conceptualizing Culture: Possibilities for Political Science." *American Political Science Review* 96 (2002): 713–28.

Whitman, Gordon. "Beyond Advocacy: The History and Vision of the PICO Network." *Social Policy* (Winter 2007): 50–59.

Williams, Rhys H. "Constructing the Public Good: Social Movements and Cultural Resources." *Social Problems* 42 (February 1995): 124–44.

———. "From the 'Beloved Community' to 'Family Values': Religious Language, Symbolic Repertoires and Democratic Culture." In *Social Movements: Identity, Culture, and the State*, edited by Nancy Whittier, David S. Meyer, and Belinda Robnett, 247–65. Oxford: Oxford University Press, 2002.

———. "Politics, Religion, and the Analysis of Culture." *Theory and Society* 25 (1996): 883–900.

Wilson, William Julius. "Revisiting Race-Neutral Politics: The Sociologist and Scholar William Julius Wilson Revises His Stance on Whether Democrats Should Put Race on the Agenda." *American Prospect* 22, no. 3 (2011): A7+. Accessed July 1, 2013. http://prospect.org/article/qa-revisiting-race-neutral-politics.

Wood, Elisabeth J. *Forging Democracy from Below: Insurgent Transitions in South Africa and El Salvador*. Cambridge: Cambridge University Press, 2000.

———. *Insurgent Collective Action and Civil War in El Salvador*. Cambridge: Cambridge University Press, 2003.

Wood, Richard L. "Higher Power: Strategic Capacity for State and National Organizing." In *Transforming the City: Community Organizing and the Challenge of Political Change*, edited by Marion Orr, 164–92. Lawrence: University Press of Kansas, 2007.

———. *Raising the Bar: Organizing Capacity in 2008 and Beyond*. Washington, DC: Neighborhood Funders Group, 2008.

———. "Religion, Faith-Based Community Organizing, and the Struggle for Justice." In the *Cambridge Handbook of Sociology*, edited by Michele Dillon, 385–99. Cambridge: Cambridge University Press, 2003.

———. "Religious Culture and Political Action." *Sociological Theory* 17 (1999): 307–32.

Wood, Richard L., and Mary Ann Flaherty. *Renewing Congregations*. New York: Interfaith Funders, 2003.

Wood, Richard L., and Mark R. Warren. "A Different Face of Faith-Based Politics: Social Capital and Community Organizing in the Public Arena." *International Journal of Sociology and Social Policy* 22 (2002): 6–54.

Wuthnow, Robert, James Davison Hunter, Albert Bergesen, and Edith Kurzweil. *Cultural Analysis: The Work of Peter L. Berger, Mary Douglas, Michel Foucault, and Jürgen Habermas*. Boston: Routledge and Kegan Paul, 1984.

Zald, Mayer N., and John D. McCarthy. *Social Movements in an Organizational Society*. New Brunswick, NJ: Transaction, 1987.

Zucker, Lynne G. "The Role of Institutionalization in Cultural Persistence." *American Sociological Review* 42 (1977): 726–43.

Locators in italics are for figures.